11/92

D0377081

By VED MEHTA

Face to Face

Walking the Indian Streets

Fly and the Fly-Bottle

The New Theologian

Delinquent Chacha

Portrait of India

John Is Easy to Please

Daddyji

Mahatma Gandhi and His Apostles

The New India

Mamaji

The Photographs of Chachaji

A Family Affair

Vedi

The Ledge Between the Streams

Three Stories of the Raj

SOUND-SHADOWS

OF THE

NEW WORLD

The Arkansas School for the Blind, Little Rock, 1949.

VED MEHTA

SOUND-SHADOWS

OF THE

NEW WORLD

W. W. Norton & Company

NEW YORK / LONDON

Published simultaneously in Canada by Penguin Books Canada Ltd,
2801 John Street, Markham, Ontario L3R 1B4

The contents of this book originated in The New Yorker.

The text of this book is composed in Garamond. Composition and
manufacturing by The Maple-Vail Book Manufacturing Group.
Book design by Guy Fleming.

First published as a Norton paperback 1987

Library of Congress Cataloging in Publication Data

Mehta, Ved, 1934–
Sound-Shadows of the New World.

Continues: Daddyji, 1972, Mamaji, 1979, Vedi, 1982, and The Ledge
Between the Streams, 1984
1. Mehta, Ved, 1934–   2. Blind—India—
Biography. I. Title.
HV2093.M43A345   1985   362.4'1'0924 {B}   85–5045

ISBN 0-393-30437-X

W. W. Norton & Company, Inc.
500 Fifth Avenue, New York, N. Y. 10110

W. W. Norton & Company Ltd.
37 Great Russell Street, London WC1B 3NU

2 3 4 5 6 7 8 9 0

To Linn

This book is as self-contained as my adolescent years in Arkansas, which it describes. But it also has, as it were, a family tie to four other books, set in a vanished India: *Daddyji* (1972), a biographical portrait of my father; *Mamaji* (1979), a biographical portrait of my mother; and *Vedi* (1982) and *The Ledge Between the Streams* (1984), which together tell the story of my childhood. All these books are part of a continuing autobiographical work, and as I put this volume to press I am sketching out a volume on my college years in California.

I wish to express my special thanks to Alice Golembiewski Phillips, who was my amanuensis and editorial assistant during the writing of this book. There is hardly a sentence in the text which did not benefit from her untiring scrutiny and alert, intuitive intelligence.

V.M.

New York
November 1985

CONTENTS

Photographs / x

I. THE CLOUD HAS SPREAD ITS DARK HAIR / 3

II. LAND OF OPPORTUNITY / 37

III. GET IN THE HOLE, BUCK / 50

IV. TRAVELLER UNKNOWN / 76

V. A DONKEY AMONG HORSES / 131

VI. ANOTHER PAIR OF HANDS / 174

VII. LYING LOW AND VENTURING OUT / 220

VIII. BROOM CLOSET / 281

IX. LIBERTY AND GENTLEMEN'S CHOICE / 307

X. A LEAF, A STEM / 354

XI. OUTSIDE THE GATE / 387

PHOTOGRAPHS

The Arkansas School for the Blind, Little Rock,

1949 / frontispiece

Ved, Little Rock, 1950 / 218

SOUND-SHADOWS

OF THE

NEW WORLD

I

THE CLOUD
HAS SPREAD ITS
DARK HAIR

INDIAN YOUTH ASKS ADMITTANCE TO ASB

A 14-year-old blind youth from Simla, India, who has completed all of the training available to him in his native country, is seeking admittance to the Arkansas School for the Blind to further his education. [I was actually fifteen.]

Members of the blind school board at a recent meeting authorized James M. Woolly, school superintendent, to investigate the youth's situation. . . .

In his letter to Mr. Woolly, a letter he typed himself in English, the youth said:

"And there is no more scope in India for my studies as I have gained from St. Dunstan's what they could teach me. Now I have great wish to come over to your school, and hope that you will be kind enough to admit me."

He indicated a desire to complete the full course offered at the Arkansas School and was also interested in university examinations offered at the completion of the course.

—*Little Rock (Ark.) Arkansas Democrat,
February 20, 1949.*

F INALLY, I WAS IN AMERICA. EVER SINCE I could remember, I had been hearing about it from my father, Daddyji, as "God's own country." He had come here from India to continue his medical studies, and now I was here as a student. I'd been trying to come for at least eight years—since I was seven years old. The morning after I arrived, I sat down at a typewriter and wrote a letter home:

544, West
113, Street,
Apt. 4A,
New York 25,
N.Y.
U.S.A.
16th August, 1949

4

My Dearest Daddyjee,

I reached New York yesterday. It was a very long Journey than we expected it to be. It took me 47 hours to get here. Mrs. John di Francesco came to receive me at the aerodrome.

Now I think I better tell you something about my journey. The Journey was quite boring and tiring. I reached London, by London timings, at 9:15 A.M. Cousin Nitya Nand was there to meet me. But the Plane did not stop there for long.

The people who met us at Aerodrome in Delhi and said they would look after me did not even come to me in the plane once, and I never even knew where they were. As a matter of fact. I—whatever I did was by myself.

I just now have had a word on telephone with Mr. Woolly. He wants me at Arkansas School for the Blind as soon as possible. He says the school will open in three weeks time from today. I rang Mr. Woolly because I came to know by Mr. and Mrs. di Francesco that there is lots of Infantile Paralysis going on in Arkansas. But Mr. Woolly has assuredly said that they are better off there than in New York. He left it to me when I wish to come I can come, but he said the sooner the better it is from his point of view. I think I shall leave for Arkansas on the 26th of this month. Mr. and Mrs. di Francesco will be going on six days holidays to Maine from the 27th. They say I am welcome to go with them if I wish to. But I am still thinking. Mr. and Mrs. di Francesco are very nice people.

I shall write you a very long letter as soon as I can get a good typewriter for long time. That I do not hope to get here in New York. Daddyjee I do not like to say anymore

5

what I feel. I am very homesick.

The bag which you bought me with a zip on it which you said will be very useful as a second bag was open on the way by breaking the zip, and all the Ivory things which you presented me were removed except one piece. Some of my clothes were also stolen. It was discovered there and then, at the New York aerodrome that the bag has been broken. It was also examined by the people over there. All the shirts which we kept in that were taken away. And instead of my things there was one hair brush and one shaving creams bottle which was not mine. I gave same back to them. The bag is absolutely spoilt. We have put down a claim for my things. But I do not know whether they will give it or not. The one piece which was left was the salt cellar. Mrs. di Francesco tells me that the price of it here in New York is 12 Dollars. She also seems to seen other ivory pieces in shops over here and she says that they are very very expensive. Only if I have had those to sell I would have made at least one and a half months living expenses in School. I have put down a claim for over One hundred Dollars because they are even more expensive over here.

With love to all and respects.

Your affectionate Son,

Ved

❧

AT the airport in New Delhi, there had been dozens of relatives all around, laughing and clapping. Suddenly, they were embracing me, and there was such a rush and confusion that people embracing me were themselves being embraced. Then Daddyji and I were walking to the Pan American airplane, dirt crunching under our feet. Daddyji fell into conversation with a couple of Sikh passengers walking just ahead of us and found out that they were going to New York on the same airplane. "This is my fifteen-year-old blind son, Ved," he said, introducing me to them. (I have been totally blind since I was four years old, as a result of meningitis.) "He's travelling alone for the first time— you see, he's going to America for his studies. I'd be grateful if you could give him assistance along the way if he needs it." I wanted to hide, out of embarrass- ment, but I had never travelled anywhere alone or gone so far away, and I said nothing.

"Most certainly, most certainly," the two Sikhs said, and clicked their tongues.

We dropped behind. "Son, you must build up your health," Daddyji said. "Ninety-one pounds for a boy five feet five is a very low weight. Even the officer who gave me permission to accompany you to the plane remarked on how thin you look for your age."

I had never been on an airplane before. There were steps going up and up and up. They were so narrow that Daddyji and I had to go single file, and they were tinny and flimsy and shook under us, creating a little storm. Inside, the floor sloped upward, and the ceiling was so low that I had to walk with my head bowed.

"Another thing—you'll have to learn not to be so shy," Daddyji was saying. His voice sounded painfully loud to me through the haze of voices in the plane.

"I'm not shy," I snapped irritably.

At my seat, we embraced quickly, like two Punjabi adults, and he hurried away, leaving me sad at my outburst. I had no idea when we might meet again.

There was a pair of seats on each side of the aisle. My seat was next to a window. I sat strapped in it, wondering how high off the ground I was and whether anyone in my family could see through the window. I tried to smile, as I always did for photographs—which, of course, I couldn't see, but which I would overhear others commenting on.

It was very hot: it was the middle of August, and we had not had any monsoon rains for days.

Daddyji had been gone no more than a few minutes when I heard the hasty rustle of a sari. It was Mamaji. She planted a kiss on my forehead, her face wet with tears. "Let God keep you," she said.

I struggled to unstrap myself, but before I could she was gone. My forehead burned. I had not been kissed since I was a small boy—since I was eight or nine, perhaps.

Almost immediately, the airplane under me roared and trembled. An air hostess who sounded very American came up and said, over my head, "Above you there are two buttons—the red one is for calling me, and the green one is a reading light."

I nodded knowingly. It is just as well she doesn't realize I can't see, I thought. This way, she won't be oversolicitous.

Several times, I thought that we had left the ground, but then the tires bumped along the runway or the plane lurched to a stop. I began to feel that we would never get off. I'd often had the same feeling during the months of preparation for going to America, when I was waiting to complete the required medical tests, to get inoculations, to have my picture and fingerprints taken, and to hear from the various authorities concerned with passport, visa, foreign exchange, and police clearance.

Finally, the airplane paused, then raced along the runway. I held my breath. Then I felt the airplane shaking in the air as it rose like a speeded-up lift cage. The airplane levelled off, but there was no letup in the roar. It all but blocked out my hearing, and I wondered how I would survive it for such a long journey.

In my flight bag I had a Braille copy of "Murder on the Orient Express," by Agatha Christie. At first, I felt awkward about reading Braille in public, but I got bored just sitting, so I took the book out and started it.

"Is that Braille you're reading?" the air hostess asked, bending over me.

I nodded sheepishly.

She sighed and went away.

The rest of the journey is a jumble of disconnected memories. I remember that I felt frightened when we landed in Karachi; all of us in my family were refugees from Pakistan, and I was wary of being in a Muslim country. I fell asleep reading. I had to go hungry for a long time, because I didn't want to confess that I didn't know how to use a knife and fork. We landed in some place, but I didn't catch its name. Everybody got off, and I waited for someone to help me, but no one came— neither the air hostess nor the two Sikhs. We went high up in the air and it got very cold, and I had to breathe very fast. My ears popped repeatedly. They hurt so badly that I thought I would go deaf. We were in Damascus. The man who was cleaning and restocking the plane helped me off and showed me to a restaurant in the airport. The waiter there did not speak English; I had to order food through an interpreter. Luckily, they had Indian food, and I ate my fill with my fingers. In one place, it was sleeting, and the airline people gave us raincoats to walk to a small waiting room, where we had to wait for two hours. We stopped in London. Cousin Nitya Nand had come from Cambridge specially to meet me, but it took so long for me to find someone to take me to a bus, for the bus to take me to Customs, and for the Customs people to clear me to go to the visitors' lounge, where Cousin Nitya Nand was waiting, that we had time only to exchange a few pieces of news before I had to get back on the bus.

After forty-seven hours, we reached New York. It was two o'clock on the afternoon of the fifteenth of August.

AT the airport, I was questioned by an immigration official. "You're blind—totally blind—and they gave you a visa? You say it's for your studies, but studies where?"

"At the Arkansas School for the Blind. It is in Little Rock, in Arkansas."

He shuffled through the pages of a book. Sleep was in my eyes. Drops of sweat were running down my back. My shirt and trousers felt dirty.

"Arkansas School is not on our list of approved schools for foreign students."

"I know," I said. "That is why the immigration officials in Delhi gave me only a visitor's visa. They said that when I got to the school I should tell the authorities to apply to be on your list of approved schools, so that I could get a student visa." I showed him a big manila envelope I was carrying; it contained my chest X-rays, medical reports, and fingerprint charts, which were necessary for a student visa, and which I'd had prepared in advance.

"Why didn't you apply to an approved school in the first place and come here on a proper student visa?" he asked, looking through the material.

My knowledge of English was limited. With difficulty, I explained to him that I had applied to some thirty schools but that, because I had been able to get little formal education in India, the Arkansas School was the only one that would accept me; that I had needed a letter of acceptance from an American school to get dollars sanctioned by the Reserve Bank of India; and that now that I was in America I was sure I could change schools if the Arkansas School was not suitable or did not get the necessary approval.

Muttering to himself, the immigration official looked up at me, down at his book, and up at me again. He finally announced, "I think you'll have to go to Washington and apply to get your visa changed to a student visa before you can go to any school."

I recalled things that Daddyji used to say as we were growing up: "In life, there is only fight or flight. You must always fight," and "America is God's own country. People there are the most hospitable and generous people in the world." I told myself I had nothing to worry about. Then I remembered that Daddyji had mentioned a Mr. and Mrs. Dickens in Washington—they were friends of friends of his—and told me that I could get in touch with them in case of emergency.

"I will do whatever is necessary," I now said to the immigration official. "I will go to Washington."

He hesitated, as if he were thinking something, and then stamped my passport and returned it to me. "We Mehtas carry our luck with us," Daddyji used to say. He is right, I thought.

The immigration official suddenly became helpful, as if he were a friend. "You shouldn't have any trouble with the immigration people in Washington," he said, and asked, "Is anybody meeting you here?"

"Mr. and Mrs. di Francesco," I said.

Mrs. di Francesco was a niece of Manmath Nath Chatterjee, whom Daddyji had known when he himself was a student, in London, in 1920. Daddyji had asked Mr. Chatterjee, who had a Scottish-American wife and was now settled in Yellow Springs, Ohio, if he could suggest anyone with whom I might stay in New York, so that I could get acclimatized to American before proceeding to the Arkansas School, which was not due to open until the eleventh of September. Mr. Chatterjee had written back that, as it happened, his wife's niece was married to John di Francesco, a singer who was totally bind, and that Mr. and Mrs. di Francesco lived in New York, and would be delighted to meet me at the airport and keep me as a paying guest at fifteen dollars a week.

"How greedy of them to ask for money!" I had cried when I learned of the arrangement. "People come and stay with us for months and we never ask for an anna."

Daddyji had said, "In the West, people do not, as a rule, stay with relatives and friends but put up in hotels, or in houses as paying guests. That is the custom there. Mr. and Mrs. di Francesco are probably a young, struggling couple who could do with a little extra money."

The immigration official now came from behind the counter, led me to an open area, and shouted, with increasing volume, "Fransisco! . . . Franchesca! . . . De Franco!" I wasn't sure what the correct pronunciation was, but his shouting sounded really disrespectful. I asked him to call for Mr. and Mrs. di Francesco softly. He bellowed, "Di Fransesco!"

No one came. My mouth went dry. Mr. and Mrs. di Francesco had sent me such a warm invitation. I couldn't imagine why they would have let me down or what I should do next.

Then I heard the footsteps of someone running toward us. "Here I am. You must be Ved. I'm Muriel di Francesco. I'm sorry John couldn't come." I noted that the name was pronounced the way it was spelled, and that hers was a Yankee voice—the kind I had heard when I first encountered Americans at home, during the war—but it had the sweetness of the voices of my sisters.

We shook hands; she had a nice firm grip. I had an impulse to call her Auntie Muriel—at home, an older person was always called by an honorific, like

"Auntie" or "Uncle"—but I greeted her as Daddyji had told me that Westerners liked to be greeted: "Mrs. di Francesco, I'm delighted to make your acquaintance."

❦

"YOU had a terrible trip, you poor boy. What a terrible way to arrive!" Mrs. di Francesco said in the taxi. "Imagine, everything stolen from a bag!"

One bag had contained clothes. The other, a holdall, had contained (in addition to some extra shirts) a number of ivory curios—statues of Lord Krishna, "no evil" monkeys, brooches with a little pattern on them—which Daddyji had bought with the idea that I could sell them at great profit. "You can take the ivory curios to a shop in Little Rock and ask the shop to sell them for you—on commission, of course," he had said. "In America, a lot of people earn and learn. Who knows? Maybe we could start an ivory-export-import business in a year or so, when I retire from government service." He was deputy director general of health services in the Indian government. "I expect there is a great deal of demand over there for hand-carved things." The fact that neither of us had ever sold even a second-hand gramophone didn't stop us from dreaming.

I didn't want Mrs. di Francesco to feel bad, so I made light of the theft. "The other bag is still full," I said.

"The ivory things must have been really valuable," she said. She had helped me fill out the insurance-claim forms. "What a bad introduction to America!"

"But it could have happened in Delhi."

She regaled the taxi-driver with the story, as if she and I were long-standing friends. "And we had to wait at the airport for two whole hours, filling out insurance forms. And he only knew the prices in rubles."

"Rupees," I said.

"Is that right?" the taxi-driver said, from the front seat. "Well, it shouldn't have happened to you, son."

I leaned toward the half-open window and listened for the roar of street crowds, the cries of hawkers, the clatter of tonga wheels, the trot of tonga horses, the crackle of whips, the blasts of Klaxons, the trills of police whistles, the tinkling of bicycle bells—but all I heard was the steady hiss and rush of cars. "In America, you can really travel fast and get places," I said.

Mrs. di Francesco took both my hands in hers and broke into open, unrestrained laughter. I have never heard a woman laugh quite like that, I thought.

"What are you laughing at?" I asked.

"I'd just noticed that all this time you had your hand in your breast pocket. Are you afraid of having your wallet stolen, too?"

I was embarrassed. I hadn't realized what I had been doing.

The taxi-driver took a sharp turn.

"Where are we?" I asked.

"On Broadway," Mrs. di Francesco said.

"Is Broadway a wide road?" I asked.

She laughed. "A very wide avenue—it's the center of the universe."

At home, the center was a circle, but here the center, it seemed, was a straight line. At home, I often felt I was on a merry-go-round, circling activities that I couldn't join in. Here I would travel in taxis amid new friends and have adventures. I tried to voice my thoughts.

"Poor boy, you have difficulty with the language," Mrs. di Francesco said, gently pressing my hand.

"English is difficult," I said, and I tried to make a joke. "When I was small and first learning English, I was always confusing 'chicken' and 'kitchen.' "

" 'Chicken' and 'kitchen,' " Mrs. di Francesco repeated, and laughed.

"I have enough trouble speaking English," the taxi-driver said. "I could never learn to speak Hindu."

"Hindi," I said, correcting him.

"You see?" the taxi-driver said.

Mrs. di Francesco laughed, and the taxi-driver joined in.

After a while, the taxi came to a stop. "Here we are at home, on a Hundred and Thirteenth Street between Broadway and Amsterdam," Mrs. di Francesco said.

Though I was carrying a bank draft for eighty dollars, I had only two dollars in cash, which a family friend had given me for good luck. I handed it to Mrs. di Francesco for the taxi.

"That won't be enough," she said.

"But it is *seven rupees!*" I cried. "At home, one could hire a tonga for a whole day for that."

"This is New York," she said. She clicked open her purse and gave some money to the taxi-driver.

The taxi-driver put my bags on the curb, shook

my hand, and said, "If I go to India, I will remember not to become a tonga driver." He drove away.

We picked up the luggage. Mrs. di Francesco tucked my free hand under her bare arm with a quick motion and started walking. A woman at home would probably have cringed at the touch of a stranger's hand under her arm, I thought, but thinking this did not stop me from making a mental note that the muscle of her arm was well developed.

We went into a house, and walked up to Mr. and Mrs. di Francesco's apartment, on the fourth floor. Mr. di Francesco opened the door and kissed Mrs. di Francesco loudly. Had a bomb exploded, I could not have been more surprised. They'll catch something, I thought. I had never heard any grownups kissing at home—not even in films.

Mr. di Francesco shook my hand. He had a powerful grip and a powerful voice. He took me by the shoulder and almost propelled me to a couch. "This is going to be your bed," he said. "I'm sorry I couldn't come to the airport. Anyway, I knew you wouldn't mind being greeted by a charming lady." He doesn't have a trace of the timid, servile manner of music masters and blind people at home, I thought.

"We had a delightful ride from the airport," I said.

Mr. di Francesco wanted to know why we were so late, and Mrs. di Francesco told him about the theft.

"What bad luck!" he said.

"But I got here," I said.

"That's the spirit," he said, laughing.

"John, thank you for starting dinner," Mrs. di Francesco said from what I took to be the kitchen.

"Oh, you cook!" I exclaimed. I had never heard of a blind person who could cook.

"Yes, I help Muriel," he said. "We don't have servants here, as they do in your country. We have labor-saving devices." He then showed me around the apartment, casually tapping and explaining—or putting my hand on—various unfamiliar things: a stove that did not burn coal or give out smoke; an ice chest that stood on end and ran on electricity; a machine that toasted bread; a bed for two people; and a tub in which one could lie down. I was full of questions, and asked how natural gas from the ground was piped into individual apartments, and how people could have so much hot water that they could lie down in it. At home, a husband and wife never slept in one bed, but I didn't say anything about that, because I felt shy.

"Do you eat meat?" Mrs. di Francesco asked me from the kitchen. "Aunt Rita—Mrs. Chatterjee—didn't know."

"Yes, I do eat meat," I called back to her. I started worrying about how I would cut it.

Mrs. di Francesco sighed with relief. "John and I hoped that you weren't a vegetarian. We're having spaghetti and meatballs, which are made of beef. Is that all right?"

I shuddered. As a Hindu, I had never eaten beef, and the mere thought of it was revolting. But I recalled another of Daddyji's sayings, "When in Rome, do as the Romans do," and said, "I promised my father that I would eat anything and everything in America and gain some weight."

Mrs. di Francesco brought out the dinner and served

it to us at a small table. "The peas are at twelve and the spaghetti and meatballs at six," she said. I must have looked puzzled, because she added, "John locates his food on a plate by the clock dial. I thought all blind people knew—"

"You forget that India has many primitive conditions," Mr. di Francesco interrupted. "Without a doubt, work for the blind there is very backward."

I bridled. "There is nothing primitive or backward in India."

There was a silence, in which I could hear Mr. di Francesco swallowing water. I felt very much alone. I wished I were back home.

"I didn't mean it that way," Mr. di Francesco said.

"I'm sorry," I said, and then, rallying a little, confessed that Braille watches were unheard of in India—that I had first read about them a year or so earlier in a British Braille magazine, and then it had taken me several months to get the foreign exchange and get a Braille pocket watch from Switzerland.

"Then how do blind people there know what time it is—whether it is day or night?" Mr. di Francesco asked.

"They have to ask someone, or learn to tell from the morning and night sounds. I suppose that things *are* a little backward there. That is why I had to leave my family and come here for education."

"The food is getting cold," Mrs. di Francesco said.

I picked up my fork and knife with trembling fingers and aimed for six. I suddenly wanted to cry.

"You look homesick," Mrs. di Francesco said.

I nodded, and tried to eat. A sense of relief engulfed

me: we had mutton meatballs at home all the time, and they didn't require a knife. But the relief was short-lived: I had never had spaghetti, and the strands were long and tended to bunch together. They stretched from my mouth to my plate—a sign of my Indian backwardness, I thought. I longed for the kedgeree at home, easily managed with a spoon.

Mrs. di Francesco reached over and showed me how to wrap the spaghetti around my fork, shake it, and pick it up. Even so, I took big bites when I thought that Mrs. di Francesco was not looking—when she was talking to Mr. di Francesco. Later in the meal, it occurred to me that I was eating the food Daddyji had eaten when he was a student abroad. I resolutely bent my face over the plate and started eating in earnest.

Mrs. di Francesco took away our plates and served us something else, and I reached for my spoon.

"That's eaten with a fork," she said.

I attacked it with a fork. "It is a pudding with a crust!" I cried. "I have never eaten anything like it."

"It's not a pudding—it's apple pie," Mrs. di Francesco said. "By the way, we're having scrambled eggs for breakfast. Is that all right?"

I confessed that I didn't know what they were, and she described them to me.

"Oh, I know—rumble-tumble eggs!" I exclaimed. "I like them very much."

They both laughed. "British— Indian English is really much nicer than American English," Mr. di Francesco said. "You should keep it. In fact, I'll adopt 'rumble-tumble.' "

I felt sad that I had come to America for my studies

instead of going to England first, as Daddyji had done. But no school in England had accepted me.

"We've heard so much about India from Uncle Manmath," Mrs. di Francesco said. "It must be a very exciting place."

"Yes, tell us about India," Mr. di Francesco said.

I felt confused. I couldn't think of what to say or how to say it.

"You look tired," Mrs. di Francesco said, patting me on the arm.

"I cannot think of the right English words sometimes," I said.

Mrs. di Francesco cleared some things off the table and said, "Don't worry. Now that you're here, your English will improve quickly."

She went to the kitchen and started washing the plates while Mr. di Francesco and I lingered at the table—much as we might at home.

I asked Mr. di Francesco how he had become self-supporting and independent, with a place of his own.

"You make it sound so romantic, but it's really very simple," he said. He spoke in a matter-of-fact way. "I spent twelve years at the Perkins Institution for the Blind, in Massachusetts. I entered when I was seven, and left when I was nineteen."

"Perkins!" I cried. "I have been trying to go there since I was seven. First, they would not have me because of the war. But after the war they would not have me, either—they said that I would end up a 'cultural misfit.' "

"What does that mean?"

"They said that bringing Eastern people to the West

at a young age leads to 'cultural maladjustment'—and they said, 'Blindness is a maladjustment in itself.' "

"But now you're here. I'll call Perkins tomorrow and tell them that the damage is already done, and that your cultural maladjustment would be much worse if you were to end up in Arkansas." He laughed.

"Do you really think they will take me? Dr. Farrell, the director at Perkins, is a very stubborn man."

"They certainly should. Unlike Massachusetts, Arkansas is a very poor state. Arkansas School for the Blind is a state school. They are required to accept all the blind children in the state free of charge. In fact, you'll probably be the only one there paying for board and tuition. The school is bound to have a lot of riff-raff. It's no place to improve your English. In Arkansas, you'll lose all your nice Britishisms and acquire a terrible Southern drawl. You have to go to Perkins. I know Dr. Farrell."

I was excited. "Perkins is said to be the best school for the blind anywhere. How did you like it? How was your life there?"

"Life at Perkins? It was probably no different from that of millions of other kids. We played and studied." He added obligingly, "It was a lot of fun."

Fun—so that's what it was, I thought. That is the difference between all the things he did at school and all the things I missed out on by not going to a good school.

"And after Perkins?"

"After Perkins, I studied voice at the New England Conservatory, where Muriel and I met. Then I came to New York, started giving voice lessons, married Muriel, and here I am."

"There must be more to tell."

"There really isn't."

"Did Mrs. di Francesco's parents not object? She is sighted."

"I wasn't asking to marry Muriel's parents. She could do what she pleased. This is America."

❧

JUST before leaving for America, I had sat alone with Daddyji in New Delhi, and he had talked to me about girls and marriage. His tone was compassionate but frank. "You are old enough so that, whether you want to or not, you will think about girls."

"I won't," I said, disingenuously.

"Don't be shy—it is biological. I wanted to bring up the subject because who knows when we'll get another chance to talk?" He fumbled for words, and then abruptly asked, "Do you think you might marry a Westerner?"

I was stunned. I was one of seven children. Pom, Nimi, Umi, and Usha, my sisters, and Om and Ashok, my brothers, all had normal eyesight. The question of their marrying a Westerner didn't even arise. They were expected to marry and settle in and around the Punjab, where we had all grown up. I alone was being asked to think about such a prospect—one that was extremely upsetting, for I, along with them, had grown up hearing Daddyji tell us that the last thing Bhabiji (his mother) had said to him when he was going away to England for *his* studies was "Don't come back with a memsahib." He used to ask us, "Can you imagine what would have happened if I had brought back a memsahib? She would have called Bhabiji 'Mrs. Mehta' and refused to touch her feet. No European can fit into our cultural pattern. In our culture, happiness in marriage can be found only within one's own caste, within one's own subcaste, within one's own group." I had completely accepted his point of view. So much so that when my big sisters argued with it—saying, for instance, that they would rather marry an Untouchable and help break down the caste barriers, as Gandhi taught—I would fight with them.

Daddyji repeated the question. "Do you think you might marry a Westerner?"

"Of course not!" I said.

Daddyji continued—now talking quickly. "I've been thinking about the whole question in respect to your particular situation, and I must confess that in your case I think you might be better off marrying a Western girl, a nice Christian girl. Oh, you could get married here, all right, but not in our caste group and education group, and therefore not well, not happily. India is a harsh land. Marriage here is like a business transaction, and parents weigh and measure their children's liabilities and assets carefully. Because of your blindness, no parents in our education group would give their girl to you."

I felt at once angry, impatient, shy, and embarrassed. I didn't want him to be talking to me about such things. I didn't want to be asked to think about such things. But I told myself that he was only doing his duty by me, that he was only talking sense. Still, I continued to feel angry and embarrassed. I was tired of trying to be sensible. I felt that I had had to learn to be sensible ever since I could remember. I would feel that I was like everyone else, but then I would have to try to be sensible, because I would realize that if I acted like everyone else—for example, went out on the road by myself—there would be terrible consequences.

"Christians in the West are very different from our Indian Christians, who have a chip on their shoulder," Daddyji was saying. "A Western Christian girl might make you a much better wife than a Hindu girl would, because Christians are taught love and compassion, while we Hindus are taught only fate and duty. That's why even Indian Christian girls make so much better nurses than Hindu girls do. I know this because I've observed them again and again in hospitals. A Western Christian girl would be sympathetic to your blindness in a way that a Hindu girl could never be."

I stopped listening. I felt I was being lectured to. But then I remembered that it was Daddyji, that I was going away, that I might not see him again for a long time, and I made an effort to concentrate on what he was saying.

"In a Western marriage, there is the possibility of intellectual companionship of equals—something that doesn't exist in an Indian marriage at all. Once you've seen that kind of marriage, you may want a companion equal to yourself, even if that means staying in the West. You see, in the West marriage is made on the basis of romantic love, by the two people involved, without the intervention of a third party—of the parents."

"I'll never stay in the West," I said. "I'm definitely going to come back. My duty and wish to serve will always call me back here. After all, this is where you all are, this is where I belong."

"That's the only way to feel, but yours is one case in which I wouldn't rule out settling in the West."

I felt confused; he seemed to be giving me so many contradictory messages. "I must confess that when I think of your children I think that a Western girl may not be a good idea." He always presented the other side. That was his nature. But children! The very thought of my having children—duplicating myself, as it were—was repugnant. We had grown up hearing Daddyji talk about Romesh Chachaji (one of his younger brothers), who had married for love, taking an Indian Christian for a wife: what grief his marriage had given to Bhabiji; how his wife hadn't fitted in; and how different his children were from my sisters and brothers and our other first cousins, who were all of the same caste and the same religion. And, of course, Romesh Chachaji's wife was an Indian. How much worse for the family and for the children, I used to think, if, in addition, she had been a foreigner—an Englishwoman, never mind an American.

I remembered that a few weeks before this conversion about girls and marriage Daddyji had heard Sister Umi, who was nineteen years old—supposedly the ideal marriageable age for a Punjabi girl—teasing me about starting an American Mehta family. He had taken me aside. "I have seen a lot of mixed marriages of English people and Indians," he had said. "The children—Anglo-Indians, as they're called—belonged neither here nor over there. It's unfair, perhaps, but that's the way things are. They're ashamed of their Indian parent, whom they consider a 'blackie.' But the English, for their part, consider the Anglo-Indians themselves to be 'blackies.' Yet Anglo-Indians consider themselves white and speak of England as home—England, to which they have never been and may never go. The truth is they have no home, no land they can call their own. I— I would remain a bachelor before I would father such a lot." He had added reflectively, "In India, at least. It hurts me to say this, because I have never believed in the nonsense of superiority of races. I have always believed in one world." Then he seemed to have further second thoughts about what he had said. "Of course, when I speak of Anglo-Indians I am speaking of the most degenerate of them. Even they are more to be pitied than despised. And, again, I suppose that once in a while—here or over there—you will meet an Anglo-Indian who is well assimilated. And in the melting pot of America the problem of the Anglo-Indian may not exist at all. The whole culture is composed of mixed marriages and mixed children."

Daddyji was now saying, "Fifteen is young, very young, to be going to a totally different culture thousands of miles away." He was silent for a moment or so, as if to underline the gravity of what he was about to say. "Marriage is, I believe, crucial to a full and rich life for anyone, and perhaps even more so in your case. So far, you have lived through the eyes of our family.

I am fifty-four—old for an Indian. My death and the marriage of your sisters and brothers will change things for you. You can't count on any of us being around to help you live your life fully. I am going to sound cruel, but it is only to impress upon you the reality of your situation. In India, trying to marry you would be like trying to marry Om without his face." Brother Om, who was eighteen, was the oldest of us brothers and therefore, by rights, the first to be married. "I bring this terrifying image to mind because I want you to understand how important most people think that eyes are in any kind of relationship. People think that men and women fall in love and make love with their eyes. I myself don't believe this. I don't believe that blindness cripples a man sexually."

THE two awkward but momentous conversations that I'd had with Daddyji before leaving home had wound a tightly coiled spring inside me, and it was suddenly released on my first day in New York, in Mr. and Mrs. di Francesco's apartment. The image of faceless Brother Om—or, rather, me—came up the moment Mr. di Francesco started talking about his marriage.

"There must be more to tell about your marriage," I said.

Mr. di Francesco laughed, and said, "There's really nothing more. Except, that is, that ours is one of those stories where the couple lives happily ever after."

"But how did you get to know each other?"

"Well, I asked her out, and things happened."

"Just like that?"

"Of course. We've been married two years. She is of Scottish parentage, I am of Italian. But in New York no one cares about things like that. It's a city of immigrants."

"But how did you come to New York?"

"Toward the end of my course of study at the Conservatory, I went to hear Ezio Pinza in Boston—he's a famous opera singer. I managed to get him to hear me sing. He was impressed. He brought me to New York and paid for my lessons for a year."

"Just like that?"

"Oh, yes. He launched me on my career, and who is to say? I may one day realize my ambition to sing at the Metropolitan Opera with him. I already have my own radio program."

"Then I can listen to you on the radio in Arkansas."

"Heavens, no. It's just a little weekly fifteen-minute program on a local radio station. But I do have a small orchestra to accompany me."

There was a knock at the door. Mr. di Francesco opened it.

"Hello, darling," Mr. di Francesco said. Then came the explosion of a kiss.

I had heard "darling" only in films, and I imagined that the newcomer must be an actress. But Mr. di Francesco was saying, "This is Jean, my accompanist. She lives next door to us, with her mother. It couldn't be more convenient." Jean shook hands with me and immediately went into the kitchen to talk to Mrs. di Francesco.

Some time later, Mr. di Francesco asked Jean to play for me. I waited, thinking that, as at home, she would make a thousand excuses and he would cajole and entreat her, but she immediately walked over to the piano and started playing. Her piano playing sounded sweeter than any Western music I had heard at Daddyji's clubs, and I had barely got used to the idea of her playing without any fuss when Mr. di Francesco walked over to the piano and started singing. His voice was unlike any I had ever heard. It filled the apartment, almost making the walls shake and the curtains flutter. His voice—he was a baritone—came not from the throat, as at home, but from somewhere deep in the chest. Six of our masterjis singing could not have made that big a sound, I thought. Compared with his chesty singing, ours is merely a throat-clearing. And he doesn't sing while sitting on the floor, as we do, but standing up—like a man, I thought.

"Could you tell what I was singing?" he asked me when he finished.

"No, I cannot follow English when it is sung."

Mr. di Francesco and Jean laughed. "That wasn't English, that was Italian," Jean said.

"I was singing an aria from the opera in which Caruso made his London début," Mr. di Francesco said. "Caruso was famous all over the world as a tenor. You must have heard of him."

I have been brought up with talk of England, America, and Italy all my life, I thought; Daddyji hardly ever sat down at table without mentioning his student days in the West. I admitted to Mr. di Francesco that I had never heard of Caruso, that I didn't know what a tenor was, or, indeed, what an opera was, exactly. I felt ignorant and ashamed of my lack of schooling, so I boasted about my sisters' education. "My sisters studied in convent schools. I'm sure they know all about tenors and operas."

"Do you know any Indian music?" Jean asked. She had a bubbly manner and seemed to take no notice of my embarrassment.

"I studied singing for some time," I said.

"We'd love to hear you sing," Mrs. di Francesco said, joining us.

I made some hurried excuses about needing a tabla and harmonium and about feeling tired. "I have some Indian records with me," I said. "Would you like to hear one of them?"

"Oh, yes, let's," Mrs. di Francesco said.

I opened my suitcase on the floor and got out a box of perhaps thirty 78-r.p.m. records I had brought along. I took out one record at random, and Mr. di Francesco put it on a radio-phonograph combination beside the piano. A chorus of women sang, in Urdu:

> The cloud has spread its dark hair,
> The cicada has started chirping,
> The cricket plays music,
> The koel sings,
> And the dew comes to have watery eyes.

I wanted to cry. The music sounded so homelike— it suddenly made the apartment seem very foreign.

"They sound like children," Mr. di Francesco said. "Is it a children's song?"

"It is women singing about spring," I said.

"It's very unusual," he said.

Years later, Mr. di Francesco told me, "Frankly, we were all in awe of you. I don't know what I'd expected, but you didn't seem like a fifteen-year-old. You had the maturity and self-confidence of someone much older. You seemed well educated—you had a deep sense of culture. You see, fifteen-year-olds here are animals. You seemed to us more like twenty or twenty-five." But on that early day in America I felt inferior and stupid, filled with awe of America, of New York, of the Americans in the apartment—of the married blind man.

That evening, I lay awake on the couch for a long time. I had never been a paying guest. I had never been alone with Yankees. I remembered that I had eaten beef, and felt sick to my stomach. At some point, someone was whispering something—I thought I was hearing things, but it was Mrs. di Francesco whispering to me. "I don't know whether you have refrigerators or not, but ours makes a horrible noise all through the night. I hope you won't mind."

"Not at all, Mrs. di Francesco," I said, turning my face up to her.

"Oh, I meant to tell you—please call me Muriel." She walked away, with a light step.

❧

IN the morning, I asked John (as he had asked me to call him), "Do you play chess? I have a special chess set for the blind with me."

"I don't know the game, but I've always wanted to learn it," he said. "How did you learn it?"

"I was taught it at school when I was a child." I got out my set and put it on a card table between us. I ran his forefinger over the raised and sunken (black and white) squares on the board and showed him the various pieces, explaining their moves and their functions. I've never taught anything to anyone before, and here I am teaching an American, I thought. I was thrilled. I could scarcely control my eagerness.

There was a knock at the door, and Jean came in. "I just heard on the radio that the polio epidemic is really bad in Little Rock," she said. "It's much worse than here."

"What is polio?" I asked. "I have never heard of that epidemic."

"You must have it in India, but know it by a different name," John said. "It's also known as infantile paralysis. It's a spinal disease, a little like meningitis. People who catch it lose the use of their arms, legs, back—whatever. They lose muscle power and sensation. Sometimes they can't walk, or even sit up."

"I have never heard of it," I said, feeling increasingly uneasy. "How do you get it?"

"No one knows, but it's quite a common disease here—especially in summer," he said. "Usually, children get it from other children at school."

I began trembling. My right leg went numb. I pinched it hard, and realized that it was only pins and needles, but I asked John to get Mr. Woolly on the telephone for me, so that I could find out if people were getting polio at his school. To my surprise, I was speaking to him immediately; a trunk call took hours at home.

"What did you say? Polio? Can't say that I've heard of anyone getting it at our school."

"Are you sure?"

"As sure as can be, son. No reason to be afraid. We're expecting you at the end of next week. You'd better get on over here, as planned. You'll need all the time you have to get used to our setup." He talked in this vein for some time. He sounded very fatherly, and I felt somewhat reassured.

❧

JOHN and Muriel introduced me to something called macaroni, which I could almost whistle through; to sausages that came in buns with all kinds of relishes; to trains that hurtled through caves; to staircases that moved up and down by themselves; to the tallest building in the world, which an airplane had run into; to a beach that had a long pavement made of wood; to an airplane in an amusement park that was yanked up so fast that my stomach almost got left behind, and dropped down so violently that it almost snapped my head off.

John telephoned Dr. Farrell, of Perkins, and Dr. Farrell promised to reconsider his decision. John also took me to meet Dr. Milton Stauffer, general secretary of the John Milton Society for the Blind, which gave financial assistance to various church-related schools overseas and to blind students who were intending to go into work for the blind in their home countries.

Dr. Stauffer said that he would try to arrange a scholarship for me, but only if Dr. Farrell would accept me in his school. Then Dr. Farrell called John back and said no, Perkins was full for the year. He concluded, echoing an old theme, sounded by other authorities in other schools, "I cannot in good conscience admit him, feeling, as I do, that bringing blind youngsters to this country at such an early age is a mistake. It leads to cultural maladjustment and compounds the maladjustment of blindness."

I had to go to Arkansas. I will just have to try to transfer to a better school from there, I thought.

John and Muriel had planned an August holiday in Maine, and they invited me to come with them.

"In Maine, we'll teach you how to swim in the sea," Muriel said. "You're not afraid of the water, are you?"

"Not at all. I have been in swimming tanks a number of times, but no one taught me to swim."

"Perhaps he'd enjoy being on a sailboat even more than swimming," Muriel said.

"I'm sure you would also enjoy sailing and fishing in Maine," John said. "Every time I get in a boat, hoist the sails, feel the rope in my hand, or lower a line, hook a fish, and feel its weight on the rod, I feel alive in a way that I never do in the city."

I didn't know exactly what a sail was, exactly what a rope was doing on a boat. The only boat I had ever been in was a rowboat, on the Punjab canals, and the only fish I had ever touched was a goldfish in a trough in the compound of our government house. But I pictured Maine as a big, exciting place: as a marvellous sea, as a marvellous hill station, as a place where I would feel independent, happy, and in command—a vast private compound for riding a bicycle. I would have given anything to go to Maine with John and Muriel, but I had to proceed to Arkansas, because Mr. Woolly insisted that I fly there at the end of my stay in New York.

II

LAND OF OPPORTUNITY

INDIAN YOUTH SELECTS ARKANSAS FOR EDUCATION

Without eyes to see the wonderful sights unfolding before him, a 14-year-old youth has come from New Delhi, India, to receive his education in Arkansas. He has arrived at the Arkansas School for the Blind here. . . .

As he prepares for school at the blind institution, he is undaunted, though just a trifle homesick.

This young man is Ved Parkash Mehle [sic], the son of a deputy director of health services in India. . . . He understands English—spoken correctly. Slurred phrases have to be repeated. . . .

When J. M. Woolly, head of the blind school, introduced Ved yesterday afternoon, Ved stood up

quickly and extended his hand in a warm welcome. But Ved did not smile, because he was in
a strange place and without eyes to see it. He had
been promised something, but all he found was an
empty building being prepared for the fall season.

"He's a little homesick," explained Mr. Woolly,
"but he'll get over that eventually."

Ved was still dressed in his Indian attire—
almost Western—but not quite. He will soon dress
as do others in Little Rock. . . .

The officials are going to see that he gets every
opportunity. Because there are international relations involved? No, because a young boy decided
to come thousands of miles to Arkansas for these
opportunities.

—*Arkansas Democrat, August 29, 1949.*

T HERE IS A HIGH—A VERY HIGH—FENCE.
There are sheep—endless lines of them. A sheep
jumps over the fence. The fence grows higher.
It's my turn. The fence is a mountain. The
sheep are staring at me. "Thank the Lord he
can't see. He doesn't know how high the fence
is." "He'll never make it, I tell you, he'll never make
it. Baa-aa." "Baa-aa-aa." *Baa, baa, black sheep.* Falling,
turning, trying to hold on to something. Falling, rolling. Nothing. Empty space. Boys having tiffin on a
cold floor. Abdul pulls at my knickers: "Shoes, you
spilled my tea! If I had a knife, I would cut off your
leg." "Sorry. It's so crowded." He's pouring tea down

my sock! He's burning me. I pull at his hair. "I'll teach you to pull big boys' hair." Daddyji: "Always 'I *shall*,' never 'I *will*.' 'Shall' means determination."

I woke with a start. I was clutching my bed. My sheets were damp with sweat. Why had I been dreaming about tiffin at Dadar School for the Blind in Bombay, where I had been sent when I was not yet five, and which I had last attended more than six years ago? I was now grown up and in America. The wretched school in Bombay couldn't touch me now. But was this school going to be much different?

I consulted my Braille watch. It was only twelve-thirty. I couldn't have been asleep more than half an hour. I must not go back to sleep, I thought, or I'll have terrible dreams. I shall stay awake. It was my first night in Little Rock, where I had arrived after spending a couple of days in Washington with Mr. and Mrs. Dickens, filing papers to try to get my visitor's visa changed to a student visa. I was alone upstairs in the older boys' sleeping hall at the Arkansas School for the Blind—a long room with thirty identical iron beds, all but mine empty. The students weren't expected for two and a half weeks. In fact, it seemed that Mr. Woolly and his family and the night watchman were the only other people in the building. I could have been in Maine, with the di Francescos, I thought. Why had Mr. Woolly made me come so early? He said he wanted me to familiarize myself with my surroundings. But how long did he think it would take someone to learn his way around the school—essentially, one simple building? Any blind person could master it in a matter of minutes. (Years later, Mr. Woolly explained, "We were all eager to meet you. We didn't know you from Adam. I'm still wondering at my brashness at having told you to come on over from India. I thought if you arrived two or three weeks before school opened, you could get used to us and we could get used to you.")

A few hours before I went to bed that first night, a longtime student at the school, a boy I'll call Wayne Tidman, had taken me around. As we walked up the circular school drive in the rain—the school was set on a hillside just to the north of a busy street called West Markham—Wayne had told me, "I live in Little Rock. I'm the only boy from the school in town now. That's why Mr. Woolly recruited me to show you around. I didn't use to live in Little Rock, but then my mother got a divorce." Wayne spoke fast, in a nasal voice, and I had to strain to follow him.

"What's a divorce?"

"You don't know what a divorce is? How old are you?"

"Fifteen."

Wayne explained a divorce to me with obvious condescension, as if he thought I had come from a really strange, backward place.

"I don't think we have it in India," I said. Then I asked, "But where is your father?"

"I don't know—I never see him."

It was my turn to feel superior.

"We're the same size, but you're much skinnier than I am, because you come from a poor country," Wayne said.

I didn't like his calling my country poor, but, of

course, he was right. So I contented myself with saying, "I think you're older than I am."

"Only a year."

We climbed some steps onto the school's front
porch.

"By the way, how did you go blind?" Wayne asked.

"From meningitis, when I was very small. And
you?"

"I'm not blind, the way you are. I have nystag-
mus." I didn't know what that was, but I didn't dare
ask.

We were now at the front door of the school. I
asked him about the building.

"The building? It was built just before the war."

"How are y'all doing?" Mr. Woolly said, coming
out of the school. "Son, what are you finding out?"

"He was asking about the building," Wayne said.

"Well, it's a typical red brick building, the kind
we have in these parts," he said, and he explained to
me, as Daddyji might, that the building was very
symmetrical. There was a three-story central section,
topped with a little clock tower, and recessed two-
story wings, which had their own smaller porches.

Wayne and I went into the central section. Opening off a central corridor that ran the length of the
section were the office (Mr. Woolly's room and an
adjoining outer room), a reception room, the auditorium, and a half-dozen classrooms for the elementary
school and the junior and senior high school. There
was a boys' staircase and a girls' staircase. Upstairs were
a library, a music conservatory, and Mr. Woolly's living quarters. Downstairs, in the basement, were the

faculty and student dining rooms and the kitchen. The west wing was built on a slightly lower level than the central corridor, and one had to go down three or four steps to get to it. At the foot of the steps, one came to a little solarium, and beyond that, along a hall, were a playroom and sleeping quarters for the little boys, and common rooms for the middle-sized boys; at the end of the hall were a lounge and, alongside it, through a swinging door, a locker room for the older boys. Upstairs were the sleeping halls for the middle-sized and older boys. A similar pattern was repeated in the east wing, which housed the girls' dormitories. Scattered through the building were single rooms for faculty members and staff.

"Is this the whole school?" I asked Wayne at one point in the tour.

"No," Wayne said, and he took me out a side door of the lounge and up a little incline to the back drive, beyond which were four little buildings, set back like a row of servants' quarters at home. On the left was the industrial-arts building, called the Shop. Next to it was the gymnasium. Next to that was the school infirmary. And on the right was a residence for junior and senior girls, called the Home Economics Cottage, where they were taught cooking, sewing, and housekeeping.

"The main building and the Cottage are so well designed that everyone in the school fits into them," Wayne was saying.

"How big is the school, then?"

"There are more than a hundred students and twenty staff members."

At home, we had worried whether the school I was going to might be for Negroes. But it seemed that there was no way to find out from that distance without risking bad feelings and jeopardizing my admission. We had reasoned that if the school turned out to be for Negroes—and so perhaps unsuitably poor for me—I could always change schools once I was in America. I now asked Wayne, "Is this school for Negroes or for whites? What color are you?"

Wayne didn't answer, and I was afraid that I had offended him. Suddenly, he said, his voice coming out almost in an angry spit, "White, you fool! What do you think?"

I was relieved, even though I worried that I might have made an enemy of my very first American school friend.

"You ain't white, you know," Wayne said after a while.

"My people are not dark-skinned, like the Dravidians, in South India," I said. "We're fair-skinned Aryans—we come from the North."

"I don't know about all that. Here you're just white or not white, and I can see that you ain't white. You can't fool me." Wayne walked me back to the boys' dormitory and left abruptly, saying, "I'm going home for supper now. I guess they fed you on the plane."

I had had only a light lunch on the plane, but I wasn't hungry. I wandered all around the older boys' section, exploring and touching everything. In the lounge were a battered wooden sofa and armchairs with shabby cushions on them. In the locker room were a long bench bolted to the floor and, on either side of it, two rows of lockers; at one end were a window and a radiator, at the other end two sinks. Beyond the sinks was the bathroom. I went out into the lounge and back into the locker room. I counted the lockers. There were thirty of them. I went out into the lounge again. Rattling around in the silence, I felt utterly alone. Then I heard someone typing in the distance. It took me a few seconds to locate the sound—it was coming from the office. I felt reassured, knowing that there was someone nearby. I went upstairs to the older boys' sleeping hall. I counted the iron bedsteads, and examined the rush-bottomed straight chairs that stood next to them. The chairs were as identical as the beds. Only one bed, near the door, was made up—it was for me.

I took off my shirt and trousers, put them on my chair, and lay down, wondering what the place would be like with thirty boys sleeping or milling around. Would I get on with them? Would they all be like Wayne—prickly and opinionated? What would they make of me?

The sleeping hall was as still as the inside of a cave. There was not so much as the rustling of a tree outside. I cleared my throat. The place felt hot and close. August in Arkansas is as bad as August in New Delhi, I thought, and there are no ceiling or table fans here.

I got up and tried to open the window at the head of my bed, but I couldn't budge it. I went back to bed. My heart began to beat faster. I'm going to get polio, I thought. I'm going to die in Arkansas. Everyone at home will cry when my body comes back on the airplane. I fell asleep. It was then that I dreamed my dream of sheep and tiffin at the school for the blind in Bombay.

When I had been awake for just a few minutes, and was still under the spell of the dream, I was startled by a noise. *Hrrr-rrr-rrr.* I couldn't make out what it was, but the sound only made the building seem hollower and more deserted. It stopped as unexpectedly as it had started. It will begin again, I thought. These must be the old ghosts from the Bombay school. They have followed me here to trip me up and torment me in America.

There was a loud rattle, as if someone were shaking the building. For a moment, I couldn't move, but then I felt that if I waited another moment I wouldn't be able to get up at all.

I sprang out of bed, slipped on my clothes, and ran downstairs, barefoot, shouting, "Who is it? . . . Anyone there? . . . Say something!"

My words echoed along the hall. I listened. Now the rattling was a hammering. I couldn't tell where the sound was coming from. It seemed to be coming from every corner at once. Then the hammering suddenly died down.

"Mr. Woolly! Mr. Woolly!" I cried, running along the central corridor.

Footsteps started from the girls' side of the building. Someone was hurriedly shuffling toward me. "Oh, it's you, the new boy from India." The voice was breathless and weak, like that of a feeble elderly man. I felt a trembling hand on my shoulder. "I'm the night watchman. What's the matter, sonny? Are you homesick?"

"That banging, that hammering!"

"Oh, that." The night watchman laughed. "Them are the steampipes. They were working on them today.

They must have left the boiler valve open, or something. The noise was coming from the steampipes, all right."

I'd never heard of steampipes; I didn't know what a boiler was for. But the idea of steam in the middle of a hot summer night seemed preposterous. I felt angry at Mr. Woolly for insisting that I come to school before the other students. I hated being alone in the boys' dormitory. I wanted to go home.

"Leave me alone!" I cried petulantly to the night watchman.

The night watchman took his hand off my shoulder and started walking away. I listened to his retreating shuffle down the central corridor. I wanted to run after him and apologize. I wished that I could ask him to come and sit at my bedside, as the servants did at home. But I stayed fixed to the spot, terrified of being left alone and yet unable to do anything about it.

I felt dizzy from the steamy heat. I had to have some air. I went to the lounge, where, I remembered, there was a side door. It was locked, but I managed to get it open. I walked out onto a little terrace and down some steps, and started going around the school building—now on a path, now on a stretch of grass—stepping carefully with my bare feet, following the walls with my facial vision, which is the ability of some blind people to perceive objects and terrain as sound-shadows by means of echoing sound and changes of air pressure around the ears. As I walked, I felt with my toes for clay flowerpots or projecting pipes or taps, which at home loomed out of the ground like so many malevolent shin bruisers. But the path was clear. It took me hardly ten minutes to circle the building. I strolled across to a wooded area behind the gymnasium. The ground was piled thick with a layer of wet leaves over a lot of dry leaves, which crackled under my feet. I found a flat stretch and lay down, thinking that it was cooler—and perhaps safer—outside than inside the eerie building. I arranged the prickly leaves under me and made myself comfortable. I fell asleep.

The sounds of birds woke me up. I felt a little cold and tried to get back into the building, but the lounge door had locked behind me. I went to the front door and boldly walked in.

The night watchman was sitting in the office. "Taking the air, sonny?" he asked kindly.

"That's right."

"You fall down, or something? Them are a lot of leaves you got stuck to your back." He came over and brushed off my back.

"Don't tell anyone that I was up—that I was out-side."

"What you say? I don't see nothing. It's gettin' to be five-thirty. It's time for me to go off duty. You be all right?"

"Yes," I said, and I marched through the central corridor.

August 29, 1949

DEAR DR. MEHTA:

Ved arrived yesterday from Washington. I was indeed sorry to hear of his loss and want you to call on me if I can be of any help in presenting his claim to the Airlines.

He seems to be a very fine lad and I am sure will apply himself to his work here. He is at the moment somewhat homesick, but that is natural. Although school does not open until September 11, I think this time will be very valuable in getting acquainted with the school and the city. As I am writing you, a young man of Ved's age and grade level is visiting with him and showing him around. The young man is a pupil here and lives in Little Rock. He will spend a great deal of time with Ved during the next two weeks.

Ved tells me he hasn't much money on account of unforeseen expenses in New York. Do not worry about it. If he needs money I will see that he has it until your bank draft arrives.

We will look into the typewriter situation and buy one whoesale for him if he wants it. [Daddyji had requested Mr. Woolly to help me get a typewriter.] However, we furnish them in the dormitories for pupil use.

In closing, I want to say again that we will look after him as if he were our own son, and we do have two of our own. I hope his mother will not be too anxious about him, nor worry about his welfare.

With personal regards, I am,

Sincerely yours,

J. M. Woolly

2 September, 1949

MY DEAR MR. WOOLLY,

I am grateful for your letter of the 29th August just received. I am glad to learn that Ved has reached Little

Rock and that your first impressions of the boy are as I had expected.

As regards how to utilize the funds for the education of Ved, you are the very best judge to decide. All I can say is that since the Partition of India, we have lost all and have to make the two ends meet from my salary, which I shall continue to get for another year before I am retired compulsorily, and, being on a non-pensionable post, I shall have to find some appointment to keep the wolf away from the door. But at the same time, I may assure you that I shall see that Ved's education does not suffer on any account, and my ambition is to make him a self-supporting citizen of the world. Your assurance that Ved will be treated like your own son has put the mind of his mother, myself, and the family entirely at ease and I cannot find words to thank you adequately for this generous offer.

I know Ved would like to have a portable typewriter of his own, as he is a very good correspondent indeed, and I shall be grateful if you buy him one as soon as the draft for 520 dollars is received by you.

With kindest regards, I remain,

Yours sincerely,

A. R. Mehta

III

GET IN THE HOLE, BUCK

ALL WORK AND NO PLAY

School is out. It's three-fifteen.
Oh, no, my friend, you still must sing.
Oh well, so what? It's only four,
And now we're free to hit the door.
Now, just a minute! Remember band.
From four to five we must demand.
Oh, my! There's wrestling until six.
(Of all the mean and dirty tricks!)
The evening now has waned away.
I guess I'll have to wait for play.

—*Kenneth Bruton, a schoolmate.*

T HE HOUR BELL IN THE CLOCK TOWER CLANGED six times on the morning of the first day of classes. "The wakeup bells are calling you, gents. It's time to face the world." It was the supervisor of the big boys, a man I'll call Mr. Warren Clay, addressing us from the door of the sleeping hall. He was an old man with a slow, almost mocking way of speaking. "Ding-dong, ding-dong. Hear that church music? Hit the road, boys! Yea, Lord, ain't no justice. But hear those birds chirping outside? The world ain't all cruel, as long as there's church music in it."

"You mean *chirp* music," George McNabb said, from his bed, on the far side of the sleeping hall. Since childhood, he had had something wrong with his sinuses, which made his voice come out in a flat, nasal whine. Although he was twenty-one, he sounded almost as old as Mr. Clay.

"Rise up, men, God damn your hide!" Mr. Clay said. He was addicted to strong language, and the boys said that it was because he was a lifelong bachelor and a retired railroad man. "The cook is cooking ham and eggs, and is going to serve you a big glass of orange juice, and Wheaties, too. Come on, champions, curry that mule. Tickle that tiger—don't let him get away!"

"We ain't never had ham and eggs," Kenneth Bruton said, from his bed. He was seventeen, but he had the high-pitched voice of a child.

"Mind your trap, Bruton," Mr. Clay said sharply— Bruton often got under his skin, for no reason we could determine—and then he said in his normal, relaxed way, "There ain't no justice."

Oather Brown, who was eighteen and, like McNabb and Bruton, was in the tenth grade, turned over in his bed, ostentatiously rustling his bedclothes, and snored loudly. There was a round of mimicking snores from several beds.

"Yea, Lord," intoned Mr. Clay. He went into his rooms, which were just outside the sleeping hall, and closed the door. It was a matter of great pride with him that he, through some fluke, had two rooms, while other staff members, including some who were married, had only one.

Presently, McNabb and Bruton (they were known by their surnames), who were inseparable, and were notorious practical jokers, went over to Max Cary. He was nineteen and was also in the tenth grade. They lifted up his bed and swung it from side to side, asking him to beg for mercy. He wouldn't, so they left his bed, with him in it, precariously balanced on two chairs.

There were yells and screams from all around. Everyone feared that he would be the next victim. My bed was next to Max's bed, and I lay very still, dreading their attack but at the same time hoping for it—I didn't want to be left out of anything. McNabb and Bruton, however, turned on Joe Wright. He was a year older than I was, but was in the fifth grade. They tipped him from his bed onto the floor. He was so good-natured that he hardly protested.

The clock struck twice, this time with a higher-pitched bell. It was six-thirty, and we had just half an hour to make our beds, get ready, and line up for breakfast. Suddenly, almost everyone was out of his bed and hurriedly fixing it up. McNabb and Bruton paused long enough to get Max's bed down from the chairs.

Mr. Clay returned, and ambled from bed to bed, inspecting and remonstrating, telling one boy to pull up his sheets, another to smooth out a bulge. Partially sighted boys said that his eyes were blue as blue and missed nothing. He prodded the few laggards to get along, muttering, "Yea, Lord, ain't no justice."

Downstairs in the locker room, there was bedlam. Some boys were whistling and joking as they hurried up other boys at the sinks or at the toilets and showers. Still other boys were standing at their lockers and applying talcum powder, deodorant, hair oil, or after-shave lotion, or pulling on their clothes. There was so little room between the lockers and the bench that if a locker door was fully open no one could get by. My locker was near the end with the sinks, and boys were always knocking into me; the simplest task, like combing my hair or putting on my socks, took longer than it ordinarily would have.

There were only three toilet stalls and one shower cubicle with three shower heads. I was reluctant to go into a toilet stall, because it was open at the top and bottom, or into the shower cubicle, because that involved taking a shower with other boys. I couldn't even get used to the idea that boys stood up half-naked at the sink to shave; at home, Daddyji shaved in paja-mas and dressing gown, sitting comfortably at a table. For a different reason, I couldn't get used to the idea of hot running water that didn't have to be husbanded and shared. I washed myself perfunctorily at the sink and got ready as best I could.

"Get in the hole, buck!" Mr. Clay said, swinging open the locker-room door. "Three minutes to line up for breakfast."

When the clock struck seven, we all rushed out of the locker room and started forming a line in the hall. Mr. Clay wouldn't let the line move forward until every last one of us was in place. Then he went ahead and we trooped after him, some boys combing their hair or buttoning their shirts. As we went along the hall, we could hear the little and middle-sized boys getting ready; their breakfast would follow ours.

We arrived in the students' dining room at the same time as the older girls, and went to the boys' side, where we found our designated chairs at tables for six. We all stood while Miss Mary Harper, the high-school English teacher and the sighted dining-room supervisor for the week, said grace at a rapid clip from the middle of the floor: "Lord, we give thanks for our daily bread, for all our joyful associations, and for the many blessed things we have here at A.S.B. Amen."

"Amen," we all repeated. I hadn't realized that one word could be said in so many different ways, or that there were so many distinct voices in the school.

There was the screech of scooting chairs as we all sat down.

Miss Harper walked over to our table to chat.

"Miss Harper, Ved doesn't believe that you can sit on your hair," Bruton announced, out of the blue. "Can he feel it?" Miss Harper was recently out of college, and Bruton teased her as if she were an older sister.

"Don't y'all be fresh," Miss Harper said.

54

"Ved, her hair is soft, and she wears it in pigtails,"
Oather said, laughing. But I noticed that, however the
boys teased her, they were always respectful.

Miss Harper moved on to the next table. A waitress served each of us a piece of dry toast and a glass of
cold milk. Before coming to America, I had hated
drinking milk; at home, milk smelled foul, because it
was served hot—it had to be boiled. But this milk was
so cold that it was almost odorless, and I drank it happily. It was as bracing as a splash of cold water on my
eyes.

"Another glass of milk?" the waitress asked, barely
pausing behind my chair.

"No, thank you," I said, automatically. I had been
brought up to consider it impolite to accept anything
at the first or second offer, and I waited for her to
return and ask me again. She never did. (I'd had similar experiences at meals in the days preceding, but I
still hadn't learned my lesson.)

Within fifteen minutes, we were through with our
simple breakfast and had returned to the dormitory.
Some of the boys went back to the locker room to finish washing and dressing. Others messed about in the
lounge or went down to the tobacco room, under the
lounge, to smoke or chew tobacco. I was on housekeeping duty for the week, and busied myself dusting
the lounge furniture and windowsills.

Mr. Clay came over to me. "How you getting
along?"

"All right, sir. It's not hard, but I've never dusted
before."

"Yea, Lord, give me that cloth!" Before I knew it,

he was dusting and wiping for me, and muttering that he was getting behind in his real duties, such as writing letters for boys and looking after their money.

Charlie Wren—he was fifteen, and in the seventh grade—was mopping the floor. "Totally blind boys can mop the floor as well as we can, sir," he said to Mr. Clay. Charlie was half-sighted, and mopping floors was a housekeeping duty reserved for boys who had some sight.

"But the bucks will miss the dead bugs on the floor," Mr. Clay said. "Yea, Lord."

"Don't listen to Bull," Oather said, coming in. Charlie was generally called Bull.

But Mr. Clay took the mop and the pail from Charlie and started mopping the floor himself.

At eight-fifteen, I went to class with Wayne Tidman. Mr. Woolly had placed me in the ninth grade, explaining, "That's where a boy of your age belongs, and Wayne Tidman is in that grade. He'll take care of you."

"Mr. Chiles is almost totally blind, you know," Wayne told me as we walked to our first class. "But he's a teacher at the school—one of the very best. He went to Hendrix College, in Conway, one of the best colleges in the world. You might say he's the best graduate of this school. I tell you, John Ed Chiles is a walking encyclopedia."

Mr. Chiles greeted me warmly—he had a very pleasant voice and a kind but precise way of speaking—and said to the class, "Ved is perhaps the only Indian in Arkansas, and certainly in Little Rock. We're mighty glad to have him with us." He showed me around the classroom. Just inside the door, on a little platform, were a chair and a desk for him, and opposite were half a dozen chairs with small desk tops attached to them. There was a bookcase full of big Braille books—they gave the room a pleasant smell of glue and thick Braille paper—and, opposite it, a couple of freestanding wooden relief maps of the United States and Europe, each state or country removable, like a piece of a jigsaw puzzle.

Besides Wayne and me, there were two other ninth graders, Evelyn Worrell and Lois Woodward, and Mr. Chiles told them to say a few words, so that I could get acquainted with them. Lois said that she was eighteen, was almost totally blind, and was from Morrilton. Her voice was so small and withdrawn that she might have been twelve years old. Evelyn said that she was fifteen, was half-sighted, and was from North Little Rock. In contrast to Lois's voice, Evelyn's was so strident and low that she could have been mistaken for a teen-age boy.

"Lois, Evelyn, and Wayne have been here since elementary school," Mr. Chiles said. "What kind of schooling did you have in India, Ved?"

"I didn't have much formal education, sir," I said. Wayne and Evelyn shifted in their seats, as if they disapproved of my being placed in the ninth grade. "At home, education for the blind is very bad."

Mr. Chiles gave each of us a Braille textbook and asked me to read out the title.

" 'An Introduction to Ciwics,' " I read.

"Not 'Ciwics,' 'Civics,' " Wayne said.

"Do you have a 'v' in your language, Ved?" Mr. Chiles asked.

I had to think for a moment. There was no Punjabi or Hindi Braille, and I didn't even know the alphabet for either of the languages. "I don't think we have a letter that sounds quite like it," I said. In fact, now that I thought about it, I realized that my family pronounced my own name one way when they were speaking to me in English and another way when they were speaking to me in Punjabi.

Mr. Chiles explained to me that the English "v" sound was made by pressing the lower lip against the upper teeth. I did what he said—pressed my lip so hard that I nearly drew blood—but still I couldn't make the correct sound.

"Vvvee," Wayne buzzed.

"Vvvee," Evelyn joined in.

"In time, with practice, you'll get it," Mr. Chiles said reassuringly, and then he asked the class, "Can anyone tell us what civics is?"

"Civics is the study of government," Wayne said.

"Yes," Mr. Chiles said. "And in this class we'll study the Constitution, its Bill of Rights, and the Emancipation Proclamation, by which Negroes were freed."

"The only nigger I have any use for is a dead nigger," Wayne said.

"Wayne, that's no way to talk," Mr. Chiles said.

"Niggers are descendants of Ham. They're from the land of Egypt. They're all damned. The Bible says so. I'm a preacher in my church—I should know."

"Negroes have rights under the Constitution, just like you and me," Mr. Chiles said.

"They aren't saved," Wayne said. "They're not in the Lord's house."

"That's enough, now, Wayne," Mr. Chiles said. "We must keep religion out of the class." He called on me. "Ved, do you know what Negroes are?"

I said I did, and asked where the blind Negroes in Little Rock went to school.

"If I were you, I'd keep my nose out of the nigger business," Wayne said.

"Blind Negroes have their own school in Little Rock," Mr. Chiles said. He changed the subject. "Can anyone tell me how many people sit in the House of Representatives?"

Neither Lois nor Evelyn knew, but Wayne provided the right answer.

As we were waiting in the corridor for our next class, Wayne said to me, in his fast twang, "If you stick your nose in the dirty nigger business too much, you'll become one yourself. Maybe you belong in the nigger school anyway. Did Mr. Woolly know your color when he accepted you?"

I felt angry, but I said nothing. I was beginning to be frightened of him.

For second period, we had junior business, with the principal, J. E. Tyson, who was sighted, and whom the boys referred to as Mr. Scarecrow or Mr. Basketball. He certainly spoke from a great height, and his voice had the intensity I associated with nervous, thin men.

"No doubt y'all have already seen the new vending

stand in the boys' solarium," Mr. Tyson said. "Mr. Woolly had it installed over the summer, so that y'all could get your feet wet in business. It has a cooler, a cash drawer, and a glass candy case, and it's well stocked. We've arranged for the juniors and seniors to take turns working at it during the recess periods, so before graduating y'all will get a turn at running it. The profits of the vending stand will be used to buy the seniors their class rings and take care of all their graduating expenses. It's probably the most practical thing some of you will get out of the school. The state rehabilitation agency has a very good program of vending stands for the blind. A vending stand may be the best way for you to earn your livelihood—unless, of course, you have an ear for piano tuning, which remains the best career open to a blind individual."

In civics, I had got the impression that Mr. Chiles might prepare us for a career in government, like Daddyji's. But now Mr. Tyson was talking as if we were only fit to work at a vending stand. I decided I didn't like junior business. Then Mr. Tyson said, "The vending stand will be a good place for you boys and girls to meet and mix." My interest was aroused.

The bell for third period rang, and the entire high school went to the auditorium for a half-hour assembly. (Periods were generally forty-five minutes long.)

Mr. Tyson told us from the stage that once every few weeks we would have a special speaker or a special program during assembly. Otherwise, assembly would be devoted to social-adjustment classes, taught by different teachers. "This is our first class," he said, and, turning to the side of the auditorium where all of us

boys were seated, he continued, "Now, boys, suppos-
ing you want to ask Mary Ann to the dance in the
gym, how would you go about it?"

A girl laughed from the girls' side of the auditorium. I'd never heard such a laugh—sweet, winging,
musical, like ice tinkling in a delicate sherbet glass.

"Who's that?" I whispered to Bruton, who was
sitting next to me.

"Mary Ann Lambert," he whispered back. "She's a
partially sighted senior. Mr. Tyson is sweet on her."
The pulse in my forehead quickened.

"Now, boys, when you're asking Mary Ann for a
date don't beat about the bush," Mr. Tyson was saying. "Don't say 'Isn't it a nice day?' or 'Can we get
together sometime?' or 'Mary Ann, are you going to
be around on Saturday?' Come right out and say, 'Mary
Ann, would you like to go to the dance with me this
Saturday?' After all, you want her to be your date. Any
questions?"

I sat wondering whether "date" had anything to
do with the delicious fruit. I had heard Englishmen
say of a girl that she was a "peach," but peaches were
soft and juicy; dates were hard and chewy. I felt too
shy to pursue the thought. Then I thought that perhaps the term came from the date on the calendar, and
wondered whether Americans asked out different girls
on different days, and how many dates they had. Perhaps a date was a girlfriend for the day, the way someone was Queen for a Day on a radio program to which
I had just been introduced. But I was afraid to voice
these questions and thoughts, in case the Americans
sitting around me laughed at them. Of one thing I felt

certain: Americans led a very fast life.

"After you finish your date with Mary Ann, be sure to thank her and ask her for a second date," Mr. Tyson was saying. "That way, she'll know that you like her and are interested in dating her."

"What Mr. Tyson really means is that if any boy asks Mary Ann for a date he'll chop his head off," McNabb whispered to Bruton from the row behind us. "He's as bold as a bulldog."

I suddenly heard Mr. Tyson call my name. "Ved, now pretend you're asking Mary Ann for a date."

I remembered in a rush Daddyji's terrifying image of the difficulty of getting me married—Brother Om without his face. I timorously stood up and turned toward the place where Mary Ann's laugh had come from. I stuttered, my voice barely audible, "Saturday night, will you come?"

There was sporadic clapping and general laughter. I felt like a fool.

"Sit down," Mr. Tyson said, from the stage. "When you ask for a date, you should sound confident, and you should remember to say where, when, and how."

Mary Ann laughed, as if the business of the date were a shared joke between her and Mr. Tyson. Mr. Tyson went on talking about the best way to ask for a date, but I stopped listening.

At ten-fifteen, we had a fifteen-minute recess, and I went with Bruton and McNabb to the vending stand. Magically, Mary Ann was already working behind the half-moon of the counter, with its candy case, filling orders for exotic snacks like Life Savers and Mounds bars, Red Hots and cheese crackers, Fritos, peanuts,

Cokes, Pepsis, 7UPs, Dr Peppers—all the while talking and laughing, running back and forth with short,
clicking steps between the cooler and the candy case,
and serving the teachers, girls, and boys, with a pert,
penetrating remark, it seemed, for everybody.

With a trembling hand, I held out a nickel and
called for a cold drink.

"Coke, you must mean," she said, barely stopping
to flip the cap off the bottle and hand it to me. She
immediately turned to someone else, saying over her
shoulder, "I liked your Indian speech to me. It was
very cute."

The word "cute" was new to me. It sounded fetch-
ing—all the more so because Mary Ann flicked it off
her tongue like a pomegranate seed. I stood there mesmerized by her—by the thump of the cooler's lid, the
whish of carbonated air from the bottles, the crackle of
candy wrappers in the candy case, the clink of coins in
the cash drawer, the general rattle-plunk of bottles and
packets along the counter. I was captivated by the speed
of her movements. She's like a goddess with many arms
and hands, I thought, and she's so lively that she could
hold her own with Sister Umi. And yet she can't be
more than a couple of years older than I am.

Then I heard Mr. Tyson's voice next to me, saying,
"The usual, Mary Ann."

"The usual, Mr. Tyson," she echoed.

I felt frightened, as if Mr. Tyson had read my mind.

The clock struck ten-thirty, and everyone immediately cleared out. I couldn't get over how orderly
everyone was; it was breathtaking.

For fourth period, Wayne, Lois, and Evelyn went

to Mr. Tyson for ninth-grade mathematics. I, however, went to fourth- and fifth-grade arithmetic class, taught by Miss Jeanne Mitchell. Since I barely knew long division, Mr. Woolly had decided to start me out there.

There were many boys my age or older who were in elementary school. Still, I hated the thought of being a laggard teen-ager and sitting with little children, so I sneaked very quietly into Miss Mitchell's classroom and sat down at a desk in the back.

One boy heard me, however, and he ran over to me and started feeling my face, chanting, "The new Red Indian in fourth grade! The new Red Indian!"

"Kenneth Grider, you go back to your seat!" Miss Mitchell, who was sighted, called to him from the front of the room. She sounded hoarse, like someone who has had to shout a lot.

But Kenneth wouldn't listen, and Miss Mitchell came over and practically yanked him away from me. "A thirteen-year-old boy should know better," she said. I was surprised at Kenneth's age; from his size and his behavior, I would have taken him for eight or nine.

Miss Mitchell called the class to order. "As some of you children may know, we have a new boy with us," she said. "He's come to us all the way from India, because they don't have a school like ours over there. So he doesn't know as much arithmetic as you children do." I felt small and humiliated. But she went on, "Mr. Woolly says he's very quick. So before you children know it he will have caught up in arithmetic with the ninth graders."

There was a low buzz in the class.

"Now, children, open your books to page seven. Kenneth, how do you multiply one-third by three-fourths?"

Kenneth didn't know.

"Little Sue, what is a denominator and what is a numerator?"

"The denominator is the divisor," Sue Harrison replied. "The numerator is the number of parts of the denominator."

Miss Mitchell looked toward me. "Did you understand that, Ved?"

"No," I said, feeling embarrassed about my grownup voice.

Miss Mitchell asked Little Sue to give me an example of how a denominator and a numerator were used.

During the period, Miss Mitchell would ask questions, and before I had even set the problem down on the special arithmetic slate for the blind, Little Sue would give the answer; she was three years younger than I was, and seemed to be something of a showoff. The class went very badly for me.

For my fifth period, I went upstairs to the conservatory for an individual piano lesson with Mr. Raymond Sykes, a partially sighted teacher. Music was a recommended subject for ninth graders.

"Do you know any piano?" Mr. Sykes asked. He was relaxed and cheerful.

"I know only the harmonium, but I can play a few scales on the piano." I haltingly played for him.

"What do you plan to do when you leave school?" he asked.

"I don't know. Go to college."

"When I was a student here, in the thirties, music and industrial arts were about the only things a blind person could do."

"Mr. Tyson seemed to think we could do little more than run a vending stand," I said.

"Oh, I think you can do more than that nowadays."

"What sort of things?" I asked, getting interested.

"Like selling insurance. But I'm not the best person to ask. You'd have to go to New York or Boston to find out. I grew up in Booneville, in western Arkansas, and the only place I know besides Booneville and Little Rock is Arkadelphia, where I studied music at Ouachita College."

There was a fifteen-minute recess, and then, at twelve-fifteen, Mr. Clay led us down for lunch. While Miss Harper said grace, I once again wondered how I would manage my food, and was relieved to find that we were served only a sandwich and potato chips. The sandwich had a strange smell and texture, and I asked about it.

"It's tuna fish," Bruton said.

I had never had tuna fish before. I didn't like it, but I ate it quickly, washing it down with cold milk. Milk seemed to be a regular item at meals.

Classes resumed at one, and Lois, Evelyn, Wayne, and I went for science to Mrs. Betty Wilkes. She was a petite, slow-speaking woman, probably no more than a few years older than Lois. She spent the entire period defining terms like "mammal" and "reptile." For the next period, the seventh, while Lois and Evelyn went to the Cottage for a class in sewing with Miss Eula Shults, Wayne and I went to Shop for a class in wood-working with Mr. Tyson. (Mr. Tyson had been pro-moted from Shop teacher to principal, but he was still temporarily teaching the subject.) In Shop, boys were learning to make bookends, leather moccasins, brooms, mops, and rubber doormats.

While Mr. Tyson was showing me how to use rub-ber treads and wire to make a doormat, Mr. Woolly walked in. "Mr. Tyson, Ved's father wants him to concentrate on his studies," he said.

"But, Mr. Woolly, Shop is the best insurance pol-icy for blind people. You know they can always find work in sheltered workshops. Anyways, he shouldn't be treated differently from other boys."

I stood there listening to Mr. Woolly and Mr. Tyson, imagining that they were having a tug-of-war over me. I myself was torn: I was frightened of ending up in a sheltered workshop, but at the same time I was excited by the buzz and whirr of the tools, many of them new to me.

Mr. Tyson got his way, and I stayed on in Shop.

For eighth period, we four ninth graders went together to English class, with Miss Harper. She read us a story by someone called O. Henry. I had never been read aloud to in English, and I could barely understand her strange accent. Moreover, she spoke at a fast clip, like an excited auctioneer I had once heard in Lahore. Anyway, I had difficulty concentrating: Miss Harper seemed to be shaking her head energetically as she read, making me wonder whether her pigtails were swinging from side to side, and how thick her hair was. I found myself thinking of Sister Umi's upcoming wedding. I thought that I had never spent such a long day, and I felt tired.

"Ved, what is the third ingredient?" Miss Harper asked, putting the book down.

I didn't know the word, and thought she was saying "Ingrid," perhaps because my sisters' favorite European actress was Ingrid Bergman, and therefore my favorite European name for a girl was Ingrid.

"The third Ingrid, Miss Harper?" I asked.

"No, ingredient," she said. "The third ingredient in the O. Henry story that I just finished reading to you."

"That's the heroine's name."

Everyone laughed.

Miss Harper shushed the class, and said, "Wayne, what is it?"

"An onion, Miss Harper."

My cheeks felt fiery hot.

After Miss Harper's class, we again had fifteen minutes of recess, and then, at three-thirty, half an hour of high-school choir practice, with Mr. Sykes, in the auditorium. Singing in a chorus was new to me. I didn't know any of the songs. All the same, I was overwhelmed by the music, and found the words, when I could catch them, very sad. I remember tears in my eyes when we sang the refrain

> O, Susanna! O, don't you cry for me,
> For I'm bound for Louisiana, with
> my banjo on my knee.

I tried to sing the refrain (the only bit I caught) louder than everyone else, in the hope that Mr. Sykes would hear me over the others—only to have him tell me not to make my voice stick out, since the point of choir was for all the voices to blend together.

Immediately after choir practice, we older boys rushed to the gymnasium.

No sooner did we enter the gymnasium than a man called out, "You there, new Indian boy!" He was Mr. R. Eugene Hartman, the partially sighted physical-education instructor for the boys. He took me by the shoulder and led me to the damp dressing room in the basement. "You're thin and frail for your age," he said. "People will walk all over you because you're blind. I'll make you tough and combative as all getout." He abruptly put a pair of trunks for me on the bench, and left.

I changed and ran upstairs. At the head of the stairs, someone was making a lot of noise, but it sounded muffled. McNabb was coming up behind me, and I asked him what was happening. (He was partially sighted.)

"That's George Conner punching a punching bag to get strong," he said. "It sounds funny because the walls and the floor are covered with mats—that's to keep you critters from getting hurt." He laughed his old man's laugh.

"Get down here on the mat and stretch out with your arms over your head!" Mr. Hartman called to me. In spite of the muffled, padded surroundings, his voice sounded sharp.

I hesitated; I didn't know where Mr. Hartman meant

me to go. He came over, put a hairy, sweaty arm around me, and propelled me to a spot between Bruton and McNabb, where, under his direction, I lay down, stretched out my arms and legs, and started breathing deeply. The mat smelled of sweat and age, and the gymnasium felt oppressively close.

Mr. Hartman went around the crowded floor blowing little trills on a whistle and pushing and shoving to make places on the mats for more boys.

"Boys, you're now in gym," Mr. Hartman said, from one end of the floor. "What does 'in gym' mean? I'll tell you. It means participating in our physical-education program, which is an ambitious one. It's intended to stimulate the favorable traits you have and expand them to their fullest. For all I know, many of you are born athletes. If you're not, I'll find out what your defects are and help you to overcome them through calisthenics. I will make many valuable alterations in your physique and personality. I will see that you develop your natural physical coördination to the fullest and, if you're any good, make you a Bronco Buster." That was the name of the school's wrestling team. "Whether you're on the team or not, the physical-education program will help you develop perseverance. That's very important for you blind people. You have to be tough and combative to get on out in the world."

Mr. Hartman barked some instructions, and everyone else seemed to understand what to do. But every two minutes he would come up to me and show me something—how to hold my ankles and try to sway from side to side, how to keep my knees straight and try to touch my toes, how to get down on my hands and toes and try to raise myself up. He was dressed only in trunks, over which his fat stomach bulged, and his body was oily with sweat. I recoiled from every contact with him.

Soon Mr. Hartman was vigorously drilling us. As he counted, *"One* and *two* and *three* and *four* and," all of us, in time to his counting, sat up without using our arms and stretched our torsos over our legs. *"Five* and *six* and *seven* and *eight."*

My heart raced like a clock gone haywire. I felt so dizzy that I thought my head was going to fly off my neck. My stomach heaved as if it were going to vomit up everything.

I felt I couldn't survive one more sit-up. *"Up* and *down* and *up* and *down!"* Mr. Hartman shouted. "Come on, boys, you can get your heads down lower!"

What seemed like aeons later, Mr. Hartman finally said, "O.K., boys, rest!"

We all lay back, panting like spent dogs.

"Have you ever wrestled?" Mr. Hartman asked, coming over to me.

I barely shook my head—or, rather, rolled it on the mat.

"You're over fifteen, but you have the body of a ten-year-old. That's a perfect combination for a champion featherweight wrestler. With some good rough training, you can be a Bronco Buster. Wrestling is the best sport for blind people, and this winter we have some wonderful wrestling meets coming up."

I felt nearly dead, and was scarcely able to take in what Mr. Hartman was saying.

"The first day, boy, is the hardest," Mr. Hartman went on. "But you'll shape up. I'll see to it." He turned to Bruton.

It was five-thirty, the end of the gym session. I somehow lifted myself off the mat and dragged myself down to the dressing room, my limbs aching, my head spinning, my heart beating so rapidly that I was afraid it would never return to its normal rhythm. In the dressing room, I sat on the bench, trembling, my head in my hands, waiting my turn at one of the three trickling shower spouts.

"Yea, Lordy, ain't no justice," Mr. Clay said, back in the lounge, as he lined us up for supper at the stroke of six. "Get in the hole, buck. Time to get down there and eat up the filet mignon that the cook has fried for you."

The light breakfast, the very light lunch, no tiffin—and Mr. Hartman—had left me ravenous. But in the dining room there was only a thin piece of meat on my plate, almost hidden beneath gravy, with French fries, peas, and a lettuce leaf. The meat was alternately tough and fatty, and I had trouble cutting it; the plate and the vegetables slid around, causing a minor tempest at the table.

Miss Harper came over, laid her firm hands on my shaky ones, and showed me how to hold the knife and fork closer to the blade and tines, how to find the end of the meat, and how to tell the slippery fat from the hard meat with my fork and then cut it off.

Miss Harper turned to Bruton and scolded him for piercing a French fry at the end and sucking it into his mouth instead of piercing it in the middle and putting it in his mouth all at once.

"The doggone fries are so heaped up I can't find the ends," Bruton said.

"You'll learn, Kenneth," Miss Harper said reassuringly, and she turned to Oather. "Watch out, Oather, your lettuce leaf is flapping from your fork. It's spraying your shirt with gravy."

"I'm just a country boy, Miss Harper," Oather said, laughing. "No matter how I saw at the darn leaf, it just won't be cut. It's stubborn, like me."

Miss Harper cut the lettuce for Oather while he grumbled away good-humoredly.

At a quarter to seven, all of us in the junior and senior high school went to the library for a forty-five-minute study hall. From everywhere in the packed room came the friendly, familiar sounds of people reading and writing—of fingers running along an embossed page and the *tick-tick* of dots being punched, of the crackle of large, thick Braille book pages being turned and the clatter of guides being moved down Braille writing slates.

Finally, we were free for the day. I sat with some boys gathered around the radio in the lounge, but I couldn't catch the words. I went into the locker room, but it was noisy. I went downstairs to the tobacco room to talk to Oather, but he was in the middle of what he called a "spit-and-argue session" with Pat Thennes. I went out on the little terrace alongside the lounge, but it was deserted. I walked over to the woods, where I had spent most of my first night at the school, but every time I took a step the leaves underfoot crunched irritatingly. I recalled my years of idleness at home, when I dreamed of going to a proper school, as my older brother and my sisters did. Each year that I grew older and was not in school, I feared that a day would come when my own brothers and sisters wouldn't want to talk to me, because I was uneducated. For me, school had come to represent all that was good, and here, at last, I was at a school in America. But I felt out of sorts.

Two birds fluttered overhead. I wondered what color they were. I wondered whether in some part of my mind I could remember the colors I had seen before I went blind, and whether, if I did, that would help me to understand Wayne's hatred of Negroes. I repeated to myself, "White, Negro, white, black." Sometimes people spoke of white as clean and black as dirty, but how could "clean" or "dirty" be applied to a whole race of people? Some people thought that the blind lived in darkness, but that was nonsense. The point was that the blind had no perception of light or darkness. Perhaps darkness was like the quiet of the night. I wondered how dark I was, how much I looked like a Negro, and what my kinship with the Negro was—where I fitted into the social puzzle. I wanted somehow or other to find out where I stood in the shading from white to black, to connect myself to the rest of the world. I ached to see, even for just a moment.

In the distance, the clock struck nine-thirty, the official bedtime. I hurried into the school building. Mr. Clay was shuffling in and out of the locker room, up and down the lounge, calling out, "Get in the hole, buck. . . . Time to turn in. Heads on the pillows. Hands out of the covers. . . . You are all old and wise, gents. . . . You know the rules. Yea, Lord, ain't no justice."

IV

TRAVELLER UNKNOWN

INDIAN YOUTH FINDS HOPE IN ARKANSAS

"We knew that as the School's first foreign student—and a prominent one at that—he would be a challenge both to the faculty and to the student body. We are awfully glad now we accepted that challenge."

Mr. Woolly said that several eastern schools, where most of the sons of foreign dignitaries go, spread the word that the Arkansis school solicited Ved as an attempt at self-promotion. T'aint so, say Ved and Mr. Woolly.

—*Arkansas Gazette, c. February 15, 1950.*

W HAT ARE WE HAVING FOR SWEET?" I ASKED
—— at dinner one evening.

❧❧❧ "You sweet on someone?" Bruton asked me.
❧❧❧ "No, I mean dessert, like a biscuit," I said.
❧❧❧ "You better ask Mr. Clay, and he'll get
you biscuits with his imaginary ham and eggs
in the morning," Bruton said, with a laugh.

Miss Harper, who was taking her turn again as
sighted dining-room supervisor, overheard us. "In India,
I guess, you call cookies 'biscuits.' Here a biscuit is a
roll." Then Miss Harper addressed the table. "Boys,
this is a good time to get yourself a date for the Saturday-night dance, if you want to."

Arlie Treadway immediately walked over to the
girls' side of the dining room and said, for all to hear,
"Vernelle, will you be my date this Saturday?"

I thought I would never be able to do that, and
then I said to myself, self-righteously, "I will never
have a date. Americans go in for temporary pleasures.
I am out for permanent pleasures. Daddyji always asked
us to concentrate on the permanent pleasures, and I
am my father's son." This got me wondering what the
fathers of the other students did, and I asked Oather
about it.

"Most of them are sharecroppers."

"What's that?"

"Why, sharecroppers! Don't you know? In the hills,
land is going cheap. Fellows can buy their land. But
in farmland, where most of us come from, a poor farmer
has quite a job buying land, so he leases it from someone who owns it but doesn't want to farm it. Sharecroppers have very little money in the bank and live

on borrowings. They charge their provisions against the day they'll bring in the crop."

"Is Mr. Chiles's father a sharecropper?"

"John Ed Chiles? Certainly not! Mr. Chiles's father owns a fair piece alongside the Mississippi River, in Pecan Point."

"Where is Pecan Point?"

"It's near Joiner."

"Where is Joiner?"

"It's near Jonesboro."

"Where is that?"

"It's near Pocahontas."

I decided I wouldn't learn exactly where Mr. Chiles came from, and I asked, "Is he really named John Ed? I wish I had a name like that." Indian names suddenly seemed drab.

"John Ed, sure enough. This is the South, ain't it, Whip?" From that day on, the boys often called me Whip or Veep, perhaps because my first two initials were V. P. and I sometimes mispronounced "v" as "w."

IN the locker room, there was a nervous, expectant air. Everyone was getting ready for the Saturday-night dance in the gymnasium. Water running in the sinks and showers kept up a steady roar. Boys were opening or slamming locker doors, banging into them, or stumbling over one another. The place smelled of damp towels and drying shoe polish, of after-shave and hair oil. People were in different stages of dress, and each of them was carrying on in his own way. Charlie Wren was idly swinging the door to the lounge and thumping out a rhythm. Max was singing "How Many Biscuits Did You Eat This Morning?" Billy Tabor was trying to drown out both Charlie and Max by doing runs on a clarinet. Oather was taking his time shaving at the sink, and a number of boys were prodding him to hurry up.

"The blind must learn patience," Oather said into the sink, washing his face. "Just be grateful y'all don't have stubble like mine." He walked away from the sink, merrily whistling.

I was crouching on the floor looking in the bottom of my locker for a pair of socks. Oather came up so quickly that his knee caught me in the back. He flung his wet arms around my neck apologetically.

"My clean white shirt! Oather, you're ruining it!" I cried.

"Sorry, Veep," he said, and moved on.

"Max! McNabb! Pat!" Bruton shouted, his voice cracking. No one answered. "There are so many of you partially sighted boys around, why doesn't one of you answer me? Bull! What color is this here damn tie?"

Charlie Wren had one good eye and could see better than many partially sighted boys. In fact, his vision seemed to us so impressive that the boys used to say that his good eye glowed at night.

Charlie left the door and went over to Bruton to inspect his tie. "It's blood red. Just right for you."

Next, he reached over and straightened my tie and, with his comb, put a few strands of my hair in place. I could be a figure in Mme. Tussaud's museum that Daddyji used to tell us about, I thought.

"Bull, you should charge money for being a mirror for the blind folks," Joe Wright said. Joe himself was partially sighted, and he was giving a shine to Big Jim Pickett. Big Jim had his shoe propped up on the bench.

"You're dumb, Joe," Big Jim said contemptuously, over Joe's head. "Have you ever heard of bulls getting paid?" He went on, in what the boys called his "leg-pulling style," "I'm telling you, if that old blind Bruton over there can't see his face in the toes of my shoes I'll ring your chimes so hard you'll never be able to think again."

"What does Big Jim expect for a nickel?" Joe whined, trying to enlist our sympathy.

Treadway, who was buffing his shoes himself with a chamois cloth, put in, "Who says Dumb Joe can think?"

"What plagues you, Joe?" Bruton asked, joining in. "You never show up at any of the dances."

"Oh, hell, what would I do at a dance?" Joe said.

Big Jim sniggered.

Boys started imagining what they would do to the girls if all the teachers and Mr. Woolly were blind.

"I'd make a picnic of Mary Ann Lambert," Max said. "I'd take all those chicks from the Cottage into the woods back there and make them see stars."

"Vernelle, too?" McNabb asked mischievously, coming into the locker room. Vernelle Stewart had the reputation of being the best-looking totally blind girl around. Partially sighted boys often talked about her thick black hair, which came down to her waist. She had the best contralto singing voice in the school, and could play at least a dozen tunes on the piano.

"You leave my girl out of this," Treadway said.

"No harm meant," McNabb said soothingly, now that he had got his barb in. When he wanted it to be, his voice was as smooth as cold milk.

Treadway left the locker room, muttering something, and McNabb turned to Max and said, "Hell, you could take Vernelle away from Treadway, couldn't you, Max? After all, everyone knows you're the handsomest boy this side of Pine Bluff."

Max hopped up and down the locker-room bench, clapping. He was known for his flamboyance. I remembered that a few days earlier we had heard someone racing a motor and blowing a horn just behind the locker room, in the back driveway. We had all run out to see who it was. There was Max, sitting in the driver's seat of a new Buick. As we were feeling the car incredulously, he drove away, right out from under our hands. He returned some time later on foot. We all asked him whose car it was, how he'd managed to get hold of it, how he could drive it, how much vision he really had, whether he had a driver's license. He wouldn't explain much. "I've always tooled around Springhill," he said mysteriously, and added, "In fact, my favorite pastime is to drive my date to a drive-in movie and spend the whole time necking." He had a way of making us all feel very jealous.

"Who are you going to dance with, Veep?" Max now asked me.

"You know I don't know how to dance," I said quietly, not wishing to be made the butt of locker-room jokes, like Joe Wright. "I'm only going because it's a school requirement."

"Don't you worry," Max said. "I'll pair you up with Peggy Lou."

The whole locker room howled. Peggy Lou (that's not her real name), who was nineteen and a grade behind me, was one of the slowest girls at school. She had a harsh, grating voice and was afflicted with club feet. She walked with an unmistakable heavy step.

"Max, cut it out," Bruton said, coming to my defense.

Max and many of the other boys set out for the girls' side to collect their dates. I went out onto the little terrace, and found Oather there. He was sitting on the wall above the steps, chewing tobacco. I joined him on the wall.

"You're one of the most popular boys at school," I said. "But the boys say that you always go alone to dances."

"I enjoy the company of my Bull Durham," he said, turning and spitting onto the grass. "There are a lot of us country boys here. We like to go to dances and have a good time dancing with all the girls. You could join us—or are you going to turn out to be a slick rascal, like Max Cary? He'll steal a kiss on the first date before he's ever even danced with the girl."

"Where? How?" I waited as tensely as if the wall we were sitting on were the edge of a precipice.

"On the grassy path to the gym—on the mouth, of course."

"Mouth!" I exclaimed. "What about germs? Don't they get sick?"

"Sick with love."

"They actually lie down on the grass?"

"You kidding? Mr. Woolly would tan their hides. They kiss standing up. That's all the chaperons allow them to do."

"You mean Peggy Lou kisses on the way to the gymnasium?"

Oather laughed. "Believe you me, she would if she could. But no one has ever asked her to a dance."

"Vernelle Stewart and Mary Ann Lambert—they kiss, too?"

"Why not? They get plenty of opportunity. Vernelle is going steady with Treadway, and Mary Ann with Max—or, you could say, with Max and Mr. Tyson. Didn't you know?"

The idea made my cheeks tingle. I couldn't imagine that they could do such a dirty thing as kiss—not nice, pretty girls like them. Peggy Lou was different. I could imagine kissing her, but the thought of kissing any other girl was frightening and overwhelming—it suffused me with shame.

The clock struck a quarter to eight—the dance was supposed to start at seven-thirty—and Oather and I and a few other stragglers rushed over to the gymnasium, now a dance hall, festooned with balloons and crêpe paper. A Strauss waltz was playing full tilt on the public-address system, and the boys with dates were dancing the first dance. Those of us without dates clustered by the wall. But then boys asked girls for a dance, and in a moment all of them, including Oather, had disappeared into the lighthearted gaiety circling the floor.

I stood alone, listening to the bustle, which sounded all the livelier because the thronged floor was so small.

I felt exposed and awkward until I reminded myself that some of the dancers, at least, were totally blind and the others had no time to give me a thought.

"Ved, would you like to dance?" It was Mary Ann Lambert speaking to *me* through the noise. She has the prettiest voice in the school, I thought. Once again, I recalled that haunting image of Brother Om without his face and, at the same time, something that Bruton had gratuitously told me: "Don't you get sweet on her, even if Mr. Tyson puts her up to it. He'll use her to catch you like a fish, and then fry you good and proper. You can ask anyone. Fishing is his hobby." Mr. Tyson is capable of anything, I thought. It was said that he would walk down the hall touching the girls' hair, sometimes right in front of Mr. Woolly, and Mr. Woolly didn't like it but was afraid to say anything to Mr. Tyson. And yet I thought that even if Mr. Tyson had never set foot in the school only the most brazen boy would have dared to go near Mary Ann Lambert. I recalled that when we boys were sitting in the lounge and heard her laughter from the vending stand echoing down the hall a certain hush would descend on us, as if everyone felt her vibrant presence but knew that she was an unobtainable sweetheart, an unearthly tease, whose mission was to thrill us all with sad longing.

"No, thank you," I now barely brought out, and, in some confusion, added, "I don't know how to dance."

"I'll teach you," she said simply.

"I'd rather not," I said, almost choking on my words.

She was gone, and instead Wayne was standing

next to me. "You're a real idiot. Do you know who asked you to dance?"

"Leave me alone," I said.

"The most gorgeous and the smartest girl in school, and for the first dance, too. Any fool would give his right arm to dance with her."

I left Wayne in the gymnasium and went back to the locker room. Joe was sitting on the bench, humming. The place had never seemed so forlorn.

"Who is it?" he asked.

"It's me," I said. I started undressing.

"Everyone is required to be at the dance on Saturday night," he said. "If you aren't, you'll get bad character marks on your report card, like me." He went back to his humming.

I went upstairs to the sleeping hall.

❧

As I was running to my civics class, I tripped on a step in the boys' solarium and hit my head against the wall. Before I reached the classroom, I could feel the blood pounding in my forehead and a bump rising. If Daddyji saw me hit my head against the wall, he would quickly blow into his handkerchief, to make it warm, and put it over the bump. The handkerchief would feel like the best medicine in the world, its warmth spreading through me like the cup of hot cocoa that Mamaji always brought me at bedtime. I felt vaguely sad.

"Wayne, wake Ved up," Mr. Chiles said, his voice

pitched unusually high, as if he were irritated.

"I'm not asleep," I said.

"Then why don't you answer the question?" Mr. Chiles asked.

"Which question? I didn't hear it," I said.

"Well, then, I think you'd better go to the infirmary and have your ears washed out. Wayne, what's the answer?"

"The Bill of Rights," Wayne said.

Mr. Chiles ignored me for the rest of the period. I thought he had been very unfair. I decided that I would speak to him after class, but the moment the bell rang he hurried out of the room.

"What happened to *you,* buddy?" Wayne asked, out in the corridor. "Mr. Chiles asked you three times what the first ten amendments to the Constitution are called."

"Really? I had no idea," I said, and I went in search of Mr. Chiles. I found him in the small reception room opposite the office, playing the piano and singing with a group of teachers. When he finished, I stumbled through an apology, mentioning my injury but not going into details, for fear of seeming to seek his sympathy.

"I suppose we both owe each other an apology," he said quietly. "I don't mind telling you that my patience was mightily tried, but I shouldn't have lost my temper."

From that day, we were like mentor and disciple. I would go up to him when he was outside taking a stroll, or stand next to him at the vending stand, and talk to him about things that were bothering me. "The boys are always cursing," I once confided to him. "They're always talking about how they want to get a girl. They don't seem to study at all. They seem so childish."

"Ours is a young and rich country, where people can afford to be children longer," he said. "But once responsibility is forced upon us Americans we mature very quickly. To understand what I mean, you just have to see the difference in an American boy before he gets a job and after he gets a job. We Americans may play hard, but when the time comes we work hard, too."

He's so intelligent, I thought. I respect him more than any other blind person I have ever met. I recalled that he was a man of means and didn't have to work, but worked because he enjoyed it—enjoyed the activity of the mind. ("The activity of the mind" was his phrase.) He was so independent, so good in mobility, so free of "blindisms," like walking with his hands out in front of him and shuffling along as if the ground would give way under his feet, that sighted people regarded him almost as one of them.

It used to trouble us older boys that Mr. Chiles, who was a kind of model for all of us, remained unmarried.

Bruton expressed our feeling by saying, "Marriage is the best thing you can wish a blind person. A sighted person can get along on his own, but no matter how independent a blind person becomes he's always going to need a hand."

It was a favorite occupation with us boys to match Mr. Chiles up with one sighted woman teacher after another. At one time, we were sure he would marry the arithmetic teacher, Miss Mitchell. We noticed that he often stood next to her at the vending stand and had a Coke with her. Then Miss Mitchell stopped coming to the vending stand, and everyone said that Mr. Chiles had become sweet on Miss Shults—he was often found coming from the direction of the Cottage. We waited, but nothing happened. Then he started jointly chaperoning our Saturday-night dances with Miss Harper, and would usually have the first and the last dance with her. We would try to dance near them (I had learned to dance a little by then), hoping to hear an exchange of endearments, but all we ever heard them talk about was whether the lieutenant governor of Arkansas could be impeached, and things like that. We fixed on her as the ideal mate for him.

Then, one Sunday afternoon, McNabb walked into the lounge and said, in his usual inflectionless voice, as if he were reciting a multiplication table, "Mr. Chiles has gone and got himself a car. He told me so himself. It's sitting right out there in the back driveway."

Joe, who was listening to a baseball game, switched off the radio. Bruton, who was snoring on the couch, woke up. Treadway came running out of the locker room. We had never heard of a blind person owning a car. This was very different from Max's attempt to impress us by taking a spin in a mysteriously obtained car. We couldn't imagine what possible use Mr. Chiles would have for a car, since he hardly ever left the school. None of the teachers did—not even the sighted ones, who were all, without exception, carless. If the source of the report had been anyone but McNabb, we would have laughed it off. But McNabb, far from embellishing stories, was known for sticking to the most indisputable, flat facts.

"Mr. Chiles must be all ready to get married," Treadway said. "He must have gotten himself a bride, who's going to drive him around. He may not be long for the school."

Practically all of us older boys rushed out—from the sleeping hall and the locker room, from the lounge and the tobacco room—to the back driveway to examine the car. We touched it all over. It was an Oldsmobile, and felt as new as a new penny. Its doors weren't locked, and we opened them. Inside, it smelled of new seats and new rubber mats. Bruton, who was a great toucher, ran his hand all over the rubber mats to see if there was any trace of dirt, but they were as clean as a sterilized needle. The tires were so new and clean that even though we stuck our fingers in the treads we couldn't detect a particle of dust. The car might have been deposited by a crane in the back driveway, straight from the factory.

We went to the vending stand to discuss the whole matter. There was Mr. Chiles, deep in conversation with Miss Harper.

"Miss Harper, can you drive?" Mr. Chiles was asking her.

"Yes, Mr. Chiles," she said. "Where shall we go?"

That night, in the sleeping hall, Bruton said, "Those two are now sure to slip away to a drive-in movie. At the drive-in, Miss Harper will be able to explain the movie to Mr. Chiles without disturbing any of their neighbors, and I'm sure that during the long, silent romantic scenes they'll neck, just like Max Cary and his Springhill dames."

We fell asleep.

🌷

EVERY day, one or another of us would go over to the car and touch it, but it seemed never to have been moved—it was as free of road dust as ever.

Then, one day, when we were teasing Miss Harper about Mr. Chiles, she said, "Y'all should know that Mr. Chiles is set in his ways, and doesn't want to be messed up by a lady friend. He never gets personal."

We all protested. Many of us were set in our ways, and we had trouble being personal with girls, but we didn't think that ruled out lady friends.

"It's so easy for y'all to daydream in this sheltered little world," Miss Harper said. We decided that Miss Harper was too independent, and not suitable for Mr. Chiles after all.

In civics and at parties, Mr. Chiles would talk about the joys of family life in small American towns, or what he called "the America behind the headlines," and about finding his own personal happiness in what he called "an America not shrouded by morbid radio programs and scandalous tabloids." "I'm not a big-time, big-town man," he once told us in civics. "I believe that blind people would be happy if they got married and settled in a small town and raised a family in its carefree atmosphere, away from big, bustling Little Rock, where each good action gets lost."

We noticed that he didn't say, "I should get married." Moreover, as time went on, we ran out of candidates at the school for Mr. Chiles's future wife, and decided that he could get married only if he left us and became a teacher at Hendrix, his alma mater. Mr. Woolly, however, soon punctured that idea by telling us that Mr. Chiles would probably need a Ph.D. to teach there, and he had only an M.A. I remember once asking Mr. Chiles why he didn't go on and get a Ph.D. "In graduate school, I went to see a professor I think the world of," he said. "The professor said, 'John Ed, you'll either get a Ph.D. with ulcers or get an M.A. without ulcers.' I thought it was a very wise remark, and I got an M.A. and got out."

We kept on hoping that the bride of our imaginations—someone who had Miss Mitchell's firm hand with children, Miss Shults's domestic skills, Miss Harper's extraordinary energy—would appear in Mr. Chiles's life, and that the two of them would go to the altar together. At the time, we thought that our castles in the air were real houses, though I remember Oather's saying, "I tell you, wedding bells ain't going to ring for Mr. Chiles. Whatever people might say, he's cursed with an independent character, like me." Years later, I learned that Mr. Chiles had gone blind as a result of retinitis pigmentosa, that he had an older sister who was blind from the same cause, and that their blindness was hereditary. So perhaps Mr. Chiles had been afraid all along to get married and raise a family.

❧

IN time, I began to catch on to the English of the dormitory and the classroom. I also stopped going to the elementary-arithmetic class and, with extra coaching from Mr. Tyson, was able to keep up with ninth-grade mathematics. In civics, I started getting marks as good as Wayne's. I discovered, however, that in many of my classes little real work got done. Much of the time was spent arguing about things that had nothing to do with our studies, like the perennial subjects of Negroes and religion. I remember that one day in our English class Miss Harper started reading "Tom Sawyer" to us. Wayne made a scathing remark about Negroes. Miss Harper told him that he had better change his attitude. Wayne quoted the Bible to her, mentioning Ham. Lois said that Ham was in the Old Testament, and Wayne, as a Baptist, should hearken to the New Testament. Evelyn said that the Old and the New Testaments had nothing to do with Negroes, since slaves had only come to America afterward. For my benefit, Miss Harper explained who Ham was, what the Old and the New Testaments were, how Christians were divided into Baptists and other denominations, and when Negroes had arrived in America. At every stage, her explanation provoked controversy. Days went by in explanations and controversy, without our making much progress in "Tom Sawyer."

Then Miss Harper learned that the book was in our library in both Talking Book and Braille, and decided that she would read "Jane Eyre" to us instead, observing, "There are no Negroes in this book, so we should have some peace and quiet in the classroom. Besides, it's one novel that every blind person should read, and it's not available in our library." Miss Harper was able to read us only fifteen or twenty pages a day, so it took us many weeks to get through it. It was wonderful to have a personal reader, and we became so engrossed in the novel that we hated to hear the bell ring at the end of the period. Now and again, Miss Harper would feel guilty about reading a novel to us during class time, and we would spend the last five minutes of the period discussing Jane's experiences in the orphanage and Mr. Rochester's character. Once or twice, she also gave us a Braille true-or-false quiz.

After some time, I began to worry that I wasn't learning enough. I would make a grammatical mistake while discussing "Jane Eyre," and everyone would laugh. Miss Harper would tell me about some rule of grammar, which would whet my appetite for more rules, but there was never any time for them in class. Once, after class, I said to Wayne, "Which is correct—'a little black dog' or 'a black little dog'? What is the rule?"

"Rule?" he said. "You have to be born an American, and then you just know that 'a little black dog' is right."

Many years later, Mr. Woolly, discussing the deficiencies of the school, told me, "When I became superintendent, in 1947, my total annual appropriation was eighty-two thousand dollars. When you came, two years after that, it was probably a few thousand dollars more, but not much more. That had to buy food. That had to pay the food-services staff. That had to pay for building-and-ground maintenance. That had to pay for heat, light, and the office telephone. That had to pay for equipment in the Shop and for instruments in the conservatory. That had to pay for refreshments at the parties, for the school bus, for trips to other states for wrestling meets. That had to pay for the infirmary and the school nurse. And that also had to pay teachers. We operated on such a shoestring that I couldn't afford to pay more than eighteen hundred dollars a year to a teacher, and a number of the teachers got only twelve hundred dollars. And they were all required to live at the school and double as house staff, with all kinds of supervisory and chaperon duties. When we did find good teachers willing to live under our conditions, they were generally straight out of college. Some of them were younger than the students they had to teach, and none of them had had any training in teaching the blind. That was hardly surprising, since in those days there were only two places in the country with a program for training such teachers. One of them was Columbia Teachers College, in New York, which was too far away for our folks. The other was George Peabody College for Teachers, in Tennessee, and the best I could do was to encourage our young teachers to take a summer session or two there. Even when we were able to improve our teaching, our facilities remained poor. They bore no comparison with those at Perkins, for instance, which was a private school. Our facilities were so cramped that we had to keep you boys and girls on a short leash, and keep you going all the time, so that you wouldn't get into mischief. But eventually I established a relationship of trust with the governor and the legislature, and we got a lot of building money. Before I retired, in 1982, I was able to build nine new buildings, with the result that nowadays students live in suites, with no more than three to a suite. There are conference rooms and a swimming pool and a hundred other facilities that were unknown in your day. But, after all that, everyone is now deciding that residential schools are not the best way to educate the blind."

❧

FROM almost my first day at school, I pined for letters from home the way I pined for Indian food. Indian food was out of the question—as far as anyone at the school knew, there was scarcely an Indian restaurant in the country—but a letter did arrive once or twice a week. I remember the thrill I would feel when, in the locker room or the halls, a boy or a teacher would stop me and say, "You're wanted in the office. You have a letter from India." I would race to the office, and Mr. Woolly or the school's secretary and bookkeeper, Mrs. Lollie Hankins, would hand me my letter and wait for me to ask to have it read. Some boys got Mr. Clay to read their letters, but he stood in the middle of the lounge and declaimed them. At first, I myself had got one of my half-sighted friends to read my letter to me, but then I had decided that it was best to keep the boys in the dark about my Indian life, in case it jeopardized their acceptance of me as one of them. Even so, if Mr. Tyson was in the office—he and Mrs. Hankins sat in a room just outside the open door of Mr. Woolly's room—I would carry the letter away unread, for fear of being overheard and being derided. I would catch Mr. Woolly or Mrs. Hankins some other time. Luckily, Mr. Tyson was a restless man, and hardly ever sat at his desk.

I wrote letters home frequently, often sending one to each member of the family in a single envelope. The envelope was fat even if there was only one letter inside, because it was not unusual for me to begin a letter one day and continue it, off and on, on subsequent days, adding and amplifying. Since I was never able to read what I had typed, I would sometimes repeat myself. That, too, would swell the envelope. One of my early letters home reads:

23rd September, 1949

MY DEAR DADDYJEE,

You shall notice the difference between my first letters from U.S.A. and this one. I am writing this letter to you on my brand new Typewriter which I got two days back, but could not get time to write to you as I was so busy with all my papers [tests]. But now it is Friday night and I can be awake till ten. And the other thing, I will not have to attend classes for the following two days.

I have received $176 for the loss of my things on my way to U.S.A., which I claimed for. A bank Draft was sent to me by the airlines People on the 12th instant. That means that the loss was fully payed within a month's time, which is absolutely amazing.

I have been extremely busy, and I am very happy that after all the work I did I got hundred per cent marks in my four papers. I competed with all the good students in our class. They all have been here since their childhood, in other words, from the kindergarten.

I have been elected secretary of my class (ninth grade). The faculty have gained a good impression of me, and all the students like to be my friends, too. In other words, I am doing well and am making good friends.

24th Sep.

I know that the subjects I have taken are the most difficult ones to manage. But unfortunately, I did not have choice. They are pretty hard, especially science. One fault in this school is not providing classes for us to learn languages, which are the easiest subjects for the Blind to manage.

I have been thinking very carefully that after spending one year in U.S.A., I should go to U.K. This thought came to me after I heard the news that the English people, like Indians, had devalued their money. That means that a pound, which was worth four dollars and three cents before, now is only worth two dollars and seventy cents.

26th Sep.

The school throws a party once a fortnight where they have dancing and other such things and where the boys are permitted to have dates with the girls for nearly three hours. I stay away from mixing, of course. They had a party about a week ago. I was not proposing to go, but it seemed very rude on my part not to go when almost every person, Faculty and students, was going. Therefore I did go and join them, but more or less minded my own business. I just listened to the music. There were plenty of students who were interested to know about India, and to best of my knowledge I told them. I was also asked to dance, but as you know, I do not know how. However, I like the thought of dancing and would like to learn. Afterwards, I took one lesson from a teacher, and I know I shall learn it somehow or other. Every person over here knows how to dance, and if one does not know it, it seems quite awful. Daddyjee, I do not think that there is any harm, is there, in learning dancing?

I would like to draw your attention now toward the boys in this school. They lead very fast life but are quite nice in their own way. They are happy go lucky. They seldom bother about any other person. It is quite a mess to mix with them because their jokes are quite fast and strange, and their way of doing everything differs from us.

The boys speak about their parents as "the old man," "the old biddy." They sound quite disrespectful. Whenever I hear them talk that way, it makes me shy. That's why I'm in a way happy that your letters are read by Mr. Woolly, and not by half-sighted boys. They would make fun of me. I propose to lead a quiet life, and that is the only good thing for a person to do at such a strange place. But however, everything is going perfectly all right. I have made two or three real good friends and with who I propose to stay friends. But I do not know what is going to happen. But there is nothing to worry about.

Daddyjee, I hope you have received my letters in which I mentioned to you about my further talks with Dr. Milton Stauffer of the John Milton Society about transferring to Perkins. I have appreciated quite a bit you not writing in your letters about any such thing, since Mr. Woolly or Mrs. Hankins reads out my letters. . . . I would like you to send me a typed letter about what you think, which I shall be able to get read by one of my half-sighted friends. I am enclosing a special envelope therefore, so that when you write to me, I will be able to know from the envelope that you have written me privately.

I propose to buy a Radio with Intermixed Record Changer for eighty dollars. Intermixed means that you can mix ten- and twelve-inch, six- and four-inch records at a time, and it shall be regulated by itself and shall keep on changing records. It can hold twelve records at a time. But I shall not buy the same unless you write to me, as well as to Mr. Woolly, that I can buy one. You know that it is always better if the Superintendent is told. He then gets little importance, and Mr. Woolly is such a man who wants feeling of little importance.

I was very pleased to read the letter from Mamajee, and please thank her for taking so much trouble, and I shall write to her next time when I write to you and other members of the family.

Love to all and especially to Ashok.

With respects,

Yours affectionately,

Ved

As a rule, I sent home mostly good news, because I didn't want to disturb anyone. I reserved my complaints for Cousin Nitya Nand, in England, who, like me, was studying far away from home, and therefore, I thought, could understand my plight. I wrote this to Cousin Nitya Nand on the twenty-seventh of September:

My Dearest Brother,

What I hate about this school is that they make us go to school right after breakfast and keep us busy until nine-thirty, when we are supposed to be in bed. We do not even have a half hour which we can call one's own. It is ridiculous. There is no account or amount of things which you have to do. Even on weekends they expect you to be attending their social adjustment parties and what not. If I have to do any extra homework or want to read some psychology book or other books, I read them in the nighttime. There is dead silence then up in the sleeping hall, but reading is not allowed though most students do it. I had to get special permission to write this letter, because it is ten o'clock, when I should be in bed.

The main object of my coming to this country was to make the best of my life. I did not want any person to feel superior to me and I didn't want to feel inferior to any person, even though I do not have my sight. I am trying my best to make a success of it here.

I shall close now thinking that you are fine and everything is going smoothly for you.

With respects,

Yours affectionately,

Ved

Weeks would go by and I wouldn't hear from Cousin Nitya Nand. When at last I did hear from him, his letters would be just a few lines, dashed off at the end of a tiring day in the library or the laboratory. But

Daddyji made a point of writing to me at least once a fortnight, and his letters were long and reflective:

3rd October, 1949

MY DEAR VED,

I am very, very glad to receive your affectionate letter of the 23rd September. It is really good that you obtained 100% marks in your four papers, but please do not over-work yourself for such results. You should certainly do your best, but health should be your first consideration. I do hope you are eating well, and all kinds of food, particularly vegetables, which are so essential to fill up your bones, and which in your growing age are so very necessary.

I am glad to note that Mr. Woolly has very kindly per-mitted you to purchase a typewriter. . . . I agreed that you ought to have a radio or perhaps a combined radio and radi-ogram so that the records of Indian music that you took with you can be played. They will not only remind you of home, but also give you a sort of background, which you may find useful in combining the melody of the East with the harmony of the West. Who knows, one day you may blossom out as a composer. Now that Sterling, to which Rupee is linked, has been devalued vis-à-vis the Dollar, fewer American films will be imported into India, and Indian films are bound to have very bright future. The composers of good music will reap a rich harvest, and I would strongly urge upon you to specialize in music, both vocal and instru-mental. This will stand you in very good stead to earn a decent living in due course. I am writing accordingly to

Mr. Woolly, and if he will permit, a radio and radiogram may be purchased for you, and one hundred dollars or so may be spent on this item.

As regards dancing, do learn it, and I am sure with an ear for music, you will become a good dancer. I only wish that in my younger days, when I had such opportunities, I might have learnt to do so, which in a country like USA is, I consider, a social necessity.

Please give my best regards to Mr. Woolly. With best wishes and love from us all, I remain,

Yours affectionately,

Daddy

P.S. I am enclosing a short letter in Hindustani in Roman script to enable you to hear our vernacular. If the sense is well-conveyed, I will write to you in this way, off and on, to keep you in touch with our vocabulary, which you may use to compose songs. Do let me know how you like it. You will have to tell the reader how to pronounce nasal "n" and soft "t" as in French and long "a" as in father.

Your Daddy

I immediately grasped the meaning of Daddyji's postscript: Instead of sending me a separate letter in the special envelope, as I'd asked him to do for our private communications, he had decided to use phonetic Hindustani. That was just as well, since a letter in English could be read by unintended eyes. The postscript said:

MERAI PIYARE VED,

Mujhe tumhári chiththi parh kar bahut khushi hui. Tum ko abhi kisi aur sckool ká khiyál nahin karná chahiye. Yeh bahut achhchhá sckool malum hotā hai aur sastá bhi hai. Purá dil lagáo. Jab main aoongá to phir badli ká khiyál karenge.

Pital aur háthi dánt ki chizon ká beopár karne ká khiyál hai. Kharch kam se kam karna aur koi vazifa mial sake to lená. Tá tá se koi jawáb nahin ayá. Aur koi ummid bhi nahin hai.

Jo ivory chizain main ne bhehi hain un ke dám wohi hain.

Khoob kháyá karo aur sehat banáo.

Namaste aur piyár.

Your affectionate

Daddy

The translation is:

MY DEAR VED,

I was very glad to read your letter. You should not think of any other school. Yours appears to be a very good school, and is also cheaper. Put your heart into the studies. And when I come, then we will consider changing the school.

I am thinking of doing some trading in brass and ivory articles. Please spend as little as you can, and please accept any scholarship that may be offered. No reply has been received from Tatas. Nor is any expected. [Daddyji had applied for a scholarship for me from the celebrated Indian company.]

I have sent you some ivory articles. The prices are marked.

Do eat well and build up your health.

Namaste and love,

Your affectionate

Daddy

It was November 19th, the appointed day for Sister Umi's marriage. For weeks, I had waited for a letter from home giving me all the details. But there was no word. Although I had been away less than three months, and constantly asked after every member of the family, there had already been a falling off of day-to-day news from home. It was as if such news were not considered fit for the notice of someone in America. But Sister Umi's wedding was the biggest family event since I left home. I couldn't understand why no one had written to me about it. I sat down and typed out a series of letters—both asking for news and giving news of myself—for one of my fat envelopes:

19th November, 1949

My Dearest Sister Umi,

Your last letter said the date for your marriage was fixed for the 19th of November. But if you were getting married today I am pretty sure you would have let me know it. Since you haven't, I assume you're not. But if you are, please accept my full good wishes. [As it turned out, Umi had indeed got married on the appointed day.] I hope you will be even more happy in your new home than you were with Daddyjee, although at first it may seem like a bit of a comedown.

Yours affectionately,

Ved

19th November, 1949

MY DEAREST SISTER NIMI,

Your last letter was so uninformative that you did not even tell me how you were. I hate to be so ignorant about what is going on with the family. When you can find nothing else to write to me about, write about what is going on in the country. For instance, what was the reaction when Nathuram Godse and his cohort were hanged. [After a long trial, Godse, Gandhi's assassin, was sentenced to die by hanging.] Because here, I am sometimes asked to give a speech and I have no way of getting any news about home. You should write to me everything new happening in the Government of India.

After coming here, something has really gone wrong with me. It seems I have forgotten how to talk. In other words, I scarcely say anything unless I have some business with someone. All I do is read and think and worry. The boys over here think I am a bookworm. In fact, they call me that. The girls think I do not like girls, and in fact I hate them. Yesterday one girl asked me if I had any sisters. I said Four. She told me I didn't act like it. Nimi, I am trying to talk, but I don't know what to say. People here are so different; their talk is so different. I don't know what

I can talk to American girls about. I don't know anything about dates, so I don't know how to behave with them. I cannot keep on praising them when I do not want to or do not think that they are worth praising. I just cannot be hypocrite.

Affectionately yours,

Ved

19th November, 1949

My Dearest Mamajee,

I am fine except that I am stiff and sore from head to foot because of wrestling. As I wrote to Daddyjee earlier, I've gone in for wrestling, and Mr. Hartman says that if I work hard on the mat I have a chance for wrestling in inter-mural matches. But I am pleased that I will not have to go to Gym for the next two days—it is the weekend. Finally, I'll be able to get some rest.

Yours affectionately,

Ved

As I soon learned from Mr. Woolly (he often shared his letters and cables from Daddyji with me), Daddyji was alarmed about my wrestling. Immediately after receiving my letter, he cabled Mr. Woolly;

1949 NOV 20 AM 7 33

VED UNDERWEIGHT DELICATE GROWING FAST STRENUOUS EXERCISES WRESTLING RUNNING INAD-

VISABLE WEIGHT INCREASING DIET REST WALKS REC-
OMMENDED

MEHTA

Daddyji followed up his cable with this letter to
Mr. Woolly, in which he elaborated on the theme of
my health:

22nd November, 1949

MY DEAR MR. WOOLLY,

I learnt from Ved's recent letter that he proposes to
become a featherweight wrestler and that he is seriously
preparing for the same by undertaking running and by
avoiding weight-increasing diet. I should hardly have inter-
fered in his selection, but I feel it my duty to acquaint you
that since his blindness, he has not remained in very good
health, and any strenuous exercise and exhaustion have had
an adverse effect upon his health. What he needs, is plenty
of nourishing diet to enable him to put on weight in this
growing period in his life. As I attach much importance to
this aspect, I sent you a cablegram, thereby enabling my
views to reach you as early as possible.

My only fear has been Ved's general health. He is rather
underweight for his height and is practically skin and bones;
and efforts appear to be necessary to make him put on weight,
to give him some reserve to avoid deterioration in his health.

It may interest Ved to know that a couple of days ago,
I met Pandit Nehru on his return from America. He inquired

about Ved's progress, and I assured him that Ved was being very well looked-after—making good progress at your school.

Yours sincerely,

A. R. Mehta

In the meantime, in reply to Daddyji's cable Mr. Woolly had written this letter:

November 21, 1949

DEAR DR. MEHTA:

I had your cable this morning and hasten to assure you that Ved is not taking undue exercise. It is true that he is working with the wrestling team, but this simply gives him a little more personal supervision in his physical activities. We were happy when Ved indicated a desire to go out for the team because we felt it would widen his perspective and make him more a part of the student body. He is not working with the team with any idea of wrestling in an interschool match this year. However, Mr. Hartman had thought he might use him a time or two late in the year in an intramural match here in school. However, if you had rather he not wrestle at all, it will be no trouble to change him from the wrestling class to the usual Physical Education class. I have checked his weight, finding he weighed in at 96 pounds in September and now weighs 106½. That in itself is encouraging.

Sincerely yours,

J. M. Woolly, Superintendent

As Mr. Woolly had suggested, I had been keen to join the wrestling team, but I soon found that the training was so rigorous that I had merely to think about it to set off heart palpitations, which sometimes lasted for an hour. I appealed to Mr. Woolly to allow me to leave the team, but he said he didn't want to naysay Mr. Hartman until he had some further word from Daddyji—Daddyji's and Mr. Woolly's letters had crossed. Then, one morning early in Decemember, Mr. Woolly called me to his office and read me this letter from Daddyji:

26th November, 1949

MY DEAR MR. WOOLLY,

Thank you for your kind letter of 21st November. . . . My only anxiety is that in this growing age, as Ved is already underweight for his height, he may not over-exert himself. He has inherited the family tendency to do things with all his might—with perhaps little or no consideration for his physical and mental well-being in the future. I myself am a victim of this tendency. I was, in my time, the only athlete in the university who excelled in sprints as well as in long-distance races, and as such, did not realize the consequences of strenuous training, which I underwent with practically no coaching, with the result that it affected my heart. Eventually I had to give up not only hockey, but also playing tennis in tournaments, and now I just play what you may call a little social tennis, though off and on I still persist in taking on younger men who are competing in championships. I have great difficulty in curbing this tendency, in spite of being a medical man myself.

Please convey my gratitude to Mr. Hartman for his personal interest in Ved. I am sure you and he know what is best for Ved. It was perhaps the overanxiety of the father who is thousands of miles away from the son that was responsible for my sending the cablegram that I did. All I can say is that Ved needs careful watching and perhaps some brake on his enthusiasm in anything he may be doing. In his case rest and recreation should play an equal part with his other activities.

In one of your letters you mentioned your wife and two sons. All good news from Ved makes us feel so grateful to you, that the family shall feel a great satisfaction to have a photograph of you and your family on our mantelpiece. May I, therefore, hope that you would very kindly oblige us by sending a copy.

With kindest regards and all good wishes, I remain,

Yours sincerely,

A. R. Mehta

After reading this letter, Mr. Woolly told Mr. Hartman that I had to be taken off the wrestling team. But my relief was short-lived, because Mr. Hartman put me on a regimen of rigorous calisthenics. So the end result was that I had none of the prestige of a school wrestler and all the pain. On top of this, I had to bear the undisguised resentment of Mr. Hartman, who felt that he had been frustrated in his ambitions for me and the team.

❧

ONE morning, Mr. Woolly came up to me at the vending stand and said, "Son, you think you can talk about your homeland and Communism to a group of ladies in town?" I must have looked puzzled, because he went on, "They belong to the Wesleyan Service Guild No. 1 of the Little Rock First Methodist Church. They read about you in the paper, and want you to come over and talk to them on November 28th. I'm sure that whatever you say to the good ladies will be appreciated. I'm sure you'll do the school and yourself mighty proud."

"I've never given a speech in my life," I said, trying to control a fit of trembling. "I'll try to figure out something to say."

"That's the boy," he said, clapping me on the shoulder. "I'll come with you, and bring along the school's public-address system."

Every evening, I would stay on in the library after study hall and try to write something out in Braille, but either I would have so many ideas that I wouldn't know where to start or my mind would go blank. I wished Daddyji had given me some training in public speaking. As the day for the talk approached, I had trouble sleeping, and when I did sleep I often woke up in the middle of the night, my heart beating fast, with a vague recollection of some unpleasant dream.

Then Mr. Woolly and I received letters from Daddyji, who gave me many pointers for my speech and wrote to Mr. Woolly:

Ved has been writing to me about a speech he is preparing to deliver to a small audience. Though his knowledge is limited, considering his age he knows quite a good bit of the topics of the day that affect India. Our Prime Minister Nehru's recent visit to America must have given him a real thrill. Pandit Nehru's visit to America was a great success and brought the two great nations—the one materially very far advanced, and the other, though economically backward, still rich in cultural heritage—closer together; such a fusion is bound to add to the peace and prosperity of the world.

Daddyji's confidence in me bucked me up. I decided that I would talk about Partition, Gandhiji, and Prime Minister Nehru—things I knew about—and bring in Communism somehow. I managed to write out an eighteen-page speech. I felt so good about it that I even dreamed of publishing it in the *Reader's Digest,* the magazine most commonly read at the school.

The day before my speech, I heard that my name had been announced on the radio. Mrs. Hankins told me that there was an article in the *Arkansas Gazette* about my pending appearance, and as a result Mr. Woolly had received calls from two other groups who wanted me to come and speak to them. I had a renewed attack of nerves.

❧

"Friends, the text for the day is Matthew, Chapter 13, Verse 57," the president of the Service Guild announced to about seventy-five women attending the meeting. "A prophet is not without honor, save in his own country, and in his own house." The loudspeaker gave a squeak, practically making me jump out of my chair on the platform.

"It's just a little feedback, son," whispered Mr. Woolly, who was sitting next to me. After the reading of the text, the president introduced me, mentioning that India was so backward in education for the blind that I had had to come all the way to Arkansas to get a proper education.

I stepped up to the microphone with my speech. I had a terrible cold. I couldn't steady my fingers—that made reading the Braille difficult. But somehow I began, half reading, half ad-libbing, "Ladies, thank you for having me here tonight." I wanted to say more of a complimentary nature, but I couldn't think of anything, so I pressed on, talking about how Gandhi and Nehru had helped us to get our independence, and how that independence had brought in its wake the Partition, which had made all of my family members and relatives refugees, along with eleven million others—Hindus, Sikhs, and Muslims. Then I turned to the subject of Communism in India. "At present, the people of India are bitterly opposed to Communism. But Communism remains a threat. There was a village near our old home in Simla where only one man could read. That's the case in most Indian villages. If that man is a Communist, the villagers are going to be Communists, for they have no other way of getting information. Being simple people, they take a man at his word. So the Indian government is now setting up free schools in the villages, where the children of these people can be taught to read and write, so that they can get information for themselves. Our other main goal is to give the people milk and food." I turned next to Communism and India's foreign policy. "Our Prime Minister Nehru would like Joseph Stalin and President Truman to meet to discuss the Korean crisis. He would like to serve as mediator. I think this is an excellent idea. It is not that Prime Minister Nehru is trying to get the United States to give in to Communism but only that we in India believe there must be a solution other than war to the present crisis. You see, we Hindus believe that there are many paths to salvation, but all of them must follow the way of nonviolence and truth."

There was a lot of clapping. I never knew women could clap so hard, but then no one, as far as I could remember, had ever clapped for me before. The president asked if there were any questions.

"What do you think about Gandhi's philosophy?" a woman asked me from the floor.

I had no profound thoughts about it, but I talked anyway. I went on to answer questions on other big topics. I have difficulty talking to girls my age, I thought, but here I am talking to women two and three times my age. I wished that Mary Ann Lambert, Vernelle Stewart, and Lois Woodward could have heard me.

"Let us now turn to page one hundred and fifty-six of the hymnal and sing," the president said. There was a flutter in the room as the women stood up and looked for the page in the hymnal. They sang:

> Come, O thou Traveller unknown,
> Whom still I hold, but cannot see,

> My company before is gone,
> And I am left alone with Thee.

I didn't know the hymn, but whenever I caught the sung words I formed them with my lips, trying not to fall too far behind.

❧

SOON after I arrived at the school, I started keeping a journal, and I continued it intermittently during my stay in Arkansas. I always typed my entries, though this meant that, as with my letters, I had no way of reading what I'd written. But, unlike my letters, the entries tended to be short, and I was able to compose them in my head before I typed them. Then again, sometimes I was too tired to care what I typed, but it didn't seem to matter, since I never imagined that anyone would ever read them. Typing the journal was for me like talking to my pillow, which could neither remember nor repeat one syllable.

My Arkansas journal remained silent for some thirty years. Then, while I was going through some old papers in preparation for writing this narrative, I happened upon it. Even though the events recounted in it were ancient personal history, as it were, I was loath to break the seal of silence, for it would mean confronting what I dimly remembered as my embarrassing adolescent self, and exposing it to the adult eyes of someone else—those of the person who would read it to me. After a struggle, I sat down with my reader and gave myself over to my unvarnished, lonely voice speaking in the middle of Arkansas.

❦

September 16, 1949

DADDYJEE wrote and told me that I should write something every day. He said that it should be material with universal appeal. I can write such material. But I don't quite understand what he expects me to do with it. Anyway, I've made a resolution to type out my reactions to the happenings of the day whenever I can. I would like to write about my impressions of America and myself—to put my memories in a neat order and explain the new country and my character. I think I will find this task very enjoyable and pleasant. I won't have too much time to devote to it, though. No doubt I'll make many mistakes in grammar and typing.

Some other entries:

September 18

On Sundays, there is no supper here. When we leave the noon meal, we pick up a bag of sandwiches. I ate mine at tea time and was very hungry all evening. So I drank a lot of water. Sometimes I wake up in the night and I'm so hungry that I could eat my bed.

September 24

There was a social hour in the gym this evening. We new students were introduced, and were required to mix with the faculty. We were judged by how good mixers we were, I think. Daddyjee is a much better mixer than I am.

Most students talked about the summer. They all seemed to have sat around on porches and listened to the radio. The blind here, outside of school, seem to be little better off than I was at home, when I was idle all day long and longed for something to do.

September 28

Choir is getting really interesting. Today we learned the words to "Skip to Maloo," "Oh Promise Me," and "Be Still My Heart." What is "Maloo"? Must somehow find out discreetly.

September 30

Lois cleared her throat in English class today. I thought of Mamajee's cough. Then I heard Mamajee clicking the knitting needles as she hummed to herself. I heard the scraping sound of Daddyjee's pumps on the bare floor as he worked his feet into them. There were raindrops on the tin roof of our Simla cottage and the hiss and rattle as the coals finally caught fire in the fireplace.

October 8

Today I went with McNabb to Stifft's Station, to take my jacket to Bumpus Cleaners. We had to cross the very busy West Markham Street in front of the school to get to it. Stifft's Station was a wondrous little place—it had only three or four shops, but you could get anything there. There was also a telephone that worked automatically when you put a nickel into it. Most surprisingly, there was no sentry at the intersection, as at home. There was just a traffic light which turned different colors, and the drivers obeyed it by themselves. What self-discipline Americans have!

October 10

After study hall, we went to the student dining room to fold Christmas seals. The tables were covered with stacks of long envelopes and sheets of what felt like stamps. McNabb explained to me that the seals said "Be Thankful You Can See," and were supposed to raise money for the Rehabilitation Center for the Blind in Little Rock.

In order to make us work faster, Mr. Woolly organized us into teams and ran contests among tables. But no matter how fast we worked, there were always more stacks of seals. We worked for four hours. At the end of the evening we were given a free Coke.

October 12

This was the third evening of folding seals. But Mr. Woolly told us that he was cancelling school tomorrow so that we could spend the whole day folding more seals. He said there was to be no school the day after, either, and we would spend that morning folding seals, too. I wish we could get on with our studies.

October 14

After folding seals, we went to the circus at Robinson Auditorium with a group called the Shriners. Most of us totally blind boys sat with partially sighted fellows so that they could tell us what was going on.

There were clowns throwing buckets of confetti, acrobats flying through the air, bears, elephants, and horses running and jumping. I wish I could say that I enjoyed it, but it was mostly a lot of noise.

October 15

This evening we had a "Backward Dance." Girls asked boys for dates. No girl asked me. Everyone walked up the steps to the gym backward, went in backward, danced backward. No girl asked me to dance, although now I know a little foxtrot and waltz.

October 16

This being Sunday, we had a special lunch of Southern fried chicken and a lot of corn bread. But Joe complained that the peas were hard. Mr. Hartman overheard him, and told Joe off. He said that the students who fussed most about the food were usually those who had come from poor families and had far worse food at home than we had at school.

October 21

I got my report card for the first six-week period today. It's not very good, but I set it down here so that I can later compare it with better report cards: English—A; Civics—C+; Junior Business Training—B; General Science—C+; Industrial Arts—Incomplete; Physical Education—B; Piano—B+; Orchestral Instruction (Violin)—Incomplete; Public School Music (Choir)—A—. I was also graded on my character, and because I can't remember the character part to copy it, I'm stapling it to this entry:

Characteristics	School Life		
	Good	Average	Poor
Co-operation		√	
Courtesy		√	
Attitude		√	
Personal Appearance		√	
Dining Room Etiquette		√	
Housekeeping			

Characteristics	Dormitory Life		
	Good	Average	Poor
Co-operation		√	
Courtesy	√		
Attitude		√	
Personal Appearance		√	
Dining Room Etiquette			
Housekeeping		√	

October 26

Today the Shriners took us to the Livestock Show. They pinned a free pass on each of us and gave us large cowboy hats. The brim of my hat extended almost beyond my shoulders. Oather, Bruton, McNabb, and I—the four of us were in one group—had trouble walking together because our hats were always bumping into each other. I wished I knew what cowboys were and why they wore such hats.

I didn't know what to expect. I thought we might

pat some cows or feed a sheep or two. Instead, the Shriner leading our group took us on some really strange rides. Everyone else called the rides amusement, but I wouldn't have gone near them if I could have seen what they were. I didn't stop screaming.

Then the Shriner took us to the sideshows and described one freakish woman after another. There was a woman with a horse's head, and one with snake scales for skin. There was also a wonderful, friendly lady who had lobster's claws for hands and feet. I asked the Shriner whether these women had been born this way, or had been dressed up for the shows. He said they were born that way. I had a fit of shudders. I asked how they lived, how they survived. The Shriner asked me a question back—how did I think horses and snakes and lobsters lived? I didn't know what to think.

November 1

In the locker room this morning, the laundry-woman said to me that she hadn't seen my underpants in the laundry pile—what did I do with them? At first, I didn't know what she was talking about, but when I finally understood, I had to tell her that I had never worn anything under my trousers. The locker room couldn't believe that I was fifteen years old and had never worn underpants.

Mr. Woolly drove me downtown and we bought some underpants in a dime-store. When I think of the incident, though, I get ashamed all over again.

November 3

Today everyone went away for fall holidays. The entire school emptied out like the bucket with a hole in it in Mr. Clay's song. I don't know how I'll get through the four days in this ghostly building.

November 6

I don't know what I would do in this country without a radio. They have such great programs during the day: "Ma Perkins," "Stella Dallas," "Lorenzo Jones," "Portia Faces Life." In the evening, there is always "Dragnet" or "Gang Busters" to listen to. I feel so sad when these shows end for the day.

November 18

We had a checkup by the dentist in the infirmary. He looked into my mouth and said that he would like to steal my teeth—I didn't have a single cavity. But he asked me how I had broken my front tooth. I told him about my roller-skating accident in Simla. He said that the tooth would give me trouble, and pulled it out. It really hurt a lot. Now Max Cary tells me that I should have kept it and had it capped. I feel very bad.

November 22

We had a Thanksgiving dance with hay on the floor, boys in blue jeans, girls in ginghams. But what is Thanksgiving? There are so many things I'd like to ask about, but won't—I don't want to remind people of my separateness.

December 1

Very excited. Am reading three new Talking Books: "A Connecticut Yankee in King Arthur's Court," by Twain; "The 500 Hats of Bartholomew Cubbins," by Seuss; "The Big Fisherman," by Douglas. I wish I could make people laugh and cry the way these writers do.

December 2

Today I gave a talk to an outstanding school in Little Rock. I spoke to the sixth-grade class for twenty minutes successfully and was asked many brilliant questions. One boy asked me what the main animal in India was. That question got me; then I thought of monkeys, and told them that in the hills we have plenty of monkeys, and how a monkey had once snatched a banana out of my hand while I was eating it. Then a girl asked me to define life. I was startled absolutely. I thought hard for a moment and then said with great confidence, "Struggling for existence." The more I think about it, the more I realize what a good answer it was.

December 8

Bruton, McNabb, George Conner, Treadway, Jackie Elam, Billy Tabor, Oather Brown, James Pickett, John Stewart, James Spakes, and Charlie Wren are all Bronco Busters. In fact, all the best-liked boys in the school are on the wrestling team. They have been given nice uniforms—gold tights with short black jersey trunks to be worn over them—and they will be travelling to nice places like Muskogee and Baton Rouge for meets. How I wish I could have gone on to be a Bronco Buster!

December 9

I got my report card for the second six-week period today. I did better in Civics, Violin, Piano, P.E., and Industrial Arts. Most of my character marks went from "average" to "good." But I went down in Science by almost a grade. My reputation is in danger.

December 10

We had a wrestling match with the Kentucky School for the Blind. The match started at 7:30 p.m. and lasted two-and-a-half hours. We won 33-12. After that, there was a reception for Kentucky in the Cottage. It lasted till midnight. The pretty girls seemed to talk only to wrestlers.

December 11

Today we had our Christmas dance. Everyone had to dance with everyone else, whether he or she could dance or not. During the punch-and-cookie time Mr. Woolly wrote our names on little slips of paper and held a drawing. He explained that on the night of the Christmas program, we had to give a present to the person whose name we got. I got Lois's name. I wonder what she would like.

December 13

This evening we had our Christmas program. There was a tree by the stage, and we all placed our presents under it. While visitors and children sat in the auditorium, everyone in the high school sat on the stage. We all had a part in the program of singing and acting and talking. After the program, Mr. Woolly handed us all our Christmas presents. I got a record from Anna Belle Morris, with a Braille note saying that it was "Devil's Trill" by Tartini—her favorite record. I gave Lois an ivory brooch, which had a lot of little elephants carved on it.

December 14

I finally went to the infirmary for cold medicine. I've had a cold almost since the day I arrived in Little

Rock. The nurse said that I have a cold because I'm underweight and I'm homesick, and that she had no medicine to help me.

December 15

In assembly today, Mr. Tyson said that in order to be on the honor roll, a student had to have no grade below B, and to receive "average" or "good" character marks. Only four people in the high school had qualified during the second six-week grading period: June Brooks and Mary Ann Lambert from the twelfth grade, George McNabb from the tenth grade, and Wayne Tidman from my grade. How I hope that I will be on it one day!

I had a letter from Daddyjee today. He said that the Reserve Bank of India had cancelled all the permits for foreign exchange it used to grant people for study abroad. Daddyjee said that we had to apply for a new permit every six months. We still haven't heard from the immigration authorities in the United States if they will approve this school for foreign students. Will I get money to stay on here? Will the school be permitted to keep me here? I'm in a big pickle.

December 25

The night watchman just brought me two presents which Mr. Woolly had kept in his office for delivery today. One present is three twelve-inch records from the Methodist group. The other is from Mr. and Mrs. Dickens. It is a beautiful gold tiepin, which must have cost them at least five dollars. Luckily, I had heard about the custom of exchanging presents at Christmas in this country and sent Mr. and Mrs. Dickens a bathmat made at our school.

January 2, 1950

Christmas vacation ended today, and everyone is drifting back to school. I thought the day would never come.

January 18

Mr. Woolly announced in assembly that Bruton and George Conner have been chosen as the school's "star grapplers." They will be going to New Orleans in March to wrestle in a tournament, and some El Dorado club will pay their way.

January 21

The United States is developing a hydrogen bomb. They say it's one thousand times more powerful than the atomic bomb. It has been said by the greatest scientists that a mere eight hydrogen bombs could finish off Russia. Just imagine!

They say scientists have invented a marvellous thing. It is called the "listening glove for the deaf." On the tip of each glove finger is some kind of electric device which is connected to a portable machine. When someone talks to the deaf person, the machine changes the sound waves into little harmless electric shocks. The deaf person can "listen" by feeling those electric shocks from the glove, much as a telegraph operator can "read" Morse code.

March 1

I just cannot figure out what I can do for my summer vacation. Whenever I think of the summer, I have a sinking feeling.

March 3

I am making inquiries about going to a small school for amateur radio operators in Little Rock this summer. That way, I will get some training in electronics, and possibly be able to talk to my family in India. Also, Mr. Woolly has written to Mr. F. E. Davis, of the Printing House for the Blind, in Kentucky, asking if I could get a summer job working at the Braille press. We are bound to set up a Braille printing press in India someday, and then my training would be useful.

March 4

They have put Romain Rolland's "Jean-Christophe" on Talking Books. They don't have it in the school library, but I think I can order it directly from the Library of Congress. I remember how sad I felt when Sister Nimi was reading it and I couldn't read it.

March 5

A state photographer came to our school and took class and group pictures. I have ordered ten copies of each picture to send home.

March 24

I went to the annual senior play, "Let's Pretend." It featured Mary Ann Lambert as a girl who leaves college to get married. This girl is sweet and lovable but unreachable by the people around her because she lives almost completely in her imagination. Whenever I heard Mary Ann Lambert's voice, I got goosebumps.

March 25

I got a record from home that the family had had specially made by going to a studio. I was able to hear everyone's voice for the first time in seven months. I couldn't control my tears.

April 7

Mary Ann Lambert gave a piano recital today. She has been taking piano at the school since she was eight, and now she's a blossoming eighteen. The recital was superb. The piece I like best was "Clair de Lune." It was composed by a French composer. That's why the name is in French. I am fixing to learn that piece.

April 12

For three days, I was confined to bed in the school infirmary. There were such terrible sores under my toes that I could not even stand. The disease has a terrible name—athlete's foot. I am telling everyone that I cut my foot on a piece of broken glass in the shower and it will take a long time to heal. I have written that home, too. I am so embarrassed.

April 19

Mr. Tyson announced in assembly today that Lois Woodward and I, from the ninth grade, and James Pickett and Mary Ann Lambert, from the twelfth grade, had made the honor roll for the last six-week period. I have been walking on air ever since.

May 1

I don't know what I'm going to do about clothes. The laundry has lost two of my shirts, and my other clothes are worn out.

May 2

I hope Brother Om does well in his B.A. exam. All his career depends on it. Sister Nimi will be graduating this year, too. I hope she's not still refusing to get married. She was very unrealistic about marriage when I left. Ashok, Usha, and Brother Om will all be home for the summer. How I wish I could be, too!

May 7

It is getting hotter and more humid by the day.

Whenever I think of the money Daddyjee is spending on me, I feel sad. He has already had to pay six hundred dollars for my tuition and board here this year. I had the extra expense of staying in New York when I arrived. Because this was my first year, there have also been other extraordinary expenses for a typewriter, a radio-phonograph combination, a battery-powered radio, a Braille wristwatch. I'm practically out of money, and I need to buy summer clothes and pay for my long-vacation room and board somewhere. I was expecting four hundred dollars for the summer, but Daddyjee's latest draft was only for three hundred. I must get a summer job.

I have applied for permission to work, to the immigration authorities, but have heard nothing. They still haven't approved this school for foreign students. Also, there has been no word from the Reserve Bank of India about sanctioning dollars for my studies next year. Oh, God, I don't know what will happen to me!

May 17

Mr. Woolly announced in assembly that the town authorities had finally installed a special traffic light for the blind to the west of the school, at the corner of West Markham and South Woodrow. Mr. Woolly said that there is a button at waist height on a pole on each side of West Markham. When you press the button, the permanent green light changes to red for fourteen seconds and a bell rings while the light is red. This means that even totally blind people lacking in mobility will be able to cross to the trolley stop or to Stifft's Station.

May 23

School closed for the summer today after the commencement exercises at 8 P.M. My sleep is ruined. Mary Ann Lambert has graduated and left the school for good. Oh, God, why did this happen to me? I have lost all reason, but I am not going to let my infatuation with Mary Ann Lambert be termed love. I won't allow myself to fall in love. I have too many responsibilities. I will never marry a half-sighted or blind girl. I shall not marry merely for love. I want to marry for more solid reasons. I want my marriage to last. My mind is in a thousand pieces. Sighs are concealed in my breathing. Tears are in my eyes. Tears are a sign of weakness. I abhor weakness.

V

A DONKEY AMONG HORSES

It may never have been said, but a philosopher can adapt himself anywhere. Especially a 16-year-old philosopher who mingles with American youngsters. . . .

Never have I seen a blind boy his age with so much self-confidence. The world to him is as though he had conquered it. He knows exactly where he is and what he is going to do.

—Feature story in the
Arkansas Democrat, June 30, 1950.

W E HAVE BEEN BUSY DEVELOPING A NEW KIND of social-adjustment program for y'all," Mr. Woolly said in assembly one spring day in 1950. "As with our earlier program, its purpose is to teach you skills that you will need to be successful in the sighted world but that you can't pick up on your own, because you can't learn by imitation, the way sighted children do. They learn how to eat, how to walk, how to sit, how to hold themselves, by imitating adults. A blind youngster must be taught everything. We are all accepted by others because of our good manners, our good habits, our good attitudes. All our relations with our fellow-man depend on them. We look upon social-adjustment programs as an integral part of your education here. Through them we hope to teach you all the skills for daily living. Learning any kind of social adjustment isn't easy. It requires practice, like learning to play the piano or the saxophone. And I must again warn you youngsters that no one on the staff has had any special training in teaching social adjustment, or even knows exactly what it is; however, all the members of the staff have been helping in the shaping of the new program, and we have worked out several courses for you. Your teachers have drawn lots to decide who will teach you which course, so they'll be learning on the job from y'all, just as y'all will be learning from them. We have initially assigned two to six weeks for each course, and we will extend the time when we feel it's necessary. These courses will meet in the periods set aside for assembly or other non-academic subjects, like junior business. All you youngsters in the junior and senior high school will be divided up in small groups for classes. Now, I want y'all to get out there and really do A.S.B proud, hear?"

❧

MISS HARPER took some of us for a general course in etiquette, personal appearance, and hygiene. "People think that because you see very little or not at all you don't care about things that sighted people do, like how you look when you eat or how your clothes look when you go out," Miss Harper said in one class. "But that's a myth. There's no reason for the blind to have bad manners or be poorly groomed." She talked to us about table manners, explaining how spoons, knives, and forks were set out on a table and in what order we should pick them up. She went on, "You shouldn't fiddle with the silverware. You shouldn't even touch it until you're served. You should keep your hands under the table until you're ready to eat. In polite society, people will generally serve you from the left, so when you hear someone approaching to serve you, shift gracefully to the right and make room. You'll probably be able to tell what you have on your plate from the smell or the sound. If not, quietly ask about it. Then pick up the right piece of silverware. Don't grope for the bowl or plate in front of you—that's a 'blindism.' Just start eating."

"You have any tips for eating soup?" Vernelle asked. "I can never keep the soup in the spoon."

"Hell, just bend down and pick up the bowl and put it to your mouth," Oather said.

"Now, that's enough, Oather," Miss Harper said,

and she continued, "Try holding the spoon level and steady, Vernelle. Then the soup won't spill."

"Miss Harper, I have the biggest trouble with them peas," Peggy Lou said. "They swim around in the gravy and I get the whole mess down my front."

"Peggy Lou, you're not alone in having trouble with peas. That's why so many of you boys and girls are getting 'Poor' on your report cards in dining-room etiquette. I think the best thing for y'all to do is to hold a piece of bread or a roll in your left hand and use it to push the peas onto your fork."

"Is that how sighted people eat?" I asked.

"Oh, no," Miss Harper said. "Most sighted people don't need to use a piece of bread as a pusher. Only crude sighted people do."

The word "crude" stung. I almost stopped listening to Miss Harper. I sat back and wondered whether it would be better to renounce altogether foods, like peas, that required pushers, and concentrate on dry, easy-to-manage foods, like roast potatoes, but I decided I couldn't do that, because that would be cowardly.

"If you're going to meet a sighted person, be sure that you're not wearing a navy-blue shirt with brown pants," Miss Harper was saying.

"Those of us who were born blind don't know what blue and brown are, and some of us don't care," Vernelle said.

"You have to learn to care," Miss Harper said. "You've just got to learn what matches what, and work out your own system for telling colors. Now, all of you know that Mr. Chiles is probably the best socially adjusted blind person in the country. He always has

the right tie on with the right shirt. You can learn to
do that, too, boys. When you put your shirts in the
laundry, you can mark them with little safety pins. If
it's a white shirt, you can put a safety pin in the top
buttonhole. If it's blue, you can put it in the second
buttonhole. You can mark your ties in a similar way."

"But how does Mr. Chiles know which ties and
shirts to buy in the first place?" Treadway asked.

"Well, he probably has a friend who has very good
taste, and once a year he probably goes with his friend
and gets everything he needs for the year. Any other
questions?"

"Miss Harper, when I went to this restaurant in
my home town and ordered an orange, the waitress
brought me half an orange with the darn spoon sticking out," Fat Earnie Barnett said. "I told her I couldn't
eat it that way. She said, 'You want me to feed you?' I
said, 'Go right ahead, Miss.' She walked away as if I'd
pulled up her skirt."

Everyone laughed.

"What did I do wrong?" Fat Earnie asked. "What
should I have done? I'd never heard of anyone eating
an orange that way."

"Now, Earnest, you wouldn't be making light of
serious matters, would you?" Miss Harper asked sus-
piciously.

"I'm not, Miss Harper. All the guys know that
oranges are my favorite."

"Well, if you can't manage the orange with a spoon,
then you've just got to pass it up, because if you start
poking around the orange with your fingers you'll give
a poor impression of all blind people," Miss Harper

said. "Y'all have got to try to keep in mind all the time that each one of you is an emissary to the country of the sighted."

"MOST sighted people shy away from handicapped people," Mr. Chiles observed, conducting one of our social-adjustment classes. "They're frightened off by anyone who's not like them, so you have to make an extra effort to make them feel that it's worth their while to get to know you. You have to convince them that you're not very different from them, that you're a likable fellow, and that they'd enjoy being around you. You've constantly got to show them that you can do things they think you can't possibly do—that you can work like them, that you're a good bet. You've got to sell yourself to them. It's an uphill struggle all the way, but you've got to do it. If you don't prove your worth to the sighted, you will live lonely, miserable lives, without sighted friends, without work, without a useful place in society."

"Why are people frightened off by us?" Treadway asked. "I don't think I'm very different from the sighted."

"Ignorance," Mr. Chiles said. "Plain ignorance. They think people who are handicapped are different from them."

The remark gave me pause. If difference is what puts sighted people off us, I thought, then my blind fellow-students, in turn, must be put off by me. In some way, I'd always known that, and from the very beginning I had taken care to seem like everyone else at the school, and kept my different, Indian background a dark secret, instinctively realizing that it would get in the way of my acceptance and add to the feeling of separateness that I carried like a burden. And my wish to win acceptance at the school was so strong that to me, often, everything in my background seemed inferior, everything in the backgrounds of the other students superior.

"But Mr. Woolly, Mr. Tyson, and Miss Harper aren't frightened off by us critters," Oather said.

"They live with us," Mr. Chiles said. "They see us every day. They take our capabilities for granted. But I'm sure that outside the school all of us have had the experience of meeting sighted people who are frightened off by us. Since most of us came here when we were little, we don't have these experiences often enough to help us keep the problem in mind."

"Then what should we do for these sighted critters?" Oather wanted to know.

"Do what we're doing here—learn social adjustment," Mr. Chiles said.

"But there are a lot of sighted people with bad social adjustment," Bruton said.

"You bet your life there are, Kenneth—half the sighted people, I'd wager," Mr. Chiles said. "But what the sighted can get away with we can't. Whenever we do anything wrong, they chalk it up to our blindness. They pity us, feel sorry for us, call us poor creatures, commit the worst sin of all—excuse us on the ground that we're blind, that we don't know any better. We have to deal—I'll go further, compete—with the sighted on their own terms."

Several boys and girls, talking at once, said that they didn't know why we always needed to seek the approval of the sighted world.

"I'll take on any sighted critter when it comes to chewing tobacco," Oather said confidently.

Everyone laughed, but after some discussion most of us acknowledged that Mr. Chiles had a point. Peggy Lou, however, asked in a grating voice, "What good is social adjustment? We'll end up making brooms and mops in sheltered workshops for the blind anyway. There who's going to care whether we're socially adjusted or not?" Her voice penetrated the room like the nasal buzz of a muted trumpet.

"Even in sheltered workshops, there will be some half-sighted or sighted supervisors, Peggy Lou," Mr. Chiles said. "That kind of talk shows that you have a bad attitude, and blind people who have a bad attitude really have a tough time out in the world. They contribute to the bad impression that sighted people everywhere have of us, because people with a bad attitude come across as embittered and angry and frustrated."

"But the longer we stay here the less idea we have of what it's like in the sighted world," Bruton said, and he added, as if he had had a new thought, "Wouldn't it be better for us to go to an ordinary, sighted public school instead of this here residential school?"

"If you went to an ordinary public school, you'd

have difficulty learning skills that blind people need,"
Mr. Chiles said. "Our social-adjustment classes are a
good example of what I mean."

Some of the students said that there could be special classes in those skills at ordinary, sighted schools.
But Mr. Chiles insisted that there were certain things
that could be learned thoroughly only in residential
schools for the blind. For the first time, I felt glad that
I hadn't gone to the Arkansas School from elementary
school on, as Mr. Chiles and most of the boys and girls
there had. I reflected that perhaps Mr. Chiles himself
might not have ended up teaching in the school—in
its way, a sheltered workshop—if he'd had more experience of the wider, sighted world.

"Whatever y'all think about the different issues
we've been discussing, there's no getting around the
fact that we are a few blind people in a big sighted
world," Mr. Chiles concluded. "If we don't succeed in
fitting into it, we'll never amount to anything."

It's true, I thought. We're like donkeys in a world
of horses. We have to prove our worth—justify our
very existence—to the horses. We have to show them
that if, for instance, we don't have their gait and mane,
can't run as fast as they can, we can lug more weight,
work harder, and put in longer hours. In another sense,
as a person from a backward, poor land I'm a donkey
even in this school.

"My mother just got married again, and now I've
got a stepfather around the house," a new student I'll
call Dale was saying. "Whenever I get up to go to the
bathroom, he puts his hand under my arm and practically lifts me up and shoves me into the bathroom.

He's really rough. Once, he made me fall and hurt myself."

"Next time, tell him nicely not to do it," Mr. Chiles said.

"I've done told him, but he don't listen."

"Well, then, you just have to keep on trying," Mr. Chiles said. "That's all that people in our situation can do."

"But I've done made up my mind to hit him the next time he does that to me," Dale said.

"Bless my stars!" Mr. Chiles exclaimed. "If you hit him, he may throw you out of the house. Then who'll take you in?"

Dale became silent. Everyone did, and I reflected that even those of us who had known only natural parents lived with the fear of being thrown out with no place to go. Perhaps because we sensed that our parents would have preferred us to be sighted, we grew up with the feeling that we were disappointments to them. Certainly many boys and girls talked as if they were a burden on their families, were unwanted and unloved. I myself wasn't free of the general feeling of insecurity around me. The fact that my family did love me, that they did want me, seemed to make little difference now that I was an alien ten thousand miles away from home, dependent on the good will of my adopted family, as it were. After all, Mr. Woolly—my stepfather, in a manner of speaking—had the power to throw me out for any reason.

❦

As part of the new social-adjustment program, each of us was assigned a faculty adviser, and had a private conference with that person, so that he or she could point out social defects too embarrassing to discuss in public. To my astonishment, some of the boys who had already had their private conferences talked about them openly in the sleeping hall, as if they wanted to boast about them.

"These individual conferences are for the birds," Max said, from his bed. "You know what Miss Shults told me? She said she didn't ever want to see me kissing Mary Ann Lambert again—that people like us doing that in public gave visually handicapped people a bad name. And you know what else she said? The staff is thinking up a social-adjustment test with questions like 'Blind people should pet in public. True or false?' " There was scattered laughter in the sleeping hall, though I, for one, wasn't sure if Max was telling the plain truth or embellishing it, as he was wont to do.

"I think the conferences are a good idea," Bruton said thoughtfully, from his bed. "My adviser, Miss Harper, told me that when I'm not talking I should keep my mouth closed. I didn't even know that I went around with it hanging open. Boy, these individual conferences are really good stuff."

"Individual conferences are no good. Mr. Hartman is no good," Treadway said, from his bed.

It was shocking to hear Treadway, a wrestler, condemn Mr. Hartman, and, indeed, some of the other wrestlers accused him of being an ingrate.

Treadway was unfazed. "You know what Mr.

Hartman said to me? 'How can you think of marrying Vernelle? You're both blind as bats.' I almost told him that it was none of his goddam business, but then I said, 'But Mrs. Hartman is totally blind.' He said, 'But I'm partially sighted, and we both have jobs at this school. But you and Vernelle will have to fight it out in the big sighted world. You'll see that it's rough out there.' "

"How *are* you going to live out there?" Big Jim Pickett asked. He usually took Mr. Hartman's side.

"Hell, I don't know," Treadway said. "I'll get a job as a piano tuner, I guess." Like most of the musically talented boys at the school, he was training to be a piano tuner.

"And Vernelle?" Big Jim asked.

"She'll be a housewife—what else?" Treadway said.

"How will you shop and buy clothes?" Charlie Wren asked. "How will you know what to wear? Out in the world, there are all kinds of decisions you need sight for."

"Hell, they can live with Treadway's mother, and she can help them," McNabb said.

"We can't do that," Treadway said. "She lives in Little Rock. There are already too many piano tuners here."

The thought of making a life outside the school seemed to put a damper on the conversation, and everyone soon fell asleep. But I remember that for days afterward Treadway would sit on the radiator in the locker room and ruminate aloud about how he and Vernelle planned to become self-sufficient. "When we get out of this school here, we'll get a sighted friend to come and shop with us. I'll get myself two good woollen suits, and she'll get herself two good woollen skirts. I'll also get myself some white shirts and a few red ties that go with any suit, and she'll get some nice blouses and things like that. We'll each get a Samsonite two-suiter—you know, the kind you can hang clothes in without wrinkling them. Then we'll head out west to Texas or California. Them are growing states, and I hear there are a lot of opportunities for a piano tuner there. Once I get a job, we'll raise a family and show Mr. Hartman we're no worse off than he and his missus are."

AT the start of one social-adjustment period, Miss Harper took us into the gymnasium and lined us up at the edge of the floor, saying, "Mr. Woolly has just come back from San Francisco, where he attended a conference of the American Association of Workers for the Blind. At the conference, he heard rehabilitation workers complain that youngsters are coming out of residential schools for the blind without mobility—without the skills to get around by themselves out on the streets. If they can't get to regular jobs, then there's no hope of their ever leading a life outside the sheltered workshops for the blind. We've therefore decided to go all out for our mobility program and help you youngsters develop your facial vision. As y'all know, facial vision is a term for the ability many of you totally blind boys and girls have to sense objects through echoes and changes in air pressure around the ear." She added,

"I'm sure the gym sounds very different to you boys and girls from the way it usually does."

But the gymnasium always sounds different, I thought. It sounds different with mats on the floor when we are doing calisthenics, without mats when we are getting it ready for a party, and with people dancing on the wooden floor during a party. At any of those times, though, it sounds full near the floor and hollow near the ceiling. Now, however, I, along with others, suddenly realized it was the other way around. The sound-shadows were floating like airy, ghostlike shapes around and above our heads.

"What is it?"

"What are they?"

"What's happening?"

"Mr. Tyson strung up some cotton-pickin' mannequins to show us what'll happen if we don't do well in mobility?" Oather asked Miss Harper.

Miss Harper laughed, and then explained that suspended on tracks from the ceiling were lightweight fibreboard panels of various sizes. The panels, which she could raise or lower by means of ropes and pulleys, formed a movable obstacle course. "The purpose of the obstacle course is to help y'all develop your facial vision," she said. "As y'all walk through it, we'll see how easily you're able to spot panels, big or small, and avoid running into them. Some of y'all may not do well at first, but the more you do it the better you should get at it."

Everyone talked at once.

"How am I going to keep from bumping into those things and getting all bruised up?" Lois Woodward asked. She was known for fretting about such matters, as if the smallest bruise could disfigure her.

"We've got plenty of obstacles around the school— why do they have to go and invent some more?" Oather asked. He went on to answer his own question. "I guess these panels are better than glass doors." When Oather was about nine, he had run into the door of the boys' solarium. His arm had gone right through its glass pane, and had never completely recovered from the injury. But this hadn't stopped him from tearing around the school like a racing car.

"I thought that people good in facial vision went blind when they were really little, and grew up having it," Treadway said. "I didn't think you could teach it later on."

"I'm not going to mention any names, but there are people standing right here who went blind when they were little who crash around like a bird in a cage," Oather said. He himself was a perfect example of what Treadway was talking about, but, as usual, he was playing the devil's advocate.

"Well, maybe their mothers didn't let them run around when they were little, so they weren't able to develop facial vision and coördination," Miss Harper said. She added that she didn't know for certain whether people were born with facial vision or could acquire it with training, but that the obstacle course was a good experiment and we should all coöperate.

"Miss Harper, why do we need classes in facial vision when we can get ourselves Seeing Eye dogs?" a boy I'll call Branch Hill asked, as if he had just woken up. The boys referred to Branch as another Dumb Joe

Wright, but, unlike Joe, Branch was totally blind.

Many of us jumped on Branch, because we thought that Seeing Eye dogs were really for blind people who didn't want to help themselves and wanted people to feel sorry for them.

"Even if you somehow get a Seeing Eye dog, you won't regret having good facial vision," Miss Harper said.

There was some more discussion in this vein, and then Miss Harper said, "Y'all are getting het up about some little old panels that will just swing away if you bump into them. Yet when you get to travelling around town you're going to meet up with all kinds of real, dangerous obstacles, like lampposts and mailboxes, ladders and scaffolding. Everywhere, you'll come across parking meters and fire hydrants, and manholes left uncovered. You'll have to learn to navigate around them, so you might as well get started here, right now, and try to train your facial vision."

I imagined the gymnasium with its obstacle course as a forest that one had to find one's way through with the perceptiveness of a dog, the cunning of a fox, the fearlessness of a tiger. I felt excited, and hoped that Miss Harper would call on me to walk through it first. But she called on Bruton.

Bruton, who was known for his prowess on the wrestling mat, sounded uncharacteristically timorous going through the obstacle course.

"No hands out in front of you, please," Miss Harper said to him. "Keep your arms at your sides. . . . You're doing fine. . . . Don't stop."

Treadway and Vernelle, perhaps becoming restive

at having nothing to do, started working out the harmony for "Button Up Your Overcoat."

"Please tell them to be quiet," Bruton said to Miss Harper, from the middle of the floor. "Their singing is interfering with my facial vision."

Miss Harper shushed Treadway and Vernelle but then said to Bruton that in the gymnasium he had only a little singing to contend with, while on the street there might be wind or jackhammers. He had to learn to put up with all kinds of noises.

Bruton bumped his head against a panel, cursed, and returned to the edge of the floor. However much Miss Harper coaxed him, he wouldn't go back out. "I'm resting now," he said.

Miss Harper called on Branch next. He went around the floor bumping into panel after panel, as if the purpose of the exercise were to score hits. People called out to him that he was doing really fine—that that was the only way to go at those blooming panels. He seemed to take their goading good-naturedly, and kept on going.

Finally, I myself was in the midst of the obstacle course. I got so caught up in the spirit of the moment, felt so happy and self-confident, that I imagined that my whole childhood of running around in Indian *gullis* and compounds, of flying kites and riding my bicycle, of living in different places and having to adjust constantly to new surroundings had been a preparation only for this obstacle course. Here was a big panel, which I was sure I could have detected even with a pneumatic drill hammering in my ear. Here was a small panel just above my eyebrow, which I was able to deftly avoid, although I didn't notice it until I was almost upon it. There, just ahead, was a panel at chin level. I easily went around it, tilting my head a little bit. As I weaved my way through the obstacle course, going now one way, now another, Miss Harper noiselessly pulled up panels so high that the gymnasium felt open, like a field, and dropped them down so close together that it felt like a thicket. Some of the panels that suddenly appeared in front of my face were even harder to detect than the slim lampposts at home, which would materialize out of nowhere when I was walking with an inattentive sighted companion, and bruise me, as if they had a will of their own. Then I would imagine that the gods were punishing me for my misdeeds, such as pinching Usha, my little sister. I now decided that if I got through the obstacle course without brushing against a single panel I would best the gods.

I skirted panels, ducked under them, sprinted past them. I put my hands in my pockets and whistled under my breath. Just ahead was a panel that hung down to my chest. I easily walked around it, but then I slipped on the short incline that framed the floor and fell. In the game of mobility, one concentrates on the signals from the region of the face only to be tripped up by things around the feet, I thought. Perhaps there is no way of besting the gods after all.

"You fell because you got overconfident," Miss Harper said primly after she had rushed over to me and I had assured her that I wasn't hurt.

In subsequent social-adjustment periods, we were made to go through the obstacle course again and again. Although the avowed purpose of the exercise was to improve our facial vision, no one ever seemed to do better or worse than before. Years later, Mr. Woolly told me, "In your time, it was the vogue to try to teach and develop facial vision. That's why we spent endless hours making every blind youngster walk through that obstacle course over and over. It was a long time before we learned that either people have facial vision or they don't—or, at least, that there is no scientific evidence that the skill can be taught. In fact, we're not sure anymore what facial vision is, or even if there *is* such a thing. The only thing we are sure of is that some blind people have an extra sensitivity—some kind of combination of all the senses they've got—that somehow enables them to detect the presence of obstacles."

ONE spring day, during social-adjustment period Miss Harper and Mr. Hartman took us out to the school's back driveway. "We want y'all to learn how to tell north from south, east from west," Miss Harper said.

"If you don't know how, you might start out walking to Kalamazoo and end up in Timbuktu," Mr. Hartman said.

There was general laughter; Mr. Hartman had a way of putting things that often got a laugh.

Miss Harper and Mr. Hartman lined us all up on the driveway and pointed us toward Stifft's Station, the little shopping strip to the west of the school. They asked us what direction the sun was hitting us from, and there was a chorus of answers:

"From behind us."

"From in front of us."

"From right overhead."

"It's hitting you from behind," Mr. Hartman said. "You're facing west. The sun rises in the east, and the morning sun is at your back now. Once you've oriented yourself by the sun, you can walk with confidence that you'll end up where you mean to go."

"What if it's cloudy or raining, and there's no sun?" someone asked. "What if it's evening?"

Miss Harper and Mr. Hartman consulted each other. "Then you've just got to stop somebody and ask," Miss Harper said, at last.

"Generally, downtown areas are laid out in a grid pattern," Mr. Hartman said. "Once you know the direction of one street, you can deduce the direction of all the other streets."

"What is 'deduce'?" Branch asked.

"Branch Hill, you are being obstreperous," Mr. Hartman said. "You're going to get poor character marks for your attitude on your report card, I can guarantee you that."

"You can't get him that way, Mr. Hartman," Bruton said judicially. "His character marks are already poor."

"Now, Bruton, you leave him alone," Miss Harper said. "Branch is improving in every way."

Presently, Mr. Hartman gave each of us a cane, saying mysteriously, "The cane is God's gift to the blind, the lame, and the halt. It's your savior—it's your Jesus Christ."

I felt my cane all over. It was a light, thin bamboo

affair with a braided leather strap at the top and a metal tip with a spring in it.

"When you walk out on the street, you must swing the cane from side to side and tap the ground in front of each foot," Mr. Hartman was explaining. "The cane will tell you whether it's safe for you to take the next step. The springed tip makes a nice sound. If you listen to the echo carefully, it will tell you what kind of terrain you're in. The spring in the tip also makes the cane bounce back, which you'll find is less tiring for your arm when you're out for a long time. Once you learn to use the cane properly, it will become your third leg—your savior."

Many of us who were naturally good in mobility said that we didn't need a cane—that we could sense in our toes when we were coming near a drop or a step, when we had to step down or up, and that *tap-tap* was how blind people on bad radio programs walked.

"There's no one of you standing here who's going to tell me that the sense in his toes is perfect," Mr. Hartman said. "Well, if you should miss a step up or down, that won't kill you. But if you pitch into a manhole you'd better say your prayers, because you're going to crack your head open and make a pretty mess. Now, if you have a cane in front of your foot it will say, 'Stop in your tracks! You're on the edge of a dangerous hole!' "

"You can say what you want, Mr. Hartman, I ain't going out there without a companion who can see some," Bruton said. "No, sirree."

"As sure as I'm standing here, fear is the greatest

obstacle to mobility," Mr. Hartman said.

"Bruton, you can't expect to have McNabb around all the time to help you," Miss Harper said.

"I'll get myself a Seeing Eye dog, like Branch," Bruton said. "A nice bitch will suit me fine."

"A cane is better than a dog or a person," Mr. Hartman said. "You don't have to feed it or be nice to it. A cane can't get sick or run away. I tell you, it's a godsend for mobility."

"The cane is as much for the benefit of the sighted drivers on the road as it is for you," Miss Harper added. "It's white, and when they see it they know that you can't watch out for them, so they must watch out for you."

Some of us protested that we preferred to look out for ourselves rather than rely on the alertness of drivers.

"It's easy to talk like that in our back driveway," Miss Harper said. "But you may not feel the same way out on the streets."

"Now I'm going to give y'all some pointers, and you boys and girls had better listen carefully, because I don't want to send you downtown for a lesson in mobility and have you come back in an ambulance," Mr. Hartman said.

"Mr. Hartman means 'hearse,' " Bruton said, in his most chilling voice.

"I ain't going out anywhere by myself," Branch said. "Mr. Woolly can kick me out of the school."

"Now, you just relax, Branch," Miss Harper said. "We'll get you walking out on the streets, if not this year, then next year, and you'll feel like a million dollars. You'll see."

"But Branch don't know what it's like to have a nickel in his pocket," Treadway said.

"Treadway, this is no time for wisecracks," Mr. Hartman said sternly, and he went on, "Now, once you've determined the direction you're walking in, the next thing you have to think about is your posture. I've noticed that many of y'all go around the school with your heads down, as if you had broken stalks for necks. No doubt you learned to do it so that if you ran into something, you'd take the blow on your thick skulls. But on the streets that won't do. There, unless you can walk good and straight you'll run into things all the time. And the only way to walk straight is to keep your head up. Now, another thing. You should always keep your back slightly arched. That way, if you should run into something like a stop sign, you'll take the blow on your belly rather than your head."

Soon Mr. Hartman and Miss Harper were marching us up and down the back driveway, telling us that our heads were too high or too low, or that there was too much arch in our backs or too little.

THE mobility classes whetted our appetite to go out onto the streets by ourselves, and I remember that one day after school Oather and I sneaked out of the gate and stood on the curb of West Markham Street listening to the cars; they rushed past like two endless trains racing in opposite directions.

"There are so many cars," I said. "Who do you suppose is in them? Where are they all going?"

Oather had just put a twist of Bull Durham tobacco in his mouth, and he didn't reply. Then he spat so expertly that I thought I heard his spit land between two speeding cars. "I ain't got the slightest idea who those bums are and where they're headed," he said, finally. "But I can tell you what little ladies they got under them."

"What are you talking about? What do you mean?"

"Well, listen. That there's a Chevy. . . . You hear that? That's a Buick. . . . My word, there goes a real, honest-to-God Pontiac Torpedo."

"But all the cars sound alike. How can you tell?"

"No, they don't. Listen!"

I was all ears.

"You hear how much quieter the engine of that Oldsmobile is than that of that there Chevrolet? . . . There goes a Chrysler Imperial—a rare bird. She really sings. . . . There goes a Ford—she's a 1946, you bet you. . . . That's an Oldsmobile. . . . That's a Dodge." He chomped his tobacco and kind of jumped in place.

I was mesmerized by the names he was reciting. Many of them were new to me. I had to admit to him that I couldn't begin to tell the engines apart.

"Whip, you stick with me and you'll get the hang of it," he said.

"How did you learn to tell the different car engines apart?"

"Well, on vacations I hang around the gas station

in my home town. When I don't recognize a make or model, I just go up to the driver and say 'Sir or Ma'am, what you got under yourself there?' and then listen to the engine."

I thought of Oather's friendliness, his quick intelligence, his country-bred humor. Now it turned out he had an additional, unsuspected gift—of recognizing the cars as if they were so many birds, each with its own call.

"I ain't saying that at first hearing I'll remember the make or model," Oather went on. "You got to hear each type of engine again and again—and again—before you can really get it fixed in your head."

Standing next to Oather on that spring afternoon on West Markham Street, I strained to hear what he heard, imagining that his gift was the poetry of good mobility. But then it struck me that however keen his hearing was he could no more travel around town alone than I could. I had travelled all the way from New Delhi to Little Rock by myself, only to be confined to one small building and its precincts for many months, and to be unable now even to cross West Markham Street and go to Stifft's Station with Oather. I felt that if I could excel in mobility and learn my way around Little Rock I would in due course be able to travel to other towns—to be the equal, in my own way, of the sighted people driving past. Indeed, I felt that I was standing on the shoulder of the road to the whole of America—that there was a whole world out there for me to discover.

"Do you know what the cars themselves are like?" I asked.

"Can't say that I do, Whip. People don't like me to touch their cars, and they never invite me inside."

❧

EACH of us was assigned a faculty member for individual mobility training out on the streets. I got Mr. Hartman. I had never warmed up to him as a person, but I couldn't imagine a better mobility teacher. I felt that even his overbearing personality, which had put me off in the calisthenic and wrestling classes, would be a boon on the streets.

I remember that our first trip was to Stifft's Station. He made me walk alone, saying, "My philosophy is sink or swim. As I'm never tired of repeating, I always send the wrestler out against the greatest odds and let him fight it out. He might get the stuffing beaten out of him at first, but he'll turn into one hell of a wrestler—that is, if he has it in him."

Mr. Hartman followed me to Stifft's Station, but he kept at such a distance that he might as well not have been with me.

On the walk, I kept my head up and my back slightly arched, as I'd been instructed, but I didn't tap my cane. The very idea of tapping it grated on my nerves like a tight bandage on a new wound. I just casually let it hang from my arm by the strap.

Walking alone, trying to stay a straight course, being mindful of lampposts and other hazards gave me a sense of liberation that I hadn't had since I was ten and learned to ride a bicycle.

I was now at the corner of South Woodrow and West Markham, opposite Bumpus Cleaners, in Stifft's Station. Some excavation was going on where the city was installing the new traffic light for the blind. I skirted it, waited for a lull in the traffic, and nonchalantly walked across the street, my hands in my pockets, my head held high, my eyes wide open to make them look as normal as possible. I wished I had an errand, like picking up some dry cleaning from Bumpus Cleaners. I felt that the errand would have made this, my first mobility lesson outside the school, into more than an exercise.

"Well, you're not disgracing yourself—I can't say that you are," Mr. Hartman said, coming up from behind. "I can't say that your posture is terrible—I can't fault it. I can't say that you can't walk a straight line, because I saw you do it. I can't say that you ran into anything—or, at least, I didn't see you if you did."

I decided that Mr. Hartman had a little bit of my countrymen in him—they generally paid compliments with the back of the hand, saying things like "Where did you steal that smart suit?" or "How many pegs of whiskey did you knock back to get that nice color in your cheeks?"

Mr. Hartman suddenly said, "Hey, your cane! You're not supposed to hook it over your arm like a shopping bag. You're supposed to hold it like a pointer. Did you tap it in front of your feet, as we told you to?"

"Yes, I did," I said, telling a barefaced lie.

"Then, man, hold your cane correctly."

I obliged.

"Now you think you're ready to take a trolley and go downtown by yourself?"

"I think so."

"Then I'll send you down there on Saturday and let you case the place on your own."

❦

ON Saturday morning, Mr. Hartman walked out with me onto the school's front drive to send me off downtown. "As you must know from your trips with partially sighted boys, the trolley goes along West Markham Street all the way to downtown and turns onto Main Street," he said. "Main Street runs north and south, while the numbered streets, which intersect it, run east and west. Now, if you're walking south on Main Street from West Markham, the numbers of the cross streets will be going up. You can count the blocks, and you'll always know what cross street you're at." As Mr. Hartman talked, I imagined Little Rock as a checkerboard set up for the game of mobility. In that game, I would use feet in place of fingers to make my moves, playing against people, cars, and obstacles.

"It seems that American towns are orderly and simple—that's a blind person's dream," I said, recalling how streets at home twisted and turned and snaked in such a way that it was hard for me ever to know exactly where I was.

"Don't go getting any such notion in your head," Mr. Hartman said. "Wait till you start moving around just here in Little Rock by yourself, boy. There are all kinds of exceptions. What should be called First Street is just the stretch of West Markham Street that runs through downtown. If a blind individual didn't know that, he could spend hours going in circles looking for First Street."

I still thought that American towns sounded relatively orderly and simple compared with those at home, but I didn't press the point. Instead, I asked, "How high up do the numbered streets go?"

"They go up to at least Ninth Street—you'll never need to go beyond that."

"And what are the names of the streets on either side of Main Street?"

"To the west is Louisiana Street. To the west of that, there are two other streets—I've forgotten their names, but you won't need to fool with either of them. We visually handicapped people only need to worry about where we can buy what we need, and where we live and work."

I said I wondered what the names and numbers of the streets were between the school and downtown.

"I don't know," Mr. Hartman said. "I've always gone downtown on the trolley." He added vaguely, "There must be houses and things there."

I decided that I would have to think of the area between the school and downtown as a mysterious trolley run until such time as I could somehow come up with the information for myself.

"You'll know when a trolley's coming because the power lines it runs on bang and rattle like Jezebel's teeth," Mr. Hartman was saying. "The trolley will stay on West Markham until the second right-hand turn, which is onto Main Street, and you, boy, get off at the stop right after that turn."

Mr. Hartman gave me three tokens—one for going downtown, one for coming back, and an extra one for any emergency. He also gave me a couple of dollars and told me to go into the Rexall drugstore on the southeast corner of Main and Fifth and buy for him and his wife a black Ace pocket comb, two sixty-watt light bulbs, a pair of brown shoelaces, and a packet of bobby pins. "You spend the morning going around the town and getting acquainted with it," he said. "I'll meet you at one o'clock at the restaurant in Pfeifer's department store. I'll buy you a milkshake." He added jokingly, "That is, if you're still alive."

"Will you be following me—watching me?"

"Boy, this is no piddling trip to Stifft's Station, with me ready to rush to your side if you land yourself in trouble. The only way you're ever going to learn to do things by yourself is to do them. Sink or swim—"

"I know—that's your philosophy."

Finally, I was on my way, thinking that it was typical of Mr. Hartman to test me by loading me up with so much last-minute information and instruction. I stepped along the front drive smartly, swinging and tapping my cane in front of my feet and feeling like a soldier going out on a dangerous mission. But as I approached the gate the *tap-tap* of the cane made me feel shy and self-conscious. "Tap-tap, here comes a blind boy from the blind school—look out!" the cane seemed to shout.

I stopped at the school gate to reflect on why I disliked the cane so much. I had always disapproved of

the boys who wore dark glasses inside the school building, as if to hide their blind eyes from visitors, because
it seemed to me that they were denying their blindness. But there was all the difference in the world
between covering up the fact of blindness with dark
glasses and not wanting to advertise it with a cane. I
conceded that a cane might be useful to blind people
less adept than I was, but I felt that in my case it could
be only an impediment to my acceptance as just another
normal person on the street or on the trolley. After all,
the point of mobility was to win that acceptance.

I stood there holding my cane. It seemed to extend
from my hand like an embarrassing appendage that,
do what I might, could not be quieted, hidden, laid
to rest—a symbol of all that was awkward and adolescent in my blindness. I whacked the cane on the ground,
thinking that it was weighing down my hopes of being
as independent as the sighted.

I held the cane poised just above the ground, in
the grip of an idea. After listening to make sure that
no one was around, I caught up the cane by both ends,
put my foot in the middle, and tried to break it. But
it would yield only to spring back. I flung it in the
gutter by the side of the drive, making a mental note
of the spot, so I could pick it up later if anyone asked
for it, and hurried across West Markham. I got across
it so easily that I couldn't imagine why I had ever
needed sighted attendants, why I had waited until that
day to strike out on my own for downtown. (Somehow, the crossing to Stifft's Station earlier that week
didn't seem to count now, because Mr. Hartman had
been tailing me.)

The sun was out in its full April glory. The air around my face was fresh, the sidewalk underfoot was smooth. I felt like bursting out in song.

I was at the trolley stop, but it was so pleasant that I decided to continue walking and explore the route. To my right, there was no steady sound-shadow of a wall or a fence to guide me along the sidewalk; there was just empty, undifferentiated space. To my left, there was a steady stream of cars going both ways at about forty miles an hour, with an occasional large vehicle whose passing sounded like the roar of an airplane and temporarily paralyzed my facial vision. But my facial vision—or whatever it is that enables the blind to perceive obstacles—soon got more or less adjusted to the noise of the traffic echoing in that undifferentiated space. Happily, I imagined that I was by the sea listening to the waves breaking at high tide.

The sidewalk suddenly ended in an abrupt drop. It's a manhole, I thought. My cane, my cane! But the drop turned out to be a high curb that had not been preceded by the usual signal of a footworn depression. I regained my balance, and although I had no idea whether I was in an alleyway or had come to the end of the sidewalk, I stepped along, if a little shakily. Soon the sidewalk resumed.

There was the clanging vibration of the trolley wires overhead and, almost a block behind, a smooth rumble with a slight whistle in it, reminiscent of the sound effects in the outer-space radio program "Dimension X." It was the trolley. A sighted teacher may be in the trolley, I thought guiltily. They may be checking up on me. It's childish to think that

I can leave the school authorities behind like my cane.

The trolley was getting closer. I felt that eyes were staring out at me, burning a hole in the back of my neck. I ran for the trolley stop, which I supposed must be just ahead, and narrowly avoided signs and posts that appeared as suddenly as the panels in the gymnasium.

The trolley passed me. I was at an intersection. I could hear the "Dimension X" rumble and whistle of the trolley on the other side of the intersection, and the light was against me.

I remembered that trolleys came at intervals of twenty minutes or more, and I put my arms out in front of me, held my breath, and stepped off the curb. I recalled in a flash what Mamaji used to say when I was riding my bicycle in the compound with my hands off the handlebars: "You'll kill yourself." I used to reply smugly, "Death only comes once." But now, with cars honking all around me, I had a vision of something much worse than death—losing a limb and being confined to a wheelchair for life. I said a quick prayer.

Somehow, I was across—and in one piece. I kept on running, and gaining on the trolley, its "Dimension X" rumble and whistle ever louder in my ear. A few feet ahead, I finally sensed the trolley stop. I heard the whoosh and clatter of the trolley door opening and the clicking of the coin box inside. I made a dash for the door but crashed into the bench at the stop, which I sensed too late to avoid. I missed the trolley.

I sat down on the bench and felt my bruises through my trouser legs. They were not too bad. I could have escaped them if I'd had my cane, I thought. Still, I prefer the private pain of my bruises to the public embarrassment of the cane. I pushed back the damp hair on my forehead. Just the day before, I had gone with Max to Stifft's Station and got a haircut. The barber had insisted that my hair was too thick on top, like a Negro's, and he had thinned it out with thinning scissors. My head felt exposed.

I repeatedly consulted my Braille watch, snapping the case open and shut, wondering if the next trolley would ever come. When it finally did, I waited for the whoosh and clatter of the door and, with my facial vision, carefully aligned myself in the middle of the opening, so that I wouldn't bump against the door—an unforgivable "blindism"—and climbed in with my hands casually at my sides. The coin box was so well situated next to the handrail that I didn't have to grope for it. I aimed my token at the slot. It dropped right in.

I put my hands in my pockets and walked along the center of the aisle, searching for an empty seat—listening for the rustle and crackle of newspapers and packages, and looking for a break in the lines of vague sound-shadows. I hoped that people in the trolley weren't watching me, didn't know I was blind. I recalled that when the boys came back from Stifft's Station they would say, "We don't give a damn about being blind, but to be blind among people who have eyes, that's what's hell." In contrast to them, I had been brought up mostly among the sighted, but just a few months in, as it were, the valley of the blind had made me self-conscious. Out in the world, there was no getting away from the feeling that we were indeed donkeys—

beasts of burden, scorned and undervalued, ever condemned to compete with natural prancers and jumpers.
No matter how we might excel in our own terms, next
to horses we would always appear to be jackasses. In
some ways, we were worse off than jackasses, because
at least they had no consciousness, no idea that they
were deficient in gait or in mane. Would that we had
their innocence! For the first time, I had an inkling of
why many of my fellow-students talked as if they would
like to go straight from the school to a sheltered workshop, and pass the rest of their days among their own
kind.

I was in front of an empty seat, and I sat down. I
found I was trembling all over. Yet I told myself that
no one had tried to show me to a seat, or had seemed
to take any notice of me. Perhaps the people did accept
me as just another passenger. Still, my face felt flushed,
and I wished I could disappear, like other passengers,
behind a newspaper. Perhaps next time I can bring
along a Braille book, I thought. But the idea of reading with my fingers in public a large, ungainly book
that, when it was open, might extend almost the width
of two seats was mortifying—something as pitiable in
its way as having a Seeing Eye dog nestling at my feet.

Several times, the trolley seemed to make a turn,
and I thought that it must be making the first of the
two right-hand turns Mr. Hartman had told me to
look out for, but then I concluded that it was probably
merely weaving and swerving in the traffic. I have taken
this trolley so many times with partially sighted friends,
yet never noticed any turns or bends, I thought. I
became anxious about missing the turns, and thought

of discreetly enlisting the help of my neighbors. A pleasant young woman was seated on one side of me. Her soft cotton dress was touching the back of my hand and a flowery, youthful scent was rising from her skin. On the other side of me, a person was muttering a prayer in a shaky, old voice. Help or no, I thought it would be fun to talk to two new people—we hardly ever met anyone from outside the school. But I held my tongue. I didn't want to be asked where I lived, why I didn't carry a cane, where I was going—to raise an alarm or to invite gratuitous solicitude. Besides, this is the first real day of my independence, I thought. I can't possibly ask for help. As it happened, the turns, when they came, were so obvious that I had no trouble recognizing them.

I was finally downtown: in a metropolis, as I thought of it, with Main Street, with M. M. Cohn's and Pfeifer's department stores, with McLellan's and Woolworth's dime stores, with the Rexall drugstore and the Lido restaurant—all the landmarks we heard advertised on the radio. I got off at the first downtown stop, at West Markham and Main. I had more than half an hour at my disposal before I was supposed to meet Mr. Hartman, so I started slowly walking up to the Rexall drugstore, trying at once to get a sense of downtown and to practice my mobility. I had walked Main Street with friends repeatedly, but I felt I was noticing some things for the first time, like the fact that there were so many shops in a block. Also, I had previously imagined that I would have difficulty telling the intersections, but I found that they almost announced themselves, being preceded by an interruption in the sound-shadows of the buildings, by a sense of openness, by an increase in the noise of the cross-street traffic, and by the footworn depression at the curb. How different walking downtown is from walking in quiet Stifft's Station, I thought. Here, there is so much traffic, and so many people are rushing in and out of doorways or barrelling along the street, hardly looking where they're going. No obstacle course could have prepared me for this. But what an excellent place to test my senses to the limit. I must make a mental note of the shops I'm passing, so that I can come back and explore further. What's this? It's a whiff of a clean paper smell—I must be passing a stationer's. Now I'm walking through a dull roasted aroma—this must be a nut shop. Here is a strong odor of leather and polish, but it's hard to tell if it's being given off by a shoeshop or a leather-goods store. Now, here is a store that's unmistakable—this peanutty exhaust could only be pumped out of a dime store.

I was at Fifth and Main, just across from the Rexall drugstore. The light was in my favor, but I didn't know how long it had been that way. Deciding to play it safe for a change, I waited.

"You have the light," a man said, nudging me.

"I know."

"Why don't you walk, then? Do you need a hand?"

"I would rather wait."

The man crossed the street, exclaiming in annoyance, "I won't help *your* kind again!"

I didn't like leaving him with a bad impression of the blind. Yet I wondered what choice I had had. There had been no quick way to explain to him the logic

behind my waiting—one explanation would have nec-
essarily involved another. Anyway, I had to concentrate on getting around, not on educating strangers,
say what Miss Harper might about each of us being an
emissary to the country of the sighted. The only way
to avoid frustrating encounters with the sighted was to
act as if I had some sight, I concluded—not for the
first time.

The traffic stopped on Main Street and started on
Fifth. I quickly crossed over.

I listened for the sweep and brush of the revolving
door to locate the Rexall drugstore, and, when there
was a pause in its turning, made a dash for it.

Inside, in the front, a clerk was busy with a woman
customer at the cash register. I stood a little to one
side, breathing in the smell of rubbing alcohol, soap,
and cough medicine, my heart beating to the screech
and click of his machine. The register drawer sprang
open. The woman got her change, gathered up some
packages, and left.

I stepped up to the register and asked the clerk
where the light bulbs were kept.

"Just look around."

I stayed put, and he looked up. "Oh. Straight to
the back—the second counter to the right." He thinks
I have some sight, I thought. I'm doing well.

By quietly asking sales assistants, by surrepti-
tiously touching things on the shelves, by listening to
other customers, I was able to find everything Mr.
Hartman had told me to buy, and to leave the shop in
good order.

I was hot, and looked forward to my reward of a

cold milkshake. Pfeifer's, which was barely a block up, was easy to locate—it had by far the busiest entrance on the block. I followed people in through a double set of swinging doors. Toward the back, through the ringing of festive bells, I heard an elevator door open, and walked to it briskly.

"The restaurant floor, please," I said, stepping in and surrendering myself to a waking dream: A champion wrestler had me now in a jackknife maneuver, now in a half-nelson lock; he tried to pin me, but I managed to keep one shoulder off the mat. No, it wasn't a wrestler at all but Mary Ann Lambert, and we were on our first date, walking hand in hand. The cane stuck out from my other hand like a symbol of painful effort— like a miserable deformity. I had to get rid of it for good—be like everyone else.

"You're doing fine," a voice said.

I jumped. It took me a second to realize that it was Mr. Hartman at my elbow, and that he must have been in the elevator the whole time.

The elevator door opened, and we got out. I fell in step with Mr. Hartman, the back of my hand barely touching the sleeve of his shirt. All of a sudden, every muscle in my body relaxed, and I feared that I was going to slump to the floor.

We sat down at a table in the restaurant.

"You get everything? You have any trouble?"

"I found everything, all right."

Mr. Hartman asked suddenly, "Where is your cane?"

"I left it in the gutter by the school gate."

"Left it at school? In a gutter? Man alive, what

were you thinking of? You got your head screwed on right?"

"A cane is a 'blindism.' "

"The first thing you've got to admit to yourself is that you *are* blind, and that there are certain things you just can't do, like walking around on the streets without a white cane. You're a hazard to yourself and to everyone else."

Mr. Hartman was getting agitated, and I thought it best to smooth his feathers. "You're right, sir," I said aloud, but to myself I said, "He's wrong. I would rather rely on my own senses than carry a wretched cane any day." I remembered what Mr. Woolly had once told me: "Some blind people who are very light on their feet, as you are—and I don't mean avoirdupois, gross weight—tend to ignore their canes. Anyway, you don't put your feet down flat, solidly on the ground. You walk lightly, on the balls of your feet—like a cat. It's not noticeable, but you do. You therefore have a knack of negotiating your way among obstacles— something we haven't seen here ever before."

The waitress brought me a strawberry milkshake with a straw sticking out of it. I put the straw between my lips and sucked on it, letting the cool, delicious milkshake go slowly down my throat. I felt weak and empty. I must have been as tense as a tightly wound top, I thought. "It must have been tougher than I admitted to myself," I said to Mr. Hartman.

"It always is, the first day you're on the road by yourself," he said. "It's like learning to walk, and there are many blind people all over Arkansas who never learn, who don't know that they can learn—who sit on their behinds in a rocker all day long being waited on hand and foot by their mamas. They don't even have the sense to come to our school to study. The state has to send agents out to find them, sweet-talk their mamas, and bring them to the school."

We walked out of Pfeifer's together, and Mr. Hartman headed south on some school business while I headed north to West Markham Street to pick up a trolley back to the school.

The sun was high, and as I walked it fell on my left shoulder, telling me—redundantly, I realized—that was indeed walking north. The sidewalk underfoot felt familiar, and I scarcely had to think about walking in a straight line or dodging obstacles—the conscious aspects of mobility. They were already becoming second nature to me, as automatic as knowing when to step up or step down.

At the stop, there were three or four buses lined up with their motors idling, but they were internal-combustion engines, and I walked alongside the buses until I came to the distinctive electric purring of the trolley's motor. I got in line and waited, making sure that I kept the proper distance from the rustling dress in front of me. I moved when the dress moved.

I reached into my pocket for the fare and remembered that I had an extra, emergency token. If I can somehow reach the school without taking the trolley, the two tokens will be good for a whole secret trip downtown, I thought. I decided that I would hitchhike back. I left the line.

I walked a block or so along West Markham in order to be clear of the confusing noise of the buses. I didn't know exactly how to flag down a car. One holds up a thumb, I thought, but how? Is the hand at an angle, or straight up? I cautiously put my arm out a little to the side and stuck up my thumb.

Cars whizzed by, little worlds in themselves, heedless of me. Maybe my thumb wasn't visible. I raised it slightly.

A car slowed down. "Where are you going?" a woman asked.

I was loath to say "School for the Blind." I didn't want her to deposit me at the school—I wanted to keep my hitchhiking adventure to myself. Anyway, I wanted her to think I had some sight. I didn't want her to be solicitous. So I fudged, and said, "Stifft's Station."

"Get in." She opened the door, and I climbed in, being careful not to grope for the seat or the door handle.

We were now driving along West Markham at a great clip.

"I bet you go to the School for the Blind," she said.

Damn my eyes, I thought—they always give me away. For once, I wished I were wearing dark glasses.

"How much can you see?" the woman asked.

My eyes don't completely give me away after all, I thought. I felt better. "Well enough to get around," I lied.

"You know, you partially sighted people are the link between the world of the seeing and the world of the blind," she said. It was the first time "partially sighted" had sounded pleasant to me. "The totally blind must have a world all their own, don't you think?"

"It's just a world minus eyes."

"But blind people develop their senses so much more acutely than you and I do. To see a blind person get around by himself with just a white cane is truly inspiring. They have so many extra senses."

"They don't have any extra senses. They live in a world of four senses but just use those senses better."

"If you were totally blind, you would know what I'm talking about."

I felt tired. I leaned back in my seat and relaxed and listened to her lecture me about blind people as the car hummed along.

"This is a nice car," I broke in at one point. "It's a Chevrolet, 1948 model, right?"

"What did you say?"

"Nice Chevrolet."

"Oh, yes. I saw this totally blind man walking along Main Street just as you or I might—" The car stopped. "Here we are, in front of the gate of your school."

God damn her extra senses, I thought, but I thanked her politely and got out.

Just inside the gate, I reached into the gutter and found my cane. In the distance, there was a *tap-bang!* . . . *tap-bang!* No doubt it was some hapless blind person finding his way on West Markham Street by banging every wretched lamppost or sign with his cane. I stood there idly tapping my cane on the driveway. It seemed to say "Blindie, blindie, blindie," telegraphing incompetence, fear, lack of self-confidence, the spring in the tip only making the depressing sound resonate like an off-key note. No one can force me to carry a cane, any more than anyone can force me to wear a certain kind of clothing, I thought. I'm a free man. Outside the school, I can do what I like, run the risks I want to. Mr. Woolly's remark about my catlike walk came back to me once more.

I again took hold of the cane by both ends and put my foot in the middle. This time, I put my whole weight on it and managed to break it in two. I threw it back in the gutter.

I took the steps in front of the building two at a time and reached the lounge out of breath. As usual, there was Joe, this time humming a nondescript tune. "Who's that?" he asked, without turning around.

"It's me," I said. "You ought to be able to recognize my step by now. You know, Oather can recognize practically every make of car by its sound."

"I'm not much for getting around," he said absently, and went back to his humming.

VI

ANOTHER
PAIR
OF HANDS

When I lost my baby, I almost lost my mind.
—*Song by Ivory Joe Hunter, 1950.*

S UMMER WAS ALMOST UPON US. THE LAWN-
mower buzzed and whirred all day long, now
in the distance, now close to the window,
drowning out teachers' voices. As it was, little
work was getting done. Some classes were
already meeting under the trees, in a picnic

atmosphere. Others were deserted or adjourned because of preparations for the senior play, the senior dance, and the senior banquet. At the vending stand or in the dining room, in class or out in the sun, seniors worried aloud about their job prospects. Everyone else talked mostly of going home for the summer holidays.

Just the mention of "home" gave me a turn. I had no plans for the summer: no place to go and no money to do anything with, even if I had had an idea of what I could do—and I didn't. I had come to the United States on a one-way ticket. It was not just that Daddyji didn't have the money for a return ticket but that I had come for education and there could be no going back while I was receiving it.

No students were allowed to stay at the school during the summer holidays, but Mr. Woolly, as an exception, had offered to let me stay on there for the summer for fifteen dollars a week. What will I do all day, I wondered. Whom will I talk to? How will I get through the day without a schedule? Once school is out, I thought, I will be free from all requirements. I won't even have to go to meals. Without something specific to do, what will get me out of bed? I knew how miserable I'd been when I was alone at the school the first couple of weeks and during the Christmas and spring holidays. It seemed that I had spent most of those holidays in bed, feeling grubby and unkempt. I would pick up a Braille book and read the same first page over and over again. I would flick on the Talking Book machine—a kind of record-player—on my bedside chair and listen to the same recording over and

over again. Even when I did manage to read on, I was
not able to focus on a story or get the names of characters straight in my head. Sometimes I would start
reading and would fall asleep and wake up a few minutes later, feeling as though I had a head full of sand.
Or if I did somehow get involved in a book—usually
a novel—I would stay up through the night and sleep
during the day, and completely disrupt the cycle of
sleeping and waking. I would wake up and not know
whether it was night or day. For days at a time, I
would even stop feeling hungry. The only thing that
kept me going was the soap operas and radio dramas,
which I tuned in to whenever I was awake. The characters in these programs were practically the only voices
I heard, and I came to think of them as more real than
friends and relatives who were absent. But, with the
fateful approach of summer, I had just heard that all
these familiar radio serials were going off the air and,
like my fellow-students, would not be back until the
autumn. It was as though everything in my life were
shutting down. The thought of rattling around in the
emptiness for three months, perhaps aimlessly going
to Stifft's Station or downtown with no money, nothing to buy, no one to go and see, filled me with terror.
I was afraid that as soon as I was alone the ghosts and
apparitions of my childhood would arrive in the night,
along with the haunting, nettling dreams.

After a lot of hesitation, I went to see Mr. Woolly
and hinted at some of my worries about staying at the
school for the summer.

"Well, there's a library," he said. "You can take

out any book you want. You have a radio and you have a typewriter. You can go and sit in the woods and think. You can always take a trip to Stifft's Station or downtown. I'm sure that you'll find a way of keeping busy."

I kept a smiling face, but teardrops started inside my head. "But I'll be all alone here," I said.

"Then do you have any ideas about what you'd rather do?" he asked.

"Perhaps I could stay as a paying guest with an American family." I had enjoyed staying as a paying guest with the di Francescos. Since then, Daddyji had been on the lookout for Americans visiting New Delhi who might take me in as a paying guest back in America, but the Americans he did meet lived, like the di Francescos, too far away from Little Rock. I simply couldn't afford the expense of getting to them.

"We might be able to find you a family here in Little Rock, but it would cost more than fifteen dollars a week, and what would you do there all day long? How would that be better than staying at the school?" He had a point. The thought of staying with sighted strangers—foreigners to boot—who would have no reason to indulge me or to understand my special problems was suddenly daunting. I decided that the best philosophy was not to wish for things that one couldn't have.

"You're right, sir. I'll stay around at the school," I said, and I left.

As I walked out of the office, one leg went numb. I stamped my foot, and some feeling returned to it.

Then the other leg went numb. I'm getting polio, I thought. Summer is the season for it.

❧

COMMENCEMENT exercises had just finished, and the auditorium was emptying fast. Everyone seemed to be hurrying away to catch the school bus, which was to take the students to the bus station for their trips home. Some of them had their parents with them and were acting in a different, somewhat constrained way, as if they were already home. I waited to say good night to Mr. Woolly, who was seeing the last stragglers out, thinking that where there had been a hundred and fifty and more of us there would soon be only nine: Mr. and Mrs. Woolly; their three boys, one ten years old, one five years old, and the third not even a month old yet; Mrs. Hankins; the night watchman; the cook; and me. No doubt a few staff members would be around sometimes, but they would come and go. We nine would form the core.

"Time to hit the hay, boy," Mr. Woolly said, clapping me on the shoulder. He went upstairs to his family. I walked back to the dormitory, mindlessly repeating to myself, "Mr. Woolly has a family. Mrs. Hankins, the night watchman, the cook, and I are solitary. There are five Woollys and four solitaries."

The sleeping hall was hot and humid. I remembered the bamboo screens and fans and jugs of fresh-squeezed limeade at home. But there wasn't so much as a shade on a window here. I climbed into the hot, scratchy bed and thought, If I only had a summer job!

All along, I had wanted a summer job, not only because I wanted something to do but also because I wanted to help Daddyji pay for my education. Whenever he and I had talked about money for my education, he had spoken of students in the West "learning and earning," but whenever I brought up the subject with Mr. Woolly he had put me off, saying, "Boy, we have trouble getting jobs for graduates of our school. People out there are really not happy about hiring blind folks. Besides, you're not really hurting for money." (Years later, he explained, "I never grasped the fact that your father had money problems, that he was a refugee from Pakistan. I don't think I even knew then what Pakistan was. I just thought that he had trouble getting money out because of foreign-exchange regulations—we had so much correspondence about them. You see, the way I saw it, at most, you were hurting for a little spending money, not for money to pay the school. Being you, you also wanted to contribute to your expenses, and that didn't seem all that important to me." His error was understandable; he perceived the social status of my family to be higher than, say, that of his own, and couldn't understand what it meant for Daddyji to have to earn in rupees and pay for my education in dollars—never mind understanding the political turmoil of Partition, which had left us refugees.) Moreover, it was not clear to Mr. Woolly whether the United States immigration laws permitted me to work. Almost from the day of my arrival, I had been corresponding with the immigration authorities on this point, but I had not received a definite answer until that April. Then I was informed that the laws barring foreigners from taking jobs in America seemed to apply only to the able-bodied. In other words, as a handicapped person I might be exempt from those laws. Thereupon, Mr. Woolly, at my insistence, had put out feelers to members of the board, to friends of the school, to the welfare officers at the Rehabilitation Center for the Blind in Little Rock, to ministers of various churches, even to the editors of the *Arkansas Democrat* and the *Arkansas Gazette,* who had frequently published stories about me. "Boy, we got the entire city looking for a job for you, but there just doesn't seem to be anything," Mr. Woolly told me. "The trouble is that you are sixteen and wanting a temporary job. Employers just don't like to assume that kind of risk for temporaries. If you were only partially sighted!"

A FEW days after the commencement exercises, as I was coming down from the library balancing several heavy boxes of Talking Books and some Braille volumes, Mr. Woolly called to me through the open door of his office. "Will you step in here, son?" he said. "I have some good news for you."

I piled the books as best I could on the filing cabinets in the outer office, and went in.

"We've found you a job," Mr. Woolly said. "Yes, we've gone and done it. It's working at the Mayflower Dairy. It's an ice-cream plant, and your hours will be from eight to five, six days a week. Your pay will be a hundred dollars a month. How do you like that? It sounds mighty nice, doesn't it?"

If this were my graduation day and I were being handed my high-school diploma, I couldn't feel happier, I thought.

"I can see you're tickled pink."

"When do I begin? Where, exactly, is the ice-cream plant? How will I get there? What will I do there?"

"Well, you had a mobility outing or two this spring. They didn't come a moment too soon. You'll be taking the trolley to Main and West Markham Street every morning and then transferring to a bus for the trip across the bridge to North Little Rock. You see, the plant is on the other side of the river. Maybe this evening the night watchman can show you the route. You think you'll be able to manage?"

I knew nothing about North Little Rock. I didn't know what "transferring" meant. I didn't even know that there was a bridge or a river in Little Rock. But I said I was sure I could manage.

"I wasn't told exactly what your job will be, but you'll probably be another pair of hands at the plant," Mr. Woolly said. "The people there are expecting you to begin tomorrow. Now, don't be late on your first day and give the school and blind folks a bad name. You hear, boy?"

"I'll be there early," I said, and I thanked Mr. Woolly repeatedly.

The rest of the day was spent in making arrangements. The school had no Braille alarm clock; Mr. Woolly therefore asked the night watchman to make sure that I was fully awake by a quarter to seven every morning. So that I would be near the night watchman's post, Mr. Woolly had me move from the dormitory into Mr. Chiles's room, next to the office. Mr. Woolly instructed the cook to serve me an early breakfast. Then he took me in his car to Pfeifer's and helped me to buy two pairs of white trousers and two white shirts for work. Then the night watchman and I took the trolley downtown and got our transfer tickets for North Little Rock. The transferring itself proved as simple as jumping off one vehicle and jumping onto another. In North Little Rock, we got off at the first stop after the bridge and walked a few hundred yards to the plant. The plant, a small, self-contained building, was closed—it was Sunday—but the night watchman showed me the door that I was to use.

That evening, as usual, Mrs. Hankins and I were alone in the faculty dining room for supper. I sat across from her at a table for six, worrying about whether I was holding my fork correctly and whether I had placed my knife just so across my plate, as we had been taught in social-adjustment class. The tap and clink of our knives and forks against out plates and the rattle and tinkle of spoons and ice in our iced-tea glasses were painfully exaggerated in the emptiness of the room. It is one thing to eat in the student dining room with the sighted supervisor occasionally looking over my shoulder, I thought, and quite another thing to have Mrs. Hankins' eye upon me all the time.

"How do you like Mr. Chiles's room?" she finally asked. "How do you like having a job?"

I wanted to tell her that I couldn't believe my good fortune: a cozy room in the heart of the building, with an attached bathroom; a night watchman within earshot, in case ghosts troubled me; something to do from morning to evening not one day and not five days but six days a week; and a whole hundred dollars a month. I wanted to say that I was touched by the note of special respect I detected in her voice, as if I were the first sixteen-year-old student at the school who had got himself a full-time job. But I said, swallowing quickly, "Words cannot express my gratitude to Mr. Woolly."

Mrs. Hankins served me a second helping. She put some salt on my food. I had a second glass of iced tea, and she squeezed some lemon into it. She's so motherly, I thought, and yet we're so reserved and solemn with each other. But then I told myself that she was much older than the women teachers, and, unlike them, she never came to the vending stand or to school parties. In her way, she was as remote from our school life as Mrs. Woolly, who mostly stayed in the superintendent's family quarters, upstairs.

"Now I'll have no one to have breakfast or lunch with," Mrs. Hankins said. "I'll miss you."

I had always missed people, but the idea that anyone could miss me was startling. I felt there was a lot I could say to Mrs. Hankins, but, as so often before, I wasn't able to get any words out.

"What will you do for lunch?" she asked.

"I hadn't thought about it," I said, and added, "Eat ice cream, I suppose." But my attempt at a joke only made me feel foolish.

The cook came in with dessert. "It's watermelon," Mrs. Hankins said. "It's all cut up. This is a real treat."

"It's for the little man—it's to celebrate his job," the cook said.

THE plant stank of ammonia. The odor was so overpowering that I could hardly breathe. There was a permanent chill in the air, and the floor was wet, slippery, and uneven.

A youngish-sounding man called Jay, who seemed to be in charge, stationed me, gasping, choking, and coughing, behind a long metal table alongside a woman I will call Gladys. I waited patiently, wondering what I'd be asked to do and how well I'd be able to do it. As a child, I'd often helped fill and crank our ice-cream maker at home, but I had no idea how ice cream was manufactured in a plant. Even when I got adjusted to the ammonia air, I still preferred to breathe through my nose rather than my mouth, but Gladys continually smacked a piece of chewing gum and, a little in the manner of Joe, sang the same refrain of a song over and over again: "When I lost my baby, I almost lost my mind." The smacking and singing in my ear were especially irritating because I had nothing to do but listen to her.

"Gladys, can I start doing something?" I finally asked.

"What's your hurry, kid?" she said, hardly pausing in her singing.

Jay's helper, Tom, dumped a load on the metal table. Its deafening clatter was oddly reminiscent of the sound that the coal made when a servant threw it onto the brick oven at home. I reached over to see what was in the load. It consisted of many items of two unfamiliar shapes—a flat bar, with rounded edges and a hard, satiny patina, on a stick, and two connected sausagelike bars, with a surface as smooth as ice, on two sticks.

"What are these things?" I asked.

"Them are Polar B'ars and Popsicles," Gladys said. "Where've you lived?"

"Are they really ice cream?" I asked.

"Chocolate-covered ice cream and flavored ice on sticks," Jay said, bringing over a pile of flattened cardboard cartons and putting them in front of me. "Gladys will put the Polar B'ars and Popsicles in paper bags, and you put them in these cartons, kid," Jay said. He showed me how to open the cartons up, pack, close, and tie them, and asked, "You think you can do it?"

"Sure. There's nothing to it," I said.

Soon Gladys and I were working as a team. She would pick up a bar by the stick, insert it in a paper bag held open in a dispenser, remove the bar in its paper home with a flick, and drop it on the table between us. I would arrange the bars in a carton with their sticks pointing in alternate directions—twelve to a carton if they were Polar B'ars, six to a carton if they were Popsicles—close the cartons, and stack them at the opposite end of the table. Jay or Tom would carry them into the walk-in freezer—it faced us—to await delivery to shops and street venders. At one point, Gladys turned to a tank behind us and filled gallon, quart, and pint containers from a spout, and I stacked them to go into the freezer, too. This slight variation in the routine came to an end when Tom dumped a fresh load of Polar B'ars on the table.

In time, I gathered that on my right was a swinging door leading to a side room where two young women, Jean and Helen, prepared and mixed the ingredients for ice cream and novelties, and poured them into buckets and trays of molds, while Tom and Jay washed the utensils under a tap, hosed down the floor, and kept the stick machine supplied with sticks. (Sticks were somehow shot into the molds in batches.) The four took turns carrying the filled buckets and trays to the freezer and depositing the finished ice cream on the table or in the tank for Gladys and me to package. (Polar B'ars required an extra step: they had to be dipped in chocolate and returned to the freezer for further hardening.)

The entire plant consisted of the two rooms and the freezer, and Gladys, Jean, Helen, Tom, and Jay appeared to have worked there together for some time and seemed like a family. In some ways, the atmosphere of the place was extremely homey: the clash and bang of the utensils as they were washed under the tap might have come from a kitchen after a meal; the stick machine sounded like a child firing a toy gun; the hum of the freezer suggested the family refrigerator. In other ways, the atmosphere was nerve-racking: the tap, whether it was in use or not, seemed to be always left on, the water splattering and running all over the floor (Gladys and I were supplied with a long plank to stand on); the noise of the stick machine exploded in the air without any warning, like strings of firecrackers; since the freezer door was directly opposite Gladys and me, every time it was opened it blasted us with cold air. Then, too, our packaging work came in fits and starts. There would be times when it seemed that every minute Jay or Tom was dumping bars on our table and Gladys piling them at my elbow in their paper bags.

My hands and arms would get stiff from the effort of packing and stacking the cartons—a job as monotonous as folding Christmas seals and stuffing them in envelopes had been at school. There were other times when there was no work, and I wouldn't know what to do with myself. I wasn't used to being on my feet, and my legs would feel as if they were falling to pieces. There was no place to sit down, and no radio or other distraction—just the infernal noise of the plant and Gladys's constant smacking and singing.

"Can I work with Jean and Helen sometime?" I asked Gladys at one point when I was idle.

"You don't got no eyes to see what you're doing. 'When I lost my baby . . .' "

"I don't like standing here doing nothing."

"You're getting paid, ain't you? 'When I lost my baby . . .'"

"But everyone else seems to be working."

"I ain't working. I got two kids at home and no man around. You think I want to come here and work my butt off?"

Helen was carrying trays of molds in and out of the freezer, and I called to her, "Helen, please come here and box and let me work at the freezer. I can do it. Believe me, I can."

"O.K.," Helen said.

She took over my place, saying, "Be careful, the floor is slippery."

"Don't worry," I said happily, pulling out large, heavy trays weighed down with ice-cold Popsicles and hardened Polar B'ars from the freezer and the table and listening to the steady motion of Gladys's and Helen's arms. It was much better than standing in one spot.

The door to the side room swung open, and I heard Jay's footsteps. He didn't say a word, but I could feel him watching me. I won't let him unnerve me, I thought.

I was walking toward the table carrying a tray, thinking that if I only showed sighted people what I could do they would let me do it, when Jay yelled "Stop!" I caught my heel in the wet cuff of my trousers and fell, scattering and mashing the Polar B'ars I was carrying.

Tom immediately threw a bucket of water on the floor. Helen started mopping up. Jean went into the freezer to get a new tray of Polar B'ars.

"What did I tell you?" Jay scolded Helen. "I didn't want to see this blind kid doing any heavy work around the place!" He turned to me and said sternly, "I don't want to see you leave your place behind that table, you hear? If you got hurt, the company would be liable."

"But why am I more likely to get hurt than anyone else?" I said, trying not to sound argumentative.

"You just fell, didn't you?" he said.

I wanted to say that that was because he had been watching me, but I immediately realized that that would only feed his anger, and said nothing.

"I'm running things here," Jay was saying. "You got to do what I tell you. I'm responsible."

It was all over. I went back to my station.

Tom dumped a tray of Popsicles on the table. The ammonia air swished and plonked as Gladys dropped the sheathed bars at my elbow.

"How old are your children, Gladys?" I asked, sweeping up several bars in my hands, arranging them against my chest like books, and dropping them into the carton in the correct position.

"Five and seven—old enough to be hell-raisers. 'When I lost my baby . . .' "

"Jean and Helen married?"

"Oh, no. 'When I lost my baby . . .' They're out looking, but I tell them, 'Make hay while you can. After that, it's cares and worries and children and mess and divorce."

Some time later, getting bolder, I asked, "Oh, Gladys, can we switch? You do the boxing for a while and I'll do the bagging. I'm sure Jay won't mind. That's not heavy work."

Jay overheard me and asked Gladys to change places and let me try. He's a kind man after all, I thought. I like him.

I enjoyed doing Gladys's job. The touch of Polar B'ar after Polar B'ar was tantalizing. I had never imagined ice cream in that form, and I got a terrific craving for it. I had worked through lunch hour, because I didn't know what else to do or where to go. I was very hungry, and I hesitantly asked Gladys if I could have a taste.

Tom, who overheard me, bounded across. He turned me around to face the tank and asked me to put my mouth under the spout.

"Why?" I asked.

"You like ice cream, don't you?" Tom asked.

"Very much," I said, remembering the pleasant salty tang of the ice cream of my childhood. No matter how carefully the cylinder in our hand-cranked ice-cream maker was sealed, some salt from the ice would always seep into the mixture, but that only helped to set off its fresh sweetness.

"Just can't get enough, right?" Tom asked.

I nodded.

In the other room, the tap was running. Helen and Jean were laughing at something. The stick machine was firing away.

Tom held my head under the spout and pressed the lever. Chocolate ice cream rushed out, and with such force that I couldn't swallow it fast enough. I glugged and choked and struggled, and Tom let go, but not before the ice cream had gushed all over my hair, my clothes, and the floor. Jean, Helen, Jay, and Gladys had gathered around me and were laughing.

"Everybody who works here has to have his turn at the spout," Jay said, hosing me down. "Otherwise, you go on having this craving and never being satisfied."

"You can go and have a turn at the spout any time you want," Tom said. "It's on the house."

I returned to my station soaked and smelling of chocolate ice cream, shivering like a Polar B'ar bag from a blast of freezer air, worn out by the effort of my first day on the assembly-line job. Still, I feel happy, I thought. Though I am allowed to do only a couple of tasks around the plant, I am accepted. After the ice-cream bath, I feel almost like one of the sighted regular hands.

I helped myself to a Polar B'ar, letting its cold vanilla center slide down my throat, as the milkshake at Pfeifer's did after my first mobility trip downtown.

❧

I HAD to travel to and from my job at rush hour. Sometimes, when I left in the morning, at seven o'clock,

I would be able to find a seat in the trolley or the bus, but most of the time both were so packed that there was scarcely room to stand. If I stood near the door, the driver would urge me to move back to clear the path for passengers getting on. Then if, on my way to the back, I bumped into passengers or stumbled over bundles placed on the floor, women would get up and offer—indeed, force me into—their seats. If I resisted, a few other people would join in the effort to stow me in a seat, as though I myself were a bundle that was in the way. Then they would stand over me and talk about me as though I weren't there, and that made me burn with embarrassment and wish that I had on a coat with a turned-up collar, so that I could sink down into it. I soon realized that there was no point in resisting, because that only created more commotion and involved more people in the scene.

Dealing with the public on the street was no easier. As I was threading my way through traffic on a wide street, calculating my distance from the oncoming cars or running through a gap in the line of cars, a stranger would bellow "Watch out!" and I would freeze to the spot, thinking that a car was about to run me down, or that I was about to crash into a perilous obstacle, or that the street was dug up and I was about to fall into a trench and crack my head open, just as Mr. Hartman had always predicted. Even if I ignored the warning and kept walking, my confidence, the sine qua non of mobility, would be undermined, and my steps would become faltering and hesitant. I wouldn't be able to cross the street in the time I had calculated, and there would be a jamming on of brakes and a honking of horns in my ear. Sometimes, in the middle of a crossing a stranger would abruptly catch hold of my arm and practically lift me off the street. I would be so tensed up for for the crossing that I would react angrily—yank my arm away. I felt that meddlesome strangers had dogged me from my childhood. When I was growing up, it seemed that people who didn't know me were always trying to give me a hand, often making me lose my balance and fall. If I screamed with rage, I would be scolded by one family member or another for not knowing how to accept help gracefully, and so contributing to my fall. Now, in the street, the stranger whose help had been spurned would fire a parting shot like "Then *get* run over!" I would be so upset, so eager to get away, that I would cross the street heedless of everything, sometimes avoiding an accident by a hairbreadth.

Whatever the nature of the interference—a shout or a hand—I would feel like lashing out at the stranger. But I would tell myself that such strangers were morally in the right, that they couldn't be expected to understand the ways of mobility, that they intended to save my life, not put it in jeopardy. Yet even if I stopped and somehow managed to explain everything to one of them—educated one of them in mobility, as it were—there would always be another ignorant stranger the next time around. So I would press on, frustrated and depressed, turning a deaf ear to would-be good Samaritans.

The interference of strangers, however, never caused me as much injury as my own willful carelessness did. Once, when I was late for work, I took a shortcut through an unfamiliar street and, even though I knew better, ran like a fiend in order to be on time. I felt the ground underfoot give way—I was falling like a stone. I landed in slush, all doubled up. My jaws snapped together with such force that I thought I had pulverized my teeth. I was so numbed by pain and shock that it took me a few seconds to realize that my teeth were all right but that I was at the bottom of a disgusting manhole.

I heard voices from above as in a hazy dream: "Where is his cane? Why doesn't he carry a cane?" and "Why do they allow blind people out on the streets alone?" Either I heard a woman faint or I imagined that one had fainted. I flailed about, trying to get out, hating myself, hating the sighted rubberneckers, hating the negligent town authorities who had left the manhole uncovered.

A man reached down and pulled me out. My clothes were wet and soiled. I ran away from him and the manhole—as usual, shutting out the people who called after me.

At the plant, Gladys, Jean, and Helen surrounded me.

"Look at you!"

"What have you done to yourself?"

"Nothing," I muttered, trying to control my tears. I stood there like a statue, the dirty water trickling down me like the ice cream on my first day of work. Tom hosed me down.

❧

AT the ice-cream plant, I would often hear, from
the side room, the sounds of Tom, Jay, Helen, and
Jean horsing around—little screams, and exclamations
like "Now, Tom, you just cut it out! I'm working!"
or "Just be a honey and keep your hands to yourself!"
Sometimes Gladys would wander into the side room
and join in the fun. They would all joke and trade
endearments and profanities in a bantering spirit. I
would be titillated and want to take part. I had never
heard words like "honey" used that way before, or known
unmarried girls who earned their own keep and breathed
the free, easy air of mixed society. The fact that the
girls were a little older than I was made them, for some
reason, only more enticing. Once or twice, I had tried
to fool around with Gladys when she was giggling with
Jean and Helen. I had been all aquiver, but she had
only pushed me away roughly and said, "Look out!
What do you think you're doing, kid?" If Gladys, who
has the hoarse voice of a fishwife, won't tolerate a little
innocent approach, I thought, what chance do I stand
with Jean and Helen, who have the sweet voices of
angels? I would stand at my station behind the metal
table and daydream about being one of the gang in the
side room and being called "honey" by the girls.

One day, while everyone was fooling around, I heard
Jay ask Jean, "Baby, what about taking in a drive-in
show tonight?"

"Why not?" she answered.

The little snatch of conversation gave me an idea.
Perhaps I can make some progress with Helen, the
friendliest of the three girls, if I arrange to meet her

outside the plant, I thought.

That afternoon, when Helen was alone in the side room I casually walked by her again and again with my hands poised to touch her accidentally. I couldn't wait to make some kind of contact with her and get her attention. I failed miserably, so I just blurted out, "I was hoping to get a date with you, Helen."

Helen laughed, as if I were trying to be funny.

"The kid wants to take you for supper to the blind school?" Jean asked, coming in. They both laughed.

I returned to my station behind the metal table, thinking that there was all the difference in the world between being accepted as a worker at the ice-cream spout and being accepted as a possible date in the side room. Still, the desire for the second kind of acceptance continued to burn.

Since I realized I could never crack Jean's or Helen's defenses, I concentrated on Gladys—especially after Tom brought his new battery-powered radio along to the plant to show us and I heard for the first time the proper tune of Gladys's song. I was immediately mesmerized by it, much as I was by the swish and plonk of our work behind the table. Thereafter, I often sang the refrain along with Gladys. Even though I sang in tune and she out of tune, and our dissonant voices sounded like a fly and a mosquito buzzing around the metal table, I liked to think of us as a pair. I even came to find her smacking of chewing gum exciting.

I used to wait for our lunch hour—from twelve to one—so that I could hear Gladys munch her sandwich. She couldn't afford to go out and buy her lunch; she brought it in a bag. She ate it slowly, crunching the pickles, as if it were her last meal. She was quite capable of taking half an hour to eat a sandwich.

I couldn't imagine getting through the lunch hour without Gladys at my side. Jay and Helen would disappear. Tom usually left the plant to meet some fellows. Jean, who skipped lunch because she was trying to lose weight, did stay around the plant, but she kept mostly to herself. The school didn't provide me with lunch and I had never been to a restaurant by myself, so I stood around with Gladys, now and again eating a little ice cream from the spout.

In later years, I would explain my infatuation with the girls at the plant, and particularly with Gladys, in terms of separation from home and family. After all, there was a great divide between the familiar and the new. There could be no going back. That door had closed when I boarded the airplane for America. I could not permit myself to pine for home or family—that was unmanly. I could not permit myself to regret the loss—the loss was already in the past. I couldn't even allow myself simply to miss anyone—I was afraid of being overwhelmed by feeling. Perhaps the explanation of my pining for gratification within the reach of my hand was no more complicated than that I was going through my adolescence.

❦

ALTHOUGH all I could concentrate on was Gladys, the unbearably sweet, motherly, divorced, experienced, possibly available co-worker, our elbows so close over the metal table that I had only to stumble for them to meet, and although the ice cream was free and clean and fresh and I could eat as much of it as I could hold, I told Tom that I wanted to strike out, have a real lunch outside the plant. (I had come to think of the ice cream as handled and grubby and of Gladys as somewhat degraded, a fit object of my low desires. I could never forget the ice cream dribbling down my hair and my clothes and onto the floor on that first day of work. In fact, no matter how often the floor was hosed down, it seemed to be sticky with ice cream. And the ammonia in the air made strawberry and chocolate ice cream smell and taste almost alike.)

The next day, Tom showed me a couple of coffee shops around the corner from the plant. After that, I started going to one or the other every noon. I would stand at a counter and eat the same ham or chicken-salad sandwich on dark bread with Coca-Cola day after day. I decided that I didn't like going to coffee shops. I had generally eaten at a table, either with my family or with students and staff at a school, and eating alone at a counter filled me with sadness. Moreover, there v.ere always incidents in the coffee shops that would leave me shaken. The waitresses would shout out the menu to me as if I were half deaf, and so attract the attention of everyone in the coffee shop. Even when they got to know me and treated me normally, I would have to contend with customers who didn't know me. I remember that once when I asked for my bill the waitress said, "A man already took care of it."

"I insist on paying for myself."

The waitress refused to accept the money. "The man done gone," she said to the coffee shop. "What does the kid want me to do—take money twice for the same ham sandwich? He should be thankful there are nice people to pay for him." I felt anything but thankful, however. I thought that I'd been an object of pity.

I remember that another time Tom took me to a new coffee shop. The waitress, instead of asking me for my order, turned to him and asked, "What does he want to eat?"

"A ham sandwich," I said, speaking up for myself. She brought me the ham sandwich, but throughout lunch she ignored me, talking to Tom as if I weren't there.

At school, dinners with Mrs. Hankins in the faculty dining room were only a little bit more pleasant. There was no question of exchanging confidences with her. I wouldn't dream of speaking openly to a member of the school staff who was perhaps two or three times my age, and she was too discreet to talk to me about school business, which was apparently her whole life. In fact, I felt too shy to talk to her about anything. Under the force of my own introspection and my daily battles with the uncomprehending world, I was turning into a silent, self-conscious, truculent boy-man.

"HAVE you ever heard of the Boys' Club?" a woman said to me in the bus late one afternoon when I was coming home from work.

"No. What is it?"

"It's for underprivileged boys."

I had to laugh. To me, "club" suggested an exclu-

sive British turf where a few select Indians were allowed
to play; Daddyji was famous for being one of the first
Indians to be accepted into such a club in the Punjab.
The idea that the underprivileged would have a club
from which the privileged might be excluded seemed
funny.

"Do they have only boys?"

"Yes, but boys can bring their dates there."

My interest was aroused. "What do they do there?"

"They swim. They play chess and cards. They sit
around and shoot the breeze."

"How do you become a member?"

"You just go there."

"What are the dues?"

"There aren't any dues. It's for poor boys."

I decided that I would go and explore, and got the
directions from her. The club was in North Little Rock,
beyond the ice-cream plant but on the same bus route.

That evening, when I got home from work I quickly
took a shower and put on fresh clothes, had my supper
alone (Mrs. Hankins sometimes skipped meals), and,
with my special chess set and Braille playing cards, set
off in search of the club. I had never travelled in the
evening, and didn't realize how infrequently the trolley and the bus ran. It took me nearly an hour to get
to the Boys' Club stop, even though, since it was after
the rush hour, we moved very quickly. (In the morning, I reckoned, it would have taken me half as long.)
Once there, I had to ask strangers for exact directions
and accept their help in crossing two unfamiliar streets.
But I managed to arrive at the club alone, thinking
that that would prove to the club authorities that I was

self-reliant, that I was a worthy candidate for membership, and that I wouldn't create a problem for them by injuring myself on the premises.

The club turned out to be only a small barracklike building set back from an outdoor swimming pool. There were a few rambunctious swimmers in the pool, and they didn't take any notice of me, but as soon as I entered the building three or four boys and two girls inside gathered around me as we at the school might surround a new student—though, unlike us, they were mostly silent.

"You're the Indian whose picture's been in the newspapers," a man said. He seemed to be the oldest person there.

"Yes," I said shyly.

"I'm Ed," he told me, standing up from his place behind a table that I later learned was used for playing cards and chess.

Another man joined us. He had come from the pool and was dripping water. I worried that he might be spoiling the floor. He shook my hand as no one had ever done before—grasping it tightly and holding it for a long time. He seemed to be trying to look right down into me. "I'm Joe Red, the director. How did you get here?"

"By bus, Mr. Red," I said.

"Joe."

I hesitated. I had hardly ever called older men only by their first names—they were "Mister" or "Uncle." Yet Ed seemed to go by only one name.

"Joe," the director repeated.

"Joe," I said, as if I were reciting the catechism.

"I would like to join this club, Joe," I added, trying to accustom myself to using his first name.

"We have problems just getting anyone to come to the club," he said. "Boys like getting into trouble better than coming here and joining in our activities." He paused, and added, "But I don't know if we have any activities that you could do." I felt disappointed, and feared that Joe would turn me away, reject me, but then he asked, "What are you interested in?"

"I know how to play chess," I said. And although I'd heard that people caught polio from swimming in public pools, and I was desperately afraid of coming down with it, I boldly went on, "I also very much want to learn swimming."

Ed wanted to know how I could play chess. I showed him and the others my chess set. Everyone looked at it as if it were a Ouija board, and asked me how I could tell white from black. I showed them the little points sticking up from the top of the white pieces. I also showed them my Braille playing cards.

They all gave me the impression of being awe-struck—of feeling that just because I could play a couple of games I was some kind of prodigy. Their reaction made me uncomfortable, since what I wanted most was to be accepted as a normal teen-ager.

"But how could he learn to swim?" Ed asked Joe.

"Like anyone else," I said, and I boasted, "I taught myself to ride a bicycle."

"You did!" Joe said. "Well, then, you can learn to swim with me and play chess with Ed. Can you come in during the day?"

"I can't. I have a job in an ice-cream plant."

"Oh," Joe said. "We usually give swimming lessons only during the day. But whenever I have a few minutes in the evenings I can help you out in the pool. You want to take a swimming lesson now?"

"I don't own a pair of trunks," I said. "But I'll buy some before coming tomorrow."

Soon Ed and I were sitting at the table, which we'd dragged outside, and playing chess by the pool. Joe was inside the club changing.

"Watch out! You've moved your queen right into the range of my bishop—I can take it," Ed said after one of my early moves.

I was horrified. Several boys and a girl were watching the game, and the girl sighed loudly. I thought that in some way her acceptance—their acceptance—of me depended on my winning, and to lose my queen that early in the game would mean that I was going to be defeated. My playing a bad game might even mean losing Ed's interest in playing with me, Joe's interest in teaching me swimming. I didn't want to be regarded as a prodigy, but neither did I want to be thought a nincompoop. At the same time, I didn't want anyone to make special concessions for my blindness—something I didn't want to say directly, in case I precipitated the very thing I wanted to avoid.

"The queen is all yours," I said, forcing an all-knowing smile, as if to say that it was a calculated move to trap his king.

"You take that move back," Ed said.

"Why? I asked.

"You didn't know my bishop was there. You didn't see it."

"Yes, yes, he didn't see," the onlookers gathered around the board said. "Let him take the move back."

"Here, I'm putting your queen back," Ed said.

I was filled with rage, but I could tell from Ed's tone that if I took my queen off the board I would antagonize him. I decided to accept my queen back, reasoning that blindness required such compromises.

Sometime later, it was my turn to move. I put my hands on the board and couldn't believe what was under my fingers. Ed had moved his rook so that my knight could take it. I thought it might be a ploy, and examined the board repeatedly, but there was no making sense of his move. Finally, I said in a small voice—uncertain whether he had made a mistake or I was about to fall into his trap—"I'm taking your rook."

"What!" he exclaimed. "I'm sorry. I didn't mean to move it there." He put his rook back.

I debated whether I should let him get away with it—he was doubling as lifeguard and so had been playing with one eye on the swimmers, who were diving, splashing, fighting. But I felt that he had become careless in his moves, as if he didn't think I was much of a match for him. Whatever the reason, I decided to hold him to his move, thinking that in that way he might learn not to make concessions for me—learn to treat me as an equal.

"A move is a move!" I cried, reaching over, moving my knight, and taking his rook.

The boys and girls watching gasped. They all think I'm being ruthless, and they're right, I thought. In buses and on the streets, when I behaved ruthlessly—yanked my arm away from a helpful stranger, for instance—I often had the impression that, at some level, I frightened people, when the truth was that I myself was frightened of appearing feeble and helpless. But the last thing I wanted was to frighten Ed. My special chess set, my having to feel the pieces instead of being able to see them at a glance, my lack of eye contact with Ed put, I felt, certain constraints on our relationship as equals, and I didn't want to add to those constraints. But all the constraints put together are a lesser evil than being patronized, I thought.

Now Ed began to play a terrible game. At one point, he actually put his knight within range of my bishop. I took it. He lost the game.

"Fella, you don't pull any punches, do you?" he said, standing up.

"I guess not," I said, feeling sorry and glad at once.

❧

SOME summer entries from my journal:

June 19

Yesterday I began swimming at the Boys' Club. I think I'm getting over my fear of catching polio from swimming in a public pool by doing the very thing I fear, just as Daddyjee taught us to do. All the same, I have to confess that there are times when I feel that polio is creeping up my legs.

June 20

Today I got my first paycheck from the ice-cream plant. I couldn't wait to hold it in my hand. For the first time I was handling money earned solely by my own effort. If I were at home, I would be expected to buy new clothes for Mamajee and my big sisters.

June 27

Mr. and Mrs. Chatterjee visited me today on their way to Mexico. I think that they were a little out-of-sorts. I had never received guests by myself before and I didn't even have a piece of candy to offer them. Mrs. Chatterjee felt hot and wanted some water. She charged into the bathroom but came right out, saying that she didn't know how I lived there without so much as a tooth mug. I laughed off the matter as best I could since I didn't know where to go looking for a glass. After a few minutes, they left, saying that they had to check into the Alamo Plaza Hotel Courts on U.S. Highway 67-70.

They are really very nice people. The whole time, Mr. Chatterjee talked about how Daddyjee was one of his oldest friends. And they both insisted that I should come and see them in Yellow Springs, Ohio, for Christmas.

June 30

At the ice-cream plant I'm learning a lot of tolerance and patience. I have to be on my feet for nine hours a day and work with average American adults, who are quite illiterate in world affairs.

July 1

I'm very worried. My temporary-stay visa expires on August 15, and Mr. Woolly says that the immigration authorities can refuse to renew it without giving a reason.

July 29

Brother Om did badly in his B.A. examination and he writes that he lost his self-confidence for a time. But now he's been selected by the government as a cadet for the marine engineering course—in fact, stood third among the fifty boys who were selected. As his letter was read out to me, my heart pounded with joy.

July 30

It has been raining for a full week. I get wet going to work and coming back from work. At work, I'm wet anyway because the ice-cream plant is generally ankle-deep in water. I must write home and ask Daddyjee permission to buy a waterproof. It's too late for this summer, though. I think waterproofs are very expensive, so it's just as well to put off buying it.

August 4

Today I gave a fifteen-minute talk about India on KLRA which was broadcast all over the state. Because the broadcast was a public service, I was not paid for it, but after it, the manager of the radio station presented me with a nylon shirt and a necktie. The manager said that they could have given me five dollars in cash—the value of the shirt and the tie—but they wanted to spare me the embarrassment of accepting cash. I told him that it had been a great honor for me to talk to the whole state.

August 7

We seem to be having an indirect war with Russia in the Far East. Because of it, it's hard to buy many things at reasonable prices. Luckily, I have been able to make some contacts with wholesalers who will sell me clothes at bargain prices.

August 8

The general feeling downtown is that the war in the Far East will not lead to the Third World War. All the same, it seems that Washington is taking all the necessary precautions in case the Russians push it on us. Let us all hope and pray that we will be able to get through this most delicate period. I wish I knew what the general feeling about the possibility of such a war is in India, which, after all, is on the doorstep of the fighting. That would help me give talks and broadcasts.

August 15

I wish people didn't pay attention to what newspapers say about me, because the reporters have a habit of twisting things around to make the articles more appealing.

❧

EVERY evening after supper, I would take the trolley and the bus and go spend a couple of hours at the Boys' Club. Ed continued to play chess with me. My fear of losing him as a chess partner had been groundless. In fact, he would now wait for me to make a mistake. Whenever I did, he would laugh gleefully, exclaiming, "We got the master that time!" There would be applause all around. Although I only played the game that I had learned when I was eight or nine, Ed always insisted on calling me a "master." The exaggerated respect that I thought put distance between Ed and me, and between the chess watchers and me, never completely disappeared. I couldn't get anyone but Ed to play with me; it was as if the boys and their dates were intimidated by me. (The Braille playing cards seemed to throw up a similar barrier.)

Whenever Joe could snatch a few minutes from his other duties, he would give me a swimming lesson—that is, if I wasn't in the middle of a chess game. In the beginning, he always called out, "Everyone out of the pool, please!" Standing there with the head man of the club, and, in only a pair of trunks (my new acquisition), feeling exposed in front of so many good eyes, I was embarrassed at Joe's calling attention to me in this way. I would try to reason that boys were rowdy, that it was a small pool, that Joe had my best interests at heart. Still, the feeling of embarrassment persisted.

In the pool, Joe would put an arm under my stomach and show me how to kick without bending my knees, how to reach out with my arms, pull them through the water, and bring them out from the elbow, and how to turn my face and inhale when an arm was up and exhale in the water when that arm was in. When I was able to swim a little by myself, he would swim alongside me, always ready to put an arm under me in case I tired or started thrashing because I thought I was sinking. At first, I worried about whether I would be able to find my way and keep a straight path in the pool, as I did in the street—particularly since I pulled better with my right arm and so had a tendency to go off to the right—but I soon discovered that some of my mobility skills were applicable in the pool; I could generally sense the side of the pool with my facial vision, for instance, and keep on a straight course by swimming alongside it.

Although I had no fear of the water, except as a carrier of polio germs, I never learned to swim particularly well. I never managed to synchronize my breathing with the motion of my arms or to pull and kick properly. At first, I blamed my "ice-cream legs and arms;" they ached constantly from the hours of standing and packing. Later on, I realized that I simply did not have good coördination in the water, perhaps because I had come to it too late. Before long, however, I was able to swim well enough to enjoy it, and Joe would leave me alone in the pool. After a while, he did not even trouble to clear it. I enjoyed playing in the water with the other boys. (Girls never came into the pool.) Sometimes they would push me off the edge of the pool, duck my head in the water, try to make me lose my sense of direction. I discovered that although I was no better at chess playing than at swimming, the swimmers had much less respect for my abilities than the chess watchers had, possibly because my physical limitations were obvious in the pool in a way that my mental limitations were not when I was concentrating on a game at the poolside. Even so, if Joe caught the swimmers teasing me he would scold them, saying things like "Don't you know any better than to treat a blind boy that way?" They would leave me alone, but I wouldn't want to swim anymore.

One evening, I protested to Joe, "I don't want to be treated differently."

"They can be a thoughtless bunch of animals."

"I'll take my chances with them."
After that, Joe mostly left us swimmers alone.

❧

JOE had a happy-go-lucky, boyish voice and the manner of a hillbilly on the radio. Yet there was something selfless about him. Once, as I was sitting at the poolside, my trunks wet, and with nothing to do, Joe came up and said that he would like to teach me fishing and hiking. "Maybe we can get your school to let you come with me and my wife, Jean, out on the Arkansas River in a rowboat one day. Hey, boy, you have a faraway look. What you thinking?

I was listening to the rattle, spring, and splash of a boy diving off a diving board, and I was wondering what a diving board was like and what prevented him from cracking his head open on the bottom of the pool.

"That boy—what keeps him from killing himself when he hits the bottom?" I asked.

Joe asked me to explain what I meant. When I did, he took me around to the deep end and showed me the pool's three diving boards. The first one I could almost have jumped onto from the poolside pavement. The second was somewhat higher. The third, however, had a series of stone steps going up to it, and Joe and I climbed them. He led and I followed, feeling a little dizzy, as if I were going up a staircase to heaven. Finally, we were on the board. It had rubber treads, but it was wet and narrow. It vibrated and trembled under our feet. I was afraid of making a misstep. We inched along, my hands on each side of Joe's ample waist.

"Don't you worry," Joe said, looking around. "The board is supposed to have a lot of give in it. Just hang on." I tightened my hold.

We were at the end of the board. Joe asked me to touch his legs, arms, and head to see how he had positioned himself for a dive. There was hardly any room to maneuver. I didn't like being so high above the pool, and the diving board was waving up and down so much that I was terrified that it was going to slip its moorings and plunge us into the water. I also didn't like the thought of touching Joe's mostly naked body all over. All the same, under his guidance, I felt his feet, which were together, with toes over the edge of the board, and his knees, which were flexed. I examined his bent waist and followed his arms, which were stretched down in front of his head with his fingers pointing toward the water. As I crouched and stood up, leaned and reached out, twisted and turned, sometimes with a foot in the air, in order to fix his stance in my head, I felt that I was doing some kind of complicated dance step with him on the edge of a precipice, or perhaps trying to keep a precarious balance on the running board of a speeding car.

"What protects your head is the way you slice into the water, the way you hold your hands," Joe was saying. "If you don't dive at this angle, you'll flop on your belly and get a water burn for sure. Now just keep your hand lightly on my feet and see how I dive off the board."

Joe rocked and leaped through my fingers, causing a minor earthquake on the board. It was all I could do to stay on. I heard him go into the water not like the heavy person he was but like a fish making barely a ripple. I felt breathless and excited.

❧

ONE evening, when I got off the bus and was getting ready to cross the very busy street in front of the Boys' Club, Joe rushed over to me, saying, "Boy, am I glad to see you!"

"You know I come every evening," I said. "Why the reception?"

Joe didn't reply immediately, but after we'd crossed the street he said, "The *Arkansas Democrat* would like to get a picture of you for a story in the Sunday paper."

I hated having my picture taken. I imagined that facial expression was conveyed mainly by the eyes, and that in pictures I came out looking sleepy or stony. Anyway, since I couldn't see pictures I had decided I had little use for them. Similarly, I wasn't sure that I liked news stories about me. At first, I may have found it flattering that reporters wanted my opinion on all sorts of questions, such as "Will India go Communist?" or "What do you think of the American educational system?" Until I started talking, I didn't know I had any opinion on such questions. Then I was impressed by the sound of my own voice and was sure that Daddyji would be proud of me if he could hear me. But whatever pleasure I might have found in the interviews was momentary, because I hardly ever knew anything about the newspaper articles based on them. No one else seemed to know about them, either. A newspaper was almost never seen around the dormitory. It was sometimes days or weeks before I knew that an article with me in it had appeared. Even then, I didn't know what it said. I simply assumed that the story had more to do with the school than with me. That March, however, the day after my sixteenth birthday, Mrs. Hankins had read me one of the stories. It was in the *Arkansas Democrat,* and I was mortified to discover that it was about a surprise birthday party that had taken place around the desk in Mr. Woolly's office.

The afternoon of my birthday, Mr. Woolly had summoned me to his office. As soon as I walked in, people had sung out, "Happy birthday to you, happy birthday, dear Ved."

I was stunned. The voices were unfamiliar, and I hadn't breathed a word even to my friends about its being my birthday; I was as shy about the day of my birth as I was about everything to do with my Indian past. Anyway, at home, except that we received a little bonus on top of our pocket money from Daddyji, our birthdays went mostly unnoticed.

After the song, Mr. Woolly introduced me to some strangers—Bishop Paul E. Martin, Mrs. Martin, a couple of their friends, and a reporter and a photographer from the *Arkansas Democrat.* It seemed that Bishop Martin had recently gone to India on some missionary business and, at Mr. Woolly's suggestion, had called on my family there.

Bishop Martin presented me with a sweater that Mamaji had knitted for me, and the photographer took some pictures.

Mrs. Martin handed me a piece of very rich cake

on a napkin and said, "The birthday cake is a gift from our friend Mrs. Maxwell Lyons, who unfortunately couldn't be here today."

After a few minutes, and more pictures, the Bishop and his party left, and I walked back to the locker room with my sweater, feeling a little exploited, and also upset with my family for unwittingly forcing me to celebrate my birthday in an office with Mr. Woolly and six total strangers.

The *Arkansas Democrat* story that Mrs. Hankins read me the next day was headlined "Blind Student from India Is Surprised," and, as if to add insult to injury, mentioned the sweater, the cake, Mrs. Lyons, and all. I could scarcely bear to hear it read. After that, I was horrified to find that even some strangers whom I encountered on the buses knew when my birthday was. They would point me out to other passengers as if I were an interesting animal in a zoo, so that I wanted to hide in the sanctuary of the school and become invisible again.

Now, as Joe and I walked to the Boys' Club, I said to him, "I don't want any part of pictures and newspaper stories. It's all very embarrassing."

"But you've got to do it for the sake of the Boys' Club," he said. "It's good publicity for us. Anyway, it's a good way of educating people about the blind and India—and all in the Sunday *Democrat*." He paused. "I already told the *Democrat* that you'd dive off our high board for the picture." Joe had taught me how to dive, and I had graduated from the low to the high diving board. Indeed, I now dived off the high board at least once every evening.

"But, Joe, I don't want to dive for a picture."

"Why not?"

I said nothing, because we were inside the Boys' Club, where a staff reporter from the *Democrat,* Van Rush, and a photographer, a Mr. Campbell, were waiting. Both of them were very friendly, and Mr. Rush started interviewing me then and there, asking me questions about my upbringing, Hinduism, India's attitude toward Communism.

After the interview, Joe got me to change into my swim trunks, and I walked over to the high diving board. As I climbed its steps, the stone underfoot and the air around me felt cold. I shivered, as if it were the middle of winter instead of the middle of summer. I recalled that during my first tries off the board I had flopped on my belly and been stung by the water, and had felt that I would never learn to dive properly—that I would get hurt, that I was too old to learn, that I should give up. I would wake up in the middle of the night with dreams of falling off cliffs or being pushed off towers. I wondered if my recently developed fear of falling through empty space was connected with my going out alone on the streets. Certainly, since I'd fallen into the manhole, I'd begun to dread that as I was walking along, the ground might abruptly give way. Now I was petrified by the thought that Mr. Campbell would be trying to fix in a picture the moment when I was falling through the air, that Mr. Rush would be writing about it, and that perhaps the bus passengers would see all of it in print on Sunday.

I was on the diving board. The rubber treads underfoot felt wet and sticky. Joe had made everybody get out of the pool, and it was quiet—quieter than it had ever been before. They're all standing below and looking up and watching me, I thought. All my life, eyes will be staring at me.

"Keep in the center!" Joe shouted gratuitously. "You don't want to fall off the side and blister yourself!"

I felt as though someone in the street had shouted "Watch out!" But I kept on walking along the board with cautious little steps. I wondered why my knees felt weak, as if they wouldn't be able to hold me up much longer. I must be careful, I thought. I mustn't step off the end, the way I stepped into the manhole.

The diving board felt increasingly unsteady, as if I were nearing the end. I took smaller and smaller steps. My toe went off the edge and I stopped short. I brought my feet together, curved my body, raised my arms over my head, shut my eyes tight, and started bounding, saying to myself, *"One, and two and—"*

"Hold it!" Mr. Campbell called up. I was barely able to keep my balance. "Look toward me. I want to get your picture on the diving board first."

There were many clicks of the camera. I felt foolish. I wished there were no Sunday papers, no Boys' Club, no people to educate.

"O.K., you can dive now." Mr. Campbell called up to me.

Getting back into position and taking a deep breath, I dived off. There was the reverberating noise of the board springing back, the click of the camera, and I was falling. Now water was pressing all around me. But I was still moving, going farther and farther down. I must protect my head, I thought. Then my out-

Ved, Little Rock, 1950.

stretched hands touched bottom. I'll never get up to the air, I thought. I thrashed frantically. What had Joe said? "It's easier coming up if you just relax." I was out in the air, but in the middle of the pool, limp and gasping. I had to get to the side.

"Don't work so hard," Joe called from somewhere above my head. "You're almost there."

I played a bad game of chess with Ed that evening.

❧

"MR. WOOLLY just told me that you've been living here—did you have a good summer?" Mr. Chiles asked a little nervously, coming in with his suitcases to take charge of his room. I thought I heard him sniff, as if to catch emanations of my stay. Without waiting for an answer, he sat down on the chair and immediately started talking about the "fine" summer he'd had, about some new ideas he'd worked out for social-adjustment classes, about all the students who'd be streaming back over the weekend—it was Thursday, and classes were to begin on the following Monday.

Mr. Chiles had surprised me by returning to school a day earlier than he was expected. I listened to him with half an ear and concentrated on gathering my belongings, which were spread out all over the room, and throwing them in a suitcase to carry to the locker room. I had to move carefully, because practically all the available floor space in what was essentially just a small bedroom was taken up by boxes of Talking Books I was reading and by my other things—and now there were also Mr. Chiles's legs and luggage.

"Mrs. Hankins tells me that you did a fine job getting around the city and working in an ice-cream plant," Mr. Chiles was saying, politely ignoring the flurry of my packing. "She says there have been stories about you in the newspapers. I'm sure you have a lot to tell."

I did. I could have told him that I had used his room and the school as a hotel, where I mostly ate, read into the night, and slept; that I had worked alongside the sighted, without a single other blind person about; that I had earned my keep; that I had gone to coffee shops by myself; that I had swum and dived and played chess with ordinary people whom I had discovered for myself. I wanted to tell him that I'd made great strides in mobility—that I now had under my feet the streets of Little Rock and North Little Rock. I was able to walk the streets without a cane, without worrying about lampposts, without having to make a special effort to feel the ground underfoot, without becoming unhinged if someone shouted "Watch out!" when I was in the middle of the street. I now felt that, with a few well-thought-out, judicious inquiries, I could go anywhere I liked. I felt like a bird that had only known a cage but had finally escaped and discovered the limitless spaces of the sky. I wanted to tell Mr. Chiles that I had also made progress in social adjustment. If, on a bus, a woman offered me her seat, I made a gallant remark about "the fair sex" and quietly but firmly declined it. If, at a crossing, a stranger tried to propel me across the street, I politely told him that it was easier for me to walk alongside than for him to push me along. If, on occasion, I fell into a manhole, I would climb out and be on my way quickly, before anyone started fussing over me. At a coffee shop or a soda fountain, I had learned to speak in a very low voice to waitresses before they spoke to me, for this often had the effect of making them speak softly. In the streets or on the buses, at bus stops or in coffee shops, I had learned to give the impression that I knew what I was doing, and that helped me to go about my business without attracting much special notice. In fact, I sometimes felt that people outside the school had started treating me as if I were partially sighted. That was all to the good, since if they were fooled into thinking that I had some sight they left me alone—treated me the way I wanted them to. Most of the things that had made up my summer were within the ken of Mr. Chiles. There was no one at school with whom I would rather have shared them. But I realized that I was no more able to talk to him about them now than I had ever been able to talk to him—or anyone else—about my home in India.

Even as I packed my suitcase and stacked the books, a seemingly permanent curtain was being drawn over my first job and my friendships at the Boys' Club. As it turned out, once I became a student again, Gladys, Helen, and Jean, Jay and Tom, Joe and Ed never came by the school, and a couple of times during the school year when I got to North Little Rock to see them all there was a constraint of experience remembered rather than experience lived. It was one of my many experiences since childhood of something vital and flowing abruptly cut off, and sadly confirmed my feeling that life was merely a passage through a series of railway stations or (now that I was in America) bus stops.

VII

LYING LOW
AND
VENTURING
OUT

When thou art at Rome, do as they do at Rome.

—*Cervantes, "Don Quixote."*

A T THE TIME, I COULD NOT HAVE GIVEN A NAME to my condition. Though I was in its grip through most of the summer and autumn, I was scarcely aware of any of its symptoms. Years later, I read through my letters, my journal, and other papers of the period and talked with the people who knew me then, trying, like a detective, to reconstruct events long past. I came away with the feeling that the condition I was going through was the slough of despond.

When I had been working at the ice-cream plant nine weeks, I arrived there one morning to discover that Jay had been fired overnight and in his place we had a tough-sounding older man. His voice had a military ring, and I wouldn't have been surprised to learn that he carried a riding crop.

The new manager made Gladys, Jean, Helen, Tom, and me line up in front of the freezer vault, and he told us in an ominous voice that the plant was not making enough profit and that he intended to turn things around, even if that meant firing us all and hiring a whole new crew. He informed us that he was instituting a new system: he would see to it that we worked our hides off until the freezer vault was filled, and then he would lay us off until all the ice cream we had made and packaged had been moved out of the plant.

"But I got two children to feed," Gladys said. "I need my weekly paycheck."

"That's your problem," the new manager said. "I'm here to run the plant and make money for Mayflower Dairy."

"How many days do you reckon we'll be laid off?"
Tom asked with feigned casualness.

"That depends," the new manager said. "It could
be one day or two days or three days a week."

We all talked at once, telling him that we'd counted
on making a certain amount of money a week.

"Quiet down!" the new manager bellowed. "If you
don't like it, you can leave. There are plenty more
hands where you came from."

The new manager arrived in the second week of
August, about a month before the beginning of the
first six-week school term. He whipped us into a frenzy
and made us overproduce for four days, then laid us off
for two. I had thought that by the end of the summer
I would have worked three full months and earned three
hundred dollars. Now there seemed to be no way for
me to reach my goal.

I began to dread being in that small plant with the
new manager. I imagined that he had the power to
blacken my short employment record and so banish me
forever from the sighted working world, to which I'd
so recently gained entry. Indeed, he appeared in my
dreams as a menacing figure—as a Muslim hooligan in
Lahore with a big knife in his hand. And yet the busier
and more productive the days at the plant were, the
emptier and lonelier the layoff days seemed in the
deserted school. When I had to go to work, I would
get up at six-thirty, perhaps because I didn't want my
pay to be docked, but when I didn't have to get to
work I would oversleep and lose the will to get out of
bed. On such days, I might wake a little after breakfast, which was cleared away promptly at seven-thirty,

and, feeling resentful, stay in bed half-awake, half-asleep, thinking that I should read something but lacking the energy even to turn on the Talking Book player at my bedside. Sometimes, in this state, I would dream about Daddyji's hand on my forehead or Mamaji's under my neck; that was the gentle way they used to wake me up when I was a child. Then I would imagine that my sisters were sitting around my bed and having a whispered conversation over me, as they used to do when I was sick. I would wake up around lunchtime. I would have no appetite, and there would seem to be no reason for me to get washed or dressed. I would stay in bed, like a small animal hibernating—so inactive that sometimes I imagined that my heartbeat had slowed. When I did get out of bed—and sometimes it wasn't until dinner—my head would be so full of lethargy that I would want only to go back to bed. On one layoff day, I made a great effort and went to the Boys' Club, and swam, dived, and played chess. But the coming and going by trolley and bus took nearly two hours, and I returned to my bed exhausted, wishing that I'd never left it. The layoff days began to disrupt my routine so that I couldn't sleep much at night, and when I did go back to work I had trouble getting to the plant on time and staying awake on the job.

On other layoff days, though, I would furiously type letters to Daddyji in New Delhi, telling him of my low spirits and asking for his advice. Day after day, I waited for an answer, thinking that a word from him would magically lift me out of the slough, only to receive a disheartening cablegram from him saying that something was obviously wrong with the ribbon on my typewriter, since the letters he was receiving from me were packets of nearly blank sheets. The realization that I had poured out my feelings to a broken typewriter deepened my depression. I couldn't bear to go over the same ground, so I just cabled him, "BLANK LETTERS UNIMPORTANT."

Then I decided I couldn't work another day under the new manager, and at the end of August I quit my job and accepted an invitation to spend a couple of days in Hot Springs as the guest of Joe and Jean Red. They had rented a cottage just ten feet from Lake Hamilton. There I did many extremely enjoyable things for the first time: I swam in the lake, and was pleasantly surprised by how soft the water was and how little resistance it offered compared with the water in the Boys' Club swimming pool; I rode in a motorboat, and was thrilled by the feeling of moving over a body of water as if in a car; I fished, and enjoyed sitting and waiting for a tug at the pole. But I came away from Hot Springs feeling sad. In the country, I had been unable to do anything by myself—everywhere, I had needed the help and indulgence of sighted people. In fact, all the time I was in Hot Springs I had longed for my familiar beat in Little Rock.

A FEW days before school opened, Cousin Yog came to Little Rock to see me. He was the eldest of my Mehta cousin-brothers, and was the trailblazer to the West for our generation of Mehtas, much as Daddyji had been for his. After earning a bachelor's degree in civil engineering at Oregon State University, in Corvallis, he had spent a year getting practical training in the state's highway department. He was now on his way back to India, to find a job and a wife. We younger cousin-brothers had always looked up to him, imagining that he combined in his person the good character traits that had been parcelled out among all the rest of us. But since coming to America I had scarcely been in touch with him; it was difficult to make calls on the school's only telephone, and he was not much of a letter writer. Anyway, Cousin Yog was six years older than I was, and I knew his younger brothers better than I knew him—I had been just twelve when he left for America. I was eager for his visit; I thought that since he knew both India and America he would be able to tell me how I should live as an Indian *in* America.

When he arrived at the school door, where I had been waiting for him, I went forward to embrace him, Indian fashion, feeling almost as if he were Daddyji come to clear up my confusions.

"Vedi, fancy seeing you here!" Cousin Yog said, breezily shaking my hand, American fashion. I tried not to show my disappointment.

Cousin Yog reclined on my bed, as if he were holding court in India, and I drew up a chair and immediately started talking to him as I had talked to no one since leaving home. I longed to see how well I remembered Punjabi, and spoke to him in our mother tongue, but he answered in English. I couldn't tell whether he had forgotten Punjabi or simply preferred English. I brought up this family member and that family friend, but he answered vaguely. Again, I couldn't tell whether he had forgotten the people or simply didn't want to remember them. Since he was older than I was, I didn't feel I could press him.

Cousin Yog was staying overnight, in a room connected through the bathroom to Mr. Chiles's room. We spent some time walking around the school building. I showed Cousin Yog the locker room, the lounge, and the sleeping hall. We went to Stifft's Station. We took the trolley downtown and strolled up and down Main Street.

In the evening, when we were again sitting in my room—he on the bed and I on the chair—I brought up the worrying question of dating. The Indian in me regarded any close contact with the opposite sex outside of wedlock as dirty and base. At the same time, from my first days at school I had wanted to have dates. I had tried hard, if furtively, to get a date. When I repeatedly failed, I had told myself that I didn't want dates anyway—that they were immoral. As long as I could remember, Daddyji had made a distinction between temporary pleasure and permanent pleasure, the one wasteful and meaningless, the other fruitful and meaningful. After each rejection by a girl, I would self-righteously tell myself that dates were mere temporary pleasures, only to ache for a date again a few minutes later.

"I find the American custom of dating quite disgusting," I now began. This was, of course, far from the truth, but I thought that he would approve of this sentiment, and praise me for remaining faithful to our

Indian principles. After all, at home, if young persons did associate with the opposite sex outside marriage they lost their reputation.

Cousin Yog's response took me aback. "Dating? Why, dating, Vedi—that's as necessary for living in America as drinking Coca-Cola." He said "Coca-Cola" in a very Indian way, emphasizing "Cola." It sounded especially funny to me because at school everyone just said "Coke." In some ways he's more Indian that I am, and in others not at all Indian, I thought. I can't make him out.

"But surely you would never go on a date, would you?" I said. I felt frightened by my boldness. It was like trying to find out whether Daddyji had ever been plagued with base desires like mine. I had taken it for granted that people I respected were above them, but something in Cousin Yog's manner—a sort of bravado—made me wonder.

"Why, Vedi, I've been going out on dates practically from the day I got to America."

His admission was so startling that I felt my ears blush. "I'm sure that Daddyji would not approve of dating," I finally said.

"Didn't you grow up hearing him say, 'When in Rome, do as the Romans do'? I'm sure that when he was in the West he had a gay old time."

"Daddyji couldn't possibly have done things like dating," I said.

"Your daddy is very worldly, you know. I'm sure he did everything."

Around the corner, in the office, the night watchman was playing his radio. Unmodulated hillbilly music echoed in the empty hall, making the building seem even lonelier than it was.

"Everything?" I cried.

"Absolutely everything."

"But I don't remember his ever talking about it."

"Things that are done in the West are never discussed at home—they don't count. I'm sure your daddy never wrote home about them. And, by the way, neither should you. They are just part of the fun of life here."

"You think people at home won't mind my keeping such things secret?"

"Certainly not. Just do as the Romans do. Behave like an American boy while you're here. You're sixteen—it's healthy at your age to get to know girls. When you get back home, you'll just turn over a new leaf."

"But I hear that if you take a girl out in this country it can easily cost you five dollars—that is, if she is a nice girl," I said, trying to strike a practical note, such as Daddyji sometimes adopted with us children when an issue was overcharged with emotion. "If she isn't a nice girl, it can cost you much more. They say American girls are very greedy and take full advantage of their sex appeal."

"You would probably take a girl out only once a week, on a Saturday night. That won't add up to too much money."

"Five dollars a week, twenty dollars a month, two hundred and forty dollars a year—it all adds up. Remember how Daddyji used to say that money saved is money earned—that he had paid for the education of at least two of his younger brothers with the money he saved by not smoking and drinking?"

"Vedi, I think you worry about money too much."

It was astonishing to hear Cousin Yog say that. In the family, he was known for being a penny-pincher; in contrast, I could never keep money in my pocket. "I can't forget that we lost everything in Partition, that we are refugees," I said, reflecting that he had come out of India in 1946, a year before Partition, and therefore was perhaps not fully aware of its effect on the family fortunes.

Cousin Yog fell silent. The hillbilly music blared on, and I felt as if we were marooned on an island with a radio that couldn't be switched off. Then Cousin Yog said, "But, come to think of it, Vedi, when you're at school you'll only be taking girls to school dances, which should cost you little more than the price of a Coca-*Cola*."

He's right, I thought. Saving money and dating are two separate issues. I must be getting them confused because I'm afraid of girls. All the same, I take life seriously. I wonder if Cousin Yog does.

"But what's the point of seeing a girl if you're not going to marry her?" I asked.

"The point of seeing American dames is to have fun," Cousin Yog said. "You never think of marrying them. You should learn to enjoy yourself."

I was appalled by Cousin Yog's talk, yet also excited by it. It was almost as if he were giving me his—and, by extension, Daddyji's—permission to have dates, to do almost anything with girls, as long as they were Americans.

"But if you do such things here you can't go back to India and get married to a nice Punjabi girl," I said hesitantly.

"Why not?"

"You'll be corrupted, unclean."

"But this is America, that is India. You have your wine, women, and song here and then you go home and have buttermilk, marriage, and children. After all, we can agree that our system of marriages arranged by the parents is the best. Nothing can take the place of the home comforts that only an Indian wife can give you. I've already written home that I will be in the market for a good Punjabi girl as soon as I get back."

When Cousin Yog went to bed that night, he left me more confused than ever. He had given me the impression that he thought that his American self and, therefore, mine were suits of clothes that we would be able to discard when we left America. I wasn't so sure.

As Cousin Yog was leaving the next morning, he spotted a story in the *Arkansas Democrat* about his visit. A reporter from the *Democrat* had hurriedly interviewed us together after Mr. Woolly alerted the paper that there was another Indian in Arkansas. "It's a wonderful headline," Cousin Yog said, and he read it aloud: "Young Cousins of India Discuss World Problems."

I didn't know whether to laugh or cry, but Cousin Yog was reading on:

Family relations in India are probably closer than in any other country in the world.

This was exemplified when Yoginder Kumar Mehta, 21, traveled 2,200 miles from Oregon to visit his first cousin,

Ved Mehta—a student in the Arkansas School for the Blind—
for only one day.

Yog, as the former is known to friends, hadn't seen Ved
since Yog left India to attend Oregon State University and
study civil engineering. After graduation, he worked a year
for that state's highway department. Then he decided to
kill two birds by visiting Ved and seeing some of the nation's
largest dams, for educational purposes.

When they got together they sounded like two professors of history, science and international government. Yog
apparently has unalterable convictions on the international
situation and puts his finger on the Communists for mud-
dling everybody's affairs.

Ved agrees, but believes gullible people of the world
can be educated out of chaos by fulfillment of promises which
the Communists merely make without keeping.

Folding up the paper, Cousin Yog said, "We'd
better get several copies of this. Both our daddies would
like to have the story."

❧

AFTER Cousin Yog left, I felt pulled this way and
that way. I wanted to have dates and do everything
he'd done, but at the same time I feared, among other
things, that I would destroy my reputation if I didn't
keep my Indian morality intact. (Years later, I realized
that the source of my confusion over the whole dating
issue was the clash between my ideal of an arranged
marriage and an all-encompassing family, on the one
hand, and my wish for romantic love and an individual

destiny, on the other. Because of my abrupt separation
from the family, Daddyji's remarks, over the years,
about the superiority of the Indian system and the
inferiority of the American system had become for me
as sacred as laws carved in stone, and, again because of
that painful separation, everything I had lost often
seemed good and everything I was discovering seemed
bad. I tended to idealize India and imagine that everything in America, by contrast, wore the face of corrup-
tion. I told myself that eschewing the pleasures that
money could buy—or women could give—was an
incomparable act of purity. And yet I was constantly
tempted by the new, frightening customs and the throb
of my own senses.) I sat down and poured out my heart
in a long letter to Sister Nimi, in whom I had always
confided, and wrote a more restrained letter to Daddyji. Since I couldn't read what I was typing—never
mind revise or edit it—I couldn't be sure whether I
was making sense, but I counted on our family close-
ness to help them understand what I was saying even
when I was saying it badly. To Sister Nimi I wrote, in
part:

I opened my soul to Cousin Yog. He told me that in
this country life is impossible without a girl, and I should
do as the Romans do. According to him, he had dated girls
from the beginning.

With one part of my mind, I consider dates to be the
lowest kind of temporary pleasure. Perhaps I feel this way
because our daddy brought us up to look for permanent
pleasures. What really troubles me, Sister Nimi, is that if
I'm not going to marry an American girl, if I am not look-

ing for a suitable match here, what's the point of dating? But then, I have not been on any dates, and maybe I have no idea how much fun they really are. For all I know, boys and girls in our country are also dating and looking for thrills, but I just didn't know it because I was visually handicapped and was not able to see them. What I do know is that if I should let my willpower slip, and succumb to one temporary pleasure, then I'll have trouble resisting the second and the third and so on, so forth.

But you will admit that we are socially very backward in India compared to America. If a virgin or a spinster is caught kissing in India she is condemned as a criminal. In this country such kissing is normal. People here go on dates every day—to shows, to dances, to picnics, to parties— with the intention of having fun. They go on long moonlight drives in deserted places. Kissing is just nothing. The folks in this country think that anything that both parties agree to is perfectly all right. Our morality is certainly better, but now I'm here, and I find that that morality does not serve me. I feel at a loss. I find myself thinking of God, thinking of that eternal thing.

Cousin Yog thought that what was holding me back from dating was my shyness. Sometimes I think he's right, there. I want to tell you something I haven't breathed a word of to anyone. The idea of going with a girl from our school doesn't completely appeal to me. After all, I don't want to marry a blind girl. And going out with an ordinary girl, a sighted girl, even if I could, doesn't appeal to me either, because I feel that she's bound to feel sorry for me, and that I wouldn't like at all. Maybe I'm wrong in this, but even if there were a one per cent chance that a girl would feel sorry for me, I wouldn't want to go out with her. Another thing, I feel that I am one in millions who has been given this opportunity to study, and shouldn't waste my time on dates. Yet I have these urges—uncontrollable urges.

I hope you'll explain everything to Daddy, especially if Cousin Yog tells him about our conversations, which I hope he won't. I don't want you to think that I am afraid of Daddy. I never want to keep anything back from him, but at the same time I don't want to add to the strain he's under.

I wish I had someone around whom I could trust with all my confidences, but it seems that in America everyone is left to face problems on his own.

I wrote to Daddyji in a totally different vein, keeping things back from him ostensibly to spare him worry, and setting the problem of my dating in the light of society's attitude that the blind weren't normal. In my letter to him I said, in part:

May I say that I enjoyed having Cousin Yog with me over here. It gave me an opportunity to share my problems with somebody who could understand the standards of our family to some extent. It also gave me a chance to talk about my country, to which I feel so close, even though it made me homesick. But Cousin Yog's ideas and my ideas about our civilization and about the West are very different. Maybe he has lived in this country so long that he has started thinking like an American. Perhaps there is nothing wrong with that, but I think like an Indian and am proud of it.

I tried to discuss with Cousin Yog some of the problems which have come staggering at me since I came to this country. But I got nowhere. He kept repeating, "When in

Rome, do as the Romans do." He advised me to act boldly like an American—to go out on dates and have a good time—but he doesn't take into account that I am a handicapped person, that the world doesn't expect handicapped people to act in a bold way. You see, we are confronted with a vast ignorance in the world about the handicapped, and the world would not understand if we acted like normal people. I couldn't begin to lead the kind of life that Cousin Yog wants me to. Until such time as I can convince the world that we are capable men and women, it's best for us to lie low. Cousin Yog doesn't understand that my experience of blindness at home has a lot to do with what I am and what I will be. The circumstances in which I will have to face life and those in which he will are absolutely different. Another thing—my every little action is noted here. I have, there-fore, to be always on guard against doing anything that would lower people's opinion of me or my country.

Reading these letters now, after the passage of some thirty-five years, I realize that I had taken my father's oft-repeated advice "Always see the other person's point of view" a little too much to heart, and so had tried to intellectualize my emotions away. Moreover, when I was less than five years old I had been sent away to the first of several substandard institutions, and there I hadn't had anyone to run to or confide in. I had had to learn to be wary. As a consequence, I had become mature in some ways long before my time and had remained infantile in other ways much too long.

No sooner had I posted the letters to Sister Nimi and Daddyji than I began fretting about what, exactly, I had said. I wondered if I should have written about Cousin Yog at all, and if perhaps I had betrayed him—

not presented his viewpoint fairly. I wondered how I would get the replies to my letters read without embarrassing the person who read them to me—not to mention myself. The first few months I was in America, people at home wrote to me mindful that their letters would have to be read aloud, and so the letters tended to be circumspect and a little bland. But lately they had dropped their guard, almost as if time and distance had made them forget my blindness and so the problem of the intermediaries. Daddyji now wrote freely about money matters and the trouble he was having finding a husband for Sister Nimi. And Mamaji, who herself needed an intermediary to translate her letters from Hindi into English, wrote about my diet and her prayers for my success.

About a month after I posted the letters, Mrs. Hankins called out to me as I was passing the door of the office, "I've got a letter for you from your dad—it's as fat as all getout." She had never sounded more disconcertingly Arkansan to my ear.

I walked toward Mrs. Hankins' desk with little steps and stood in front of it, my heart beating fast. The sheaf of papers crackled in her hand like the airmail stationery in Daddyji's office. Daddyji must have dictated it to his steno, I thought. So maybe it's all right for Mrs. Hankins to read it.

"It's dated the twenty-fifth of September," she began, and she read:

MY DEAREST VED,

In your letter to me dated the 28th August was enclosed a letter solely meant for Nirmil, and as such, was passed on

to her. She has been rather worried over the views expressed
by you in that letter, and she has passed on the same to me
to reply to. I have carefully read your letters, and, knowing
you as I do, I am not alarmed by them. You have expressed
your possible ignorance about the situation in India in the
words, "For all I know, boys and girls in our country are
also dating and looking for thrills, but I just didn't know
it because I was visually handicapped and was not able to
see them." Well, I may assure you that your brothers and
sisters were always frank and open hearted with you and
never concealed anything from you, nor did I do so, as I
have always treated you as normal. Promila, Nirmila, and
Urmila, and Sheila and Leila [Cousin Yog's two sisters]—and
their friends—cannot imagine this dating business. In Indian
society, such things are not done, because Indian religion
and philosophy tell us that they do not bring any happiness.
If you date a girl and so to speak get a taste of it, you want
to do it over and over again. It is just like any intoxicant.
You feel in a way happy under its influence and want to
take more of the same. But no sooner is that short period of
intoxication over than reaction sets in and you feel much
more unhappy than you did before you took the intoxicant,
and the longing comes back again and again to repeat the
thrills of the cheap pleasure. Perhaps such an experience is
necessary in America to select a suitable companion by
experiment, but in our culture marriages are more or less
arranged by the parents, who are well experienced in life
and have a maturer judgment, and take into consideration
not only "love," as it is understood ordinarily, but also the
social and economic background of the two families. My
point is that we in India minimize the risks in marriage by
finding a partner for our child who is as much like him or

her as possible. Once married, like anywhere else, the law of compensation and compromise must apply—given the fact that no one is perfect.

Insofar as I could take in the words through the haze of my apprehension, I was glad that it was Dad-dyji rather than Sister Nimi who was writing. He is saying intimate things, but in a fairly abstract way, I thought. I noticed that Mrs Hankins was reading faster and faster. I thought that with anyone else that might have had to do with the length of the letter, but not with her, for she was a reflective person and generally read letters to me deliberately, as if she grasped the fact that she had to fully understand what she was reading in order for me to understand it. I imagined that she was reading quickly because she sensed that the letter was extremely personal and that I was feeling awkward. I tried to relax my shoulder muscles and assume a casual posture. She read on:

According to our Hindu religion, there are four periods of life: the first, bachelorhood, or celibacy; the second, married life; the third, social service; and the fourth, renunciation of worldly things. Each of these periods is meant to last twenty-three to twenty-five years. You are passing through the first period. During it you should devote all your time to study and to gaining knowledge. This is the time when all of the organs of your body develop to maturity.

I felt like snatching the letter from her hand and running out of the office, even if it meant never finishing the letter. But I was no more capable of moving than a statue. I was able to bear what she was reading only because my natural curiosity was getting the better of me.

From the physiological point of view, I may acquaint you with the fact that there are excretions in the body such as perspiration, urine, and faeces which must be thrown out of the system to keep it in a healthy state, and there are secretions like saliva and semen which it is not necessary to throw out—in fact, they are reabsorbed into the system and are necessary for the development of various organs, particularly the brain. From this, please do not conclude that the loss of a little saliva or a little semen is harmful—not at all—but it is the habitual discarding of such valuable elements which is not very desirable. Another very important point that you must take into consideration while thinking about such a subject is the valuable time which can be devoted to studying worthwhile books, to developing one's faculties for the practice and appreciation of music, etc. I am sure you realize that you would not have gained the knowledge and the respect that are yours in Little Rock but for your keeping away from temporary cheap pleasures like dating, and, instead, saving time for doing worthwhile things. The picture of dating painted by Yog is a wrong one. Yog's ideas are very immature, and I am afraid he got mixed up with a crowd who talk much of dating girls and spending hundreds of rupees on them. Such things are not welcomed in good American families—those of doctors, engineers, professors, and other professional people.

Even in India, there is some cheap sex, but only among factory workers and certain hill peoples. Amongst such people a version of dating occurs, but even that very, very secretly. Amongst them, the standards of morality are so low that venereal diseases are common.

I think Yog's idea that you are shy is entirely wrong. I know you are simply reserved, and have high principles. People like us, who are reserved and principled and who have an eye to their future, grow up self-confident. Certainly, with people like us, such character traits have borne good results. I'm sure moral character is also appreciated in America. I would strongly recommend that you not be carried away by Yog's ideas.

Do not have any hesitation to write about sex matters to me. There is nothing unnatural about them, because sex is a normal physiological phenomenon which enters into all of our lives. All that we have to do is to understand its implications—not be frightened by it—and to remain disciplined.

You have talked of the backwardness of our country in the letter to Nirmil. We certainly are underdeveloped so far as the material wealth is concerned, but so far as our moral and spiritual stature is concerned, we are rich. Our old culture and philosophy are respected and appreciated everywhere. Gandhi's nonviolence, truth, and moral laws are looked up to all over the world. Please do understand that we in India are morally well advanced. Down through the ages, our Bhagavad Gita's message has been to do one's duty and keep to the path of good action and truth, and let the results take care of themselves. This message has proved to be the best the world has received. Your own motto, "Do your best and leave the rest to God," is the correct interpretation of the Gita's philosophy. I think I had better not sermonize any more, and leave it to your own good sense to decide for yourself what is best for you. All I would say to

you is that the opportunities which are coming your way—
to gain knowledge and to improve your prospects, to make
worthwhile contacts and to gain respect—should not be
missed.

As regards your marriage, you should not have any fixed
ideas about it. You should be open hearted, and should look
at it from all points of view. There will be plenty of time
when you and I can discuss this subject.

Please do not worry about me at all. As long as I know
that my children are remaining true to their principles, I
feel quite confident of their future. Their good reputation
gives me great satisfaction.

With all good wishes and love,

Yours affectionately,

Daddy

Mrs. Hankins made a lot of noise refolding the
letter, as if she were as much at a loss for words as I
was. She handed it to me across the desk. "It's a very
nice letter," she observed, with a touch of shyness.
"Your dad is a fine gentleman."

I nodded, suddenly becoming aware of Mr. Lord—
as I'll call the man who had succeeded Mr. Tyson as
our principal—shuffling papers, and of Mr. Woolly
dialling a number on the telephone in his office, which
was next door. They have certainly overheard some of
the letter, if not all of it, I thought. There is no privacy in this damn place.

I hurried away with the letter in my hand, trembling like a kite in a gusty wind.

For the rest of the day, I thought of little but how

to reply to Daddyji's letter. There was so much more about sex I wanted to know, but I was utterly overwhelmed by the subject and by the geographical distance that separated us. Besides, I felt small, inadequate, and base in comparison with the lofty sentiments of his letter. In the end, I simply wrote to him that his long letter had taught me much, and left it at that.

THERE were many changes at the school that year. Some of them, like the new aluminum awnings over the building's four doors, which provided welcome shelter from the rain if we were standing by the door and talking during recess, were for the better. Others, like a change in the character of our small class, were for the worse. Evelyn Worrell, who was a difficult person, was becoming more difficult by the day, and Wayne Tidman was spending more and more time away from school, preaching; indeed, he planned to quit school soon for the ministry. Then, too, our cozy class of four had been changed by the arrival of two new members—Joyce Boyle and Peggy Stevens, both of whom had just come to the school.

As tenth graders, we were required to take English literature, English grammar, world history, and algebra, and I had also signed up for beginners' French, biography writing, Dictaphone typing, Braille music, piano, accordion, and choir. I felt I should take French because I had fought for the introduction of a foreign-language course into the syllabus. I felt I should take biography writing because I couldn't wait to learn to write. I felt I should take typing because I considered it a necessity for journalism—something I was getting increasingly interested in. I felt I should take all the music courses I could because, among other things, I wanted to play accordion in the school band. (The band had an open slot for an accordion player.) Aside from being on the wrestling team, only membership in the band provided a chance for a student to travel; the band regularly performed in the local mental hospital and other state instututions. Not only that but every member received five dollars for an engagement.

The load of schoolwork proved crushing. I would often stay awake worrying that I was falling behind in my subjects, but I couldn't bring myself to drop any of them. Then I got involved in a time-consuming writing project that I supposed could make Daddyji and me rich. I read somewhere that the *Reader's Digest* paid a thousand dollars for an article, and I imagined that because of the Korean War its editors would be eager to publish articles on Asian countries. I typed out some of my thoughts on India, copied out some passages about India from Braille books, and embellished these with gobbets of memorized information from letters of Daddyji's that were written with the intention of helping me with my public speaking. I imagined that there was enough material for a series of articles on Indian philosophy, Indian religions, Indian customs, Indian monuments. I dispatched the material to Daddyji and asked him to work it up into half a dozen articles, thinking that if we sold all of them we would make our fortune. I didn't hear from him for a while, and I felt anxious, suddenly unsure whether we had even one publishable sentence. I got hold of old Braille issues of the *Reader's Digest*. The more I read them, the more preposterous the whole idea seemed. And then Daddjyi wrote to say that we would have to wait to do the articles until we could meet and talk. In the meantime, I was getting further and further behind in my subjects.

❧

SOMETIME during the first weeks of the new school year, Mr. Hartman came up to me while I was changing my clothes after his class and said, "I see that you've put on a little weight over the summer. You look fit as a fiddle. What about trying out for the wrestling team again?"

I felt flattered, but I smiled noncommittally. Wrestling had great glamour at the school, but to go out for it again I would have to give up the one free hour I had between eight-fifteen in the morning and seven-thirty in the evening. Anyway, I hated Mr. Hartman's relentless way of drilling us in gym.

"What about it?" Mr. Hartman pressed.

"I wish I could, but I just don't have the time," I said.

"Don't have the time, man—for wrestling!" He stamped away, his footsteps almost bristling with annoyance. He believed that what blind people needed in order to survive was, above all, physical prowess.

The next day, I wasn't feeling up to gym, and I skipped it. When I happened to run into Mr. Hartman that evening, he didn't return my greeting. He was famous for holding grudges against boys who didn't take gym as seriously as he did.

I didn't like being in anyone's bad graces, especially his—I felt I owed my proficiency in mobility to him. I found myself saying, "I think I would like go to out for wrestling after all, Mr. Hartman." I could have bitten off my tongue, but the words were out.

"Boy, I always thought you had it in you," Mr. Hartman said immediately. "Wrestling will toughen you up. Then you can do anything in the world out there." He continued, striking one of his favorite themes, "I've never heard of one of us blind folks getting ahead because of books. What we need is a strong physique and a bull head, which you can only get in gym or on the wrestling mat with me."

He has never sounded so friendly, I thought. His voice felt as warm to my ears as roasted chestnuts to the fingers on a cold day. I felt happy in spite of myself.

"But, boy, I want to tell you one thing," he went on, abruptly sounding stern. "I don't have any respect for people who quit. I took it mighty ill when you quit wrestling last year. Now that you're going out for it again, you got to stick it out, come hell or high water. You hear?" He had a high, nasal voice, as penetrating as a police siren, and my heart thumped irregularly—so hard that I felt it in the veins of my neck. I hadn't had palpitations like these in the year since I quit wrestling. "With a few weeks of good workouts, you should shape up as a vigorous hundred-and-ten-pounder," Mr. Hartman was saying. He turned away and went upstairs to his room, his footsteps echoing sternly.

❧

"Y'ALL know that Ved has come out for wrestling as a hundred-and-ten-pounder, so we are going to be tough to beat in that class," Mr. Hartman said to the wrestlers as I lay on the mat, panting like a dog. I had already done an hour of calisthenics in regular gym, and I was so sore that I could barely move my head. I also felt weak with hunger. Our already meagre rations had recently been cut down, because of budgetary problems. Mr. Hartman had said, "The state is cutting back on all state institutions. The prisons, the mental institutions, the schools—we're all in the same dinghy with a hole in it."

Mr. Hartman now walked over to me and stood in a spot above my head and reeled off the conditioning exercises that we wrestlers would have to work up to. We would regularly have to run a mile and a half around the gymnasium floor and then do x number of pushups, y number of sit-ups, z number of chin-ups. The numbers Mr. Hartman was reciting seemed so high that I could scarcely take them in.

"Now, boys, let's start your conditioning with some breathing exercises," Mr. Hartman said. "Breathe in . . . breathe out. Breathe in . . ."

I inhaled and exhaled as if to a metronome. I mentally dozed off, and daydreamed that I was one of those wrestlers on the floor around me who had been doing conditioning exercises from the first grade on.

For the rest of the time, I did the conditioning exercises in a half-drugged state, not being sure at all, for instance, that my arms and legs were actually moving when Mr. Hartman was having us do pushups.

I came away from wrestling practice feeling dizzy, and with hardly enough energy to chew the food at the supper I'd been waiting for. After supper and night study hall, I dropped into bed.

&

FOLLOWING one particularly rigorous wrestling practice, I stayed after the bell and said to Mr. Hartman, my words tumbling out as though if I hesitated I would become tongue-tied, "I don't feel well. I may have to quit wrestling—I mean, stop coming for a while."

He growled as if he were about to attack, the rumble growing louder and fiercer. "If you're not man enough to stick by your decision to become a wrestler, I don't give a damn about you," he said. "If people get to know that you don't stick by your word, they won't give a damn about you, either. No one will respect you."

I hated the thought of losing Mr. Hartman's respect. "You're right, Mr. Hartman," I said. "It was just a silly idea."

&

I CONTINUED to go to wrestling practice, but sometimes my heart throbbed so wildly that I was afraid I was going to have a seizure.

One afternoon, I went to see Mr. Woolly and told him that I thought I was having some heart trouble.

"Heart trouble at age sixteen is pretty unusual," he said, but he immediately got a Dr. Fred William Harris on the telephone and arranged for me to go and see him.

"We usually see only old folks here," Dr. Harris said kindly as he guided me through an office full of modern machinery. "You're too young for heart trouble. Can you tell me what, exactly, is wrong?"

"I've got wrestling heart trouble," I said. "I get palpitations when I'm wrestling."

Dr. Harris wanted to know more. When I explained the situation, he said, "At your age, little palpitations from wrestling shouldn't matter. Are you afraid of your wrestling coach?"

"Fear is not in my vocabulary," I said, quoting Daddyji and feeling like a hypocrite.

Dr. Harris examined me with a stethoscope. He made me take off my clothes and stand in front of a machine. He made me lie down, and applied some ice-cold jelly to my legs and arms. He put some suction cups on the wet spots.

"There is nothing to worry about," he said as I got back into my clothes. "I think you can go on wrestling, and do whatever you want."

A month or so after my visit to Dr. Harris, Treadway and I were standing in the gym in a wrestling position, our heads bent forward and each of us with a hand pressed against the back of the other's neck, waiting for Mr. Hartman to give us the starting signal, "Go for it, boys." Instead, Mr. Hartman came over to me and said, "Ved, I'm taking you off the wrestling team as of this minute." I thought I had done something wrong and Mr. Hartman was punishing me, but he went on, "Boy, you can rejoin the team whenever you feel better. Another thing—if you're not feeling up to par, you can skip gym, too."

I couldn't believe what he was saying. I wondered if there had been a touch of sarcasm in Mr. Hartman's tone, but then decided not. I felt like jumping and clapping my hands, but in a non-physical way.

I expected Mr. Hartman to run me down as someone who didn't stick by his word, berate me for being a quitter, but he continued to treat me with the same respect as if I were still training for the wrestling team. At the time, I could think of no explanation. Recently, I came upon several letters bearing on my sudden release from wrestling which Daddyji had saved. One was from me—typed immediately after my visit to Dr. Harris— telling Daddyji that because of my own foolishness I had got caught in wrestling, and that I could see no way of quitting it and keeping Mr. Hartman's respect, since Dr. Harris had given me a clean bill of health. A slightly later one was a copy of a letter from Daddyji to Mr. Woolly, asking him to request Dr. Harris to send Daddyji the results of my medical examination. A third was a letter from Dr. Harris in response to Daddyji's request. This one read:

DEAR DOCTOR MEHTA,

On October 25, 1950, we asked that your son Ved be brought to our office for a complete cardiac work-up. In addition to our physical examination, we did an electrocardiogram and fluoroscoped his chest.

Ved has a minor organic heart condition that we do not think is serious at this time. The outstanding finding on the electrocardiogram is low voltage of the q.r.s. couples of the limb leads with a slight deviation from normal in the T waves. All complexes in the precardial leads are within normal limits.

I recommended to Ved and Mr. Woolly, Superintendent of the Blind School, that he be allowed to participate in the usual activities at school.

Ved is a very fine young man and his scholarship and general good bearing have reflected credit to himself and his Country. Be assured of our interest in your son, and should anything unusual develop, I personally shall notify you.

Most sincerely yours,

Fred Wm. Harris, M.D.

Finally, there were copies of a couple of letters from Daddyji to Mr. Woolly appealing to him in the strongest terms to "debar" me from wrestling but without telling me why, because, he said, he didn't want me to become conscious of my health, and my heart.

When I discussed this correspondence with Mr. Woolly, he observed that although Dr. Harris's letter was equivocal he himself had told Mr. Hartman that the school ran some medical risks in keeping me wrestling. The use of the word "medical" had won the day.

❧

THAT year, some new teachers had come to the school. They were so odd that we found it difficult to get along with them. There was, for instance, Mr. Lord. He had a funny quirk of speech. He sprinkled everything he said with "from it," "to it," "with it," "for it," "up it." His "it"s didn't mean anything. He just used them when he seemed to be thinking about what to say. "Now, you boys and girls . . . with it," he would say, "have to work hard . . . from it. I don't want to catch any of you boys . . . up it, straying over to the girls' side . . . to it, for it." Sometimes the "it"s were preceded by pauses, and then we could easily identify them as mere verbal crutches. But often his meaning was lost in a verbal fog. I remember once Treadway told us that he had asked Mr. Woolly where he had found a "from-it principal," and Mr. Woolly had laughed and said, "Mr. Lord studied in Texas for a while. They talk peculiar over there."

Mr. Lord taught algebra to us tenth graders. The others in the class had a good background in mathematics. I didn't, and mathematics was one subject that seemed to require years of drilling and accumulated knowledge; in mathematics, I couldn't paper over the gaps in my education. Even when I thought I understood an equation, the understanding would vanish a few minutes later in a quicksand of confusion, and Mr. Lord's explanations, couched as they were in "it"s, only compounded that confusion. "Boys and girls," he would say, "numbers . . . to it, are symbols. Letters are symbols of symbols . . . from it. One is . . . to it, a known quantity . . . for it. So it is that $2a$ is two times the value of a . . . for it, with it."

One day, I got a C-plus on an algebra test and went to see Mr. Lord in the office.

"I'm having trouble with algebra," I said.

"You're doing all right . . . for it. I haven't noticed anything . . . with it."

"But I got a C-plus on the test."

"That's a good grade for it . . . for it."

"But I've never got such a low mark—except, that is, in gym, or in Shop when we had to make brooms."

"That's right . . . to it."

"But I don't like it."

"You'll get used to it . . . for it, with it."

"But I want to improve, do better."

"Plenty of boys and girls get C's and D's on tests, and they're fine people . . . from it, and . . . to it, you're an Indian . . . with it, for it."

I realize as I write this that Mr. Lord sounds like a caricature, but at the time he was far from it. He and algebra haunted my waking hours with premonitions of failure.

❧

ALSO new to our school that year was a teacher I'll call Miss Holt. She taught us singing and piano, and was as volatile and prima donna-ish as her predecessor had been calm and modest. Miss Holt sometimes practiced singing in the evening in an empty classroom downstairs, off the school's central corridor. When she did, some of us would stand outside and listen. She had an angelic voice, and it made our hearts quicken.

We once asked Mr. Chiles why she wasted her time teaching at our school when—so we imagined—she could have gone to New York or Boston and sung in an opera house.

"Maybe Miss Holt is more interested in her religion than in her singing," he said. She had just graduated from Ouachita College, in nearby Arkadelphia, and was known to be a devout Baptist and an avid Bible reader.

I remember that once she caught a couple of us listening to her outside the classroom she was singing in.

"How dare you listen to my warming-up exercises!" she cried. The strange thing was that practicing where she did was an open invitation to people to listen to her; her voice carried all along the halls.

WE took choir with Miss Holt. Although Mr. Woolly was very keen that we should have a good choir, which could perform in assembly when we had guest speakers and on special occasions like Christmas, everyone's schedule was so full that he made choir an optional activity. Then most students decided not to take it, because it meant giving up the free period between the end of academic classes, at three-thirty, and the beginning of gym, at four-fifteen. I urged boys to join the choir.

"To heck with choir," Oather said. "I'd rather spend the time chewing tobacco."

"But the choir is good for the school, and it's so nice to sing," I said.

"O.K., Whip, I'll give it a try," Oather said finally. He, too, liked to sing, and he had a good bass voice. "But I don't like the sound of Miss Holt. I bet she got on her high horse when she was little, and she's never got off it."

Eventually, most of the other students also joined the choir.

During one of the first choir-practice sessions, we were singing "America the Beautiful." Miss Holt was at the piano on the little stage, and we were all standing by our seats on the floor of the auditorium. When we came to "America, America, God shed His grace on thee," everyone except Miss Holt stopped, as if by common consent.

For a few moments, Miss Holt didn't realize that hers was the only voice echoing in the auditorium. When she did, she banged the piano shut and cried, "What's the matter with y'all?"

"The pitch, Miss Holt—it's way too high," several of us said.

"Forget it—even the girls are having trouble," Charlie Wren said.

"I didn't come to this blind school to have my teaching questioned!" Miss Holt fumed. "Who's the teacher here!"

Everyone gasped—her outburst was so unjustified.

Because of my efforts on behalf of the choir, the students had elected me its vice-president. I felt I should speak up, so I said, "Miss Holt, we can't help it. The pitch—"

"Ved, if you say another word I'll send you out!" she interrupted me.

People in the choir started grumbling.

"Choir is an optional activity," Bruton said.

"Anyone who talks back will get bad character marks on his report card!" Miss Holt cried from her piano bench.

"But no one is talking back, Miss Holt," I said.

"Ved, leave the auditorium this minute."

I had hoped that Miss Holt would calm down so I could plead our cause. But I realized now that she was very worked up. I felt I had no choice but to leave.

From the door, I heard the students singing "America the Beautiful" on her pitch, their voices cracking with the effort.

Later that day, many students were saying that they were going to wait until the end of the six-week period, when Miss Holt's character marks were in, and then drop choir. I tried halfheartedly to talk them out of it, because I knew how much Mr. Woolly wanted the school to have a good choir. I didn't get very far.

The next day, Miss Holt announced in choir, for no apparent reason, "I just want everyone to know that I have a policy of never giving an A-plus."

Everyone, including people who never got A's, wanted to know why not.

"I think only God is smart enough to get A-plus," Miss Holt said flatly.

We protested.

"I'd like to know which one of you thinks he's as smart as God," Miss Holt said challengingly.

"You can gripe all you want, but it won't do you any good, because Miss Holt is on the side of God," Wayne Tidman said. It was strange to hear him say that. Although he spent a lot of time preaching in his church, he still raked in A-pluses term after term.

"But God is not a student here," some of us objected.

Miss Holt stuck to her guns. "I've talked to the faculty, and all A-pluses are going to be outlawed," she said. "That is what the good Lord wants, and that'll be the school policy."

Her announcement fell like a bombshell. Since most students had decided to drop choir, getting an A-plus in choir or not was a one-time matter. But not to get A-pluses in any classes at all meant that we couldn't set them off against our poor marks to improve our over-all average.

"I tell you," Oather said to me after the session, "this school is going down, down, down. In all the years I've been here, Whip, I haven't seen or heard anything like this. No, sirree. There's no school spirit left."

I imagined that my spirits were linked with the school spirit, and I felt depressed and demoralized. Still, as the end of the first six-week period approached I redoubled my efforts in all my subjects, in the hope of getting good marks. But when the report cards came out I was disappointed. I got a B in both algebra and choir, and only one A-plus, in French. (Despite Miss Holt's efforts and claims, A-pluses were not outlawed.) Also, under the report-card heading "School Life" I received "Poor" in coöperation, courtesy, and attitude—no doubt Miss Holt had helped to pull down my character marks. Meanwhile, there was so much talk of a wholesale exodus from the choir that Mr. Woolly ended up making attendance mandatory.

❧

LIKE many students at the school, I looked to music for a possible livelihood, and was taking individual piano lessons from Miss Holt. She taught in one of three practice rooms in the conservatory. She was as gentle during individual lessons as she was strident in choir. In fact, she didn't let the "America the Beautiful" ruckus affect my piano lessons with her in any way. Even when she criticized me for shifting on the bench, for wiggling my feet, for neglecting to press the keys with my fingertips as she had told me to do, she never raised her voice.

One morning after I'd been going to her for a month or so, she stopped me in the middle of a scale I was playing and said softly, "You look unhappy. Are you often unhappy?"

"Well, occasionally," I said.

"Sometimes you really look gloomy." She scooted her chair closer to my bench.

"I'm sorry. I don't mean to." I resumed playing the scale.

"Just a minute," she broke in, and she asked, "What is your religion?"

I was taken aback. We had never had a personal conversation before, and I wondered what she was driving at. "I suppose I am a Hindu," I said. "At least, I was born one."

"But what does being a Hindu *mean?*"

"It's hard to say. We didn't ever go to temples or have special prayers. Hinduism is just a way of life, I think." I groped for words, feeling that perhaps I was immature in religious matters.

"Are your parents religious?"

I was really stymied. Mamaji was religious, but Daddyji dismissed her religion as superstition. Daddyji talked sometimes as if he believed in God and at other times as if he didn't.

"Sort of," I now said.

"Do you know anything about Christianity—about Jesus, our Saviour?"

"As a child, I attended Dadar School for the Blind, which was run by American missionaries, and everyone there used to tell me that I should live like Jesus. I actually became a Christian in my heart, so that I could be like my friend Deoji and the nurse who looked after me in the hospital. They were Indian Christians."

"But you were never baptized?"

"I don't know what that is. I just lived like a Christian, but I always remained a Hindu." I thought I sounded a little confused, and I stopped.

"Baptism is being saved—being shown the light of God, casting off all superstitions, fighting off the Devil." She continued, in compassionate tones, "I'm sorry that you haven't seen the light yet. But because of your blindness—your suffering—you're closer to Jesus and more ready to be saved than many lost sheep."

I started idly drumming my fingers on the bench, thinking that there were so many terms in Miss Holt's speech that I didn't understand—"Saviour" and "lost sheep" as well as "baptism." It's just like baseball games on the radio, I thought—you have to be born here to understand such things.

"I must help you to be baptized," Miss Holt was

saying. "I must save you from being damned forever
to Hell and fire. It's not too late. You just have to say
yes to Jesus. One simple word—'yes.' That's all He
asks."

In the next practice room, Pat West was playing
"Star Dust" on his trumpet. In the third practice room,
Billy Tabor was working through the "Twelfth Street
Rag" on his clarinet. Someone was practicing on the
piano in the auditorium below, and a few disconnected
piano notes drifted in. Ordinarily, I would scarcely
have paid attention to such background noise—it was
just part of being in the conservatory—but now I found
it as disturbing as what Miss Holt was saying. I
drummed my fingers harder on the bench.

"After you're saved, you can go home and bring
the light to those heathen who would otherwise have
no way to enter the Kingdom of Heaven," Miss Holt
said.

I was afraid that by the mere act of asking a question I might seem to be giving in to Miss Holt. Still,
I found myself asking, " 'Yes to Jesus'—what does that
mean, exactly? What does it involve?"

" 'Yes to Jesus'?" she echoed rapturously. "That
means you accept Jesus as your Saviour, your Lord."

"But Jesus was a man and he's dead."

"But He was the Son of God, who gave His life for
us, for the human race. He took the sins of believers
on Himself. It says in the Bible, 'God so loved the
world, that He gave His only begotten Son, that who-
soever believeth in Him should not perish, but have
everlasting life.' "

"What about those who don't believe in Him?" I

asked, trying to forestall her until the bell downstairs sounded the end of the period. I was afraid that giving in to her would somehow mean losing my religion and nationality. I wanted to rush out and get help from Pat West and Billy Tabor, without having the slightest idea of what kind of help I needed.

"Those who don't believe in Jesus? They're damned to burn in Hell forever," Miss Holt said, a little impatiently.

"All of them?"

"Yes, all of them."

Pat West was on the recapitulation section, and his trumpet was getting very loud. His high notes made the door and window in our practice room buzz and rattle. I wished the conservatory were soundproof, so I could think.

"How unfair of Jesus," I finally said. "How can He condemn a Hindu? How can He condemn someone who's never heard of Him?"

"But you're hearing about Him from me, now," she said emphatically, ignoring the larger issue, as if in raising it I were merely being obstreperous. "A person who hears and then turns away—he has no excuse. He's damned for sure. Don't you understand, Ved? Jesus is calling you through me to come to Him."

To the clashing runs of trumpet and clarinet was now added the thump-thump of Pat's foot on the floor, making our practice room shake.

Miss Holt suddenly cried, "Stop it! That drumming—the Devil has entered your fingers!"

My hand stopped in midair. I had lost all awareness of drumming my fingers. Anyway, Pat's foot was

making much more noise than I was. Miss Holt reached
over and took my hand in both of hers. She pressed it
fervently. "He's touching you with His light," she said
eerily. I remember thinking that I didn't know what
light was like—or, rather, that I had known it so long
ago, when I could see, that knowledge of it was buried
deep inside me. I certainly associated it with the heat
of the sun or a lamp—with any kind of warmth. Miss
Holt's hands felt warm, flushed, as if her fingers were
glowing. Perhaps God *is* in them, I thought.

"Will you let me pray for you?" she asked. Her
voice was so high and faraway that she could almost
have been a medium at a séance. She moved her chair
right up against the bench and said, almost in my ear,
"Did you hear my question?"

I started. Why does she keep on asking me questions, I thought. Why doesn't she leave me alone to
sort it all out?

"Say something. Why don't you say something?"
She sounded angry.

The room was suffocatingly hot. My forehead was
covered with sweat. A drop of sweat fell on my free
hand. Though she still had my other hand in her warm
grasp, a chill went through me.

"The period is going by," she said in a calm voice.
She slid off her chair, knelt on the bare floor, and pulled
at my hand. "Come kneel with me. Let's pray together."

I stayed put. "I can't, Miss Holt," I said. She let
my hand fall. "It's too much for me. I have to think."

"Think!" she cried. "What is there to think about
when He is calling you?"

The bell rang downstairs. The trumpet, the clarinet, the thumping, the piano in the auditorium stopped.

I stood up.

"I'll pray for you," Miss Holt said, getting up from the floor. "I know that God in His mercy will show you the light. But you must pray, too. It says in the Bible, 'Seek, and ye shall find; knock, and it shall be opened unto you.'"

Just then, there was a rap at the door. Miss Holt answered it. It was Little Sue Harrison, coming for her lesson.

I sidled out of the practice room and ran down the stairs three steps at a time, bumping into Billy Tabor and sending his clarinet case banging down the stairs.

❧

EVERY time I went to Miss Holt for my lesson, she would ask me "Will you be saved for Jesus?" or "Are you ready?" or "Why don't you come to my church with me this Sunday and get baptized?" I could feel her steady, evangelical gaze upon me. Each time, I would put her off with some excuse, such as "I need time" or "I'm praying for guidance." The excuses were true, yet they made me feel guilty. I came to dread my lessons with her. I could scarcely play a simple scale without making mistakes. I would strike two keys simultaneously or miss a note. She would stop me and spend the rest of the lesson passionately talking about the boundless joys of salvation and the excruciating, unremitting pain of damnation.

I once guardedly broached the subject of Miss Holt and her religion with Oather. He didn't take piano, so he knew Miss Holt only from choir. But I felt I could talk to him about her in confidence, and that was important to me, because I assumed that I was the only object of Miss Holt's compassion and that if word about her campaign to convert me got out I would be the laughingstock of the dormitory. "Miss Holt wants to save me," I said to Oather. "Are you saved?"

"Saved? Hell, no."

"But you're a Christian."

"Not Miss Holt's kind. I'm just an honest, God-fearing fellow who cusses and chews tobacco, dances and plays poker. In Miss Holt's book, I've already gone to the Devil."

"Is Treadway saved?"

"I don't think so. I doubt if most of the boys in the dormitory are saved."

"What will happen if I go to Miss Holt's church?"

"I think she's one of those Baptist Holy Rollers. She'll get you rolling on the floor and tell you to say anything you want—that you will speak with the tongues of angels." The idea that I might find myself saying anything that came into my head excited and terrified me at the same time. "Once you give in to Miss Holt about rolling around, she'll really have you."

I decided that I was no better or worse than other boys, and that I should try to resist Miss Holt's evangelical efforts.

❧

ONE day in Mr. Chiles's world-history class, when we were discussing the principle of separation of church and state, I thought I saw a glimmer of what was wrong with Miss Holt and her Baptist Church.

"If I were running this country, I'd make the Baptist Church the national church," Wayne said.

"Wayne, do you know how many Protestant denominations there are in this country?" Mr. Chiles asked. "Do you know what would happen if you tried to set one above the others?"

"There's just one way to God, and my church knows it," Wayne said.

"Now, Wayne, everybody thinks that," Mr. Chiles said. "Evelyn probably thinks her church knows the way to God. Joyce probably thinks her church knows it. Each person thinks that his or her beliefs are right and everyone else's are wrong. But what is probably true is that all of us are standing in a circle trying to reach God at the center but taking our own particular path to Him."

"But all paths can't be right," Wayne said stubbornly. "Even a fool will grant that some must be dead wrong. If I believed in your circle theory, I'd quit preaching in my church."

I found the idea of the circle very satisfying, however, and asked Mr. Chiles how different religions fitted into his circle theory.

"In my opinion, they, too, are part of the circle, since they, too, are looking for a path to God," Mr. Chiles said. "I'm a sincere Christian and I believe the way is through Christ, but I also believe that you, Ved, as a Hindu, may find your way to God if you lead life on the up and up."

I felt inspired, and decided that Mr. Chiles was

one of the smartest men I'd ever encountered. I knew I was young, but I considered myself a good judge of people.

❧

EVERY Sunday morning, all of us were taken in the school bus and dropped off at the church of our choice in Little Rock. That was a school requirement. We had to sit through Sunday school and the church service. Then we were picked up and driven back to school in time for lunch.

After Mr. Chiles's discussion of the circle, I went to Mr. Woolly and asked to be excused from the requirement, on the ground that I was a Hindu.

"Boy, I don't like to treat you differently," Mr. Woolly said. "If I do, I'll be courting trouble from the faculty and students."

"It's against my religion," I said boldly. I didn't think it was, but I wanted to press the point because I liked to sleep late on Sundays and I had trouble staying awake during the service—I didn't understand the Bible lessons or the sermons.

"If I let you off the hook, I'm going to hear from Miss Holt and I'm going to hear from Wayne Tidman. There are people here who think that going to church is mighty important, you know."

Nevertheless, my argument that I was a Hindu carried the day.

The next time I went for my piano lesson, Miss Holt assailed me almost before I sat down and opened the piano. "I hear that you won't even be going to church anymore—that you're willfully divorcing yourself from Jesus."

I fended her off. "But I'm a Hindu." I had heard that Benjamin Franklin said that Jesus had never claimed to be the Son of God but was only a great man through whom God worked, and I now said, "I agree with Benjamin Franklin. Jesus is not the Son of God at all. He was just a great man."

"Then *go* and burn in Hell!" she said passionately.

Miss Holt seemed to be laying a curse on me. Only the night before, she had appeared in my dreams as a mad dog. The dog had pinned me to the ground and started tearing at my throat. Now I decided that I had to fight her with all the forces at my command, and I said, "But there are hundreds of millions of Hindus who are not saved. Surely they can't all be damned."

"But they are."

"All my family, all my relatives?"

"They, too."

"So be it. Then *I* don't mind being damned."

I expected Miss Holt to lash out at me, but she said in the gentlest of tones, "Jesus, in His infinite mercy, brought you to Little Rock to show you the light. He will save you yet."

ONE Saturday afternoon, a number of us were lounging around the vending stand, and Oather was working behind it. Charlie Wren asked him for a Coke, and Oather flipped open the cooler.

"Darn it, Bull, we're clean out of Coke," Oather

said to him. "Could you bring me a case from outside? They're stacked just next to the door, I do believe."

Charlie went out, and returned with a case. "God damn it!" he exclaimed. "I caught my pants on the case, and now I've got a big snag."

"Go wash your cotton-picking mouth," Oather said, taking the case from Charlie. "You're among the fair sex."

"God damn your case!" Charlie said defiantly, and he cursed some more under his breath.

"Charles!" It was Miss Holt. In the confusion, none of us had heard her distinctive, clicking step in the hall. "Charles, you promised, and just a day ago, too." She continued, "What am I going to do with this school?" She turned and went back down the hall, her heels clicking furiously.

"That lady is going to go and have a good cry," Oather said, stacking the bottles in the cooler.

"What did you promise her?" people around the vending stand asked. "What did you say, Bull?"

Charlie ran out of the solarium, the automatic door closing behind him.

"I wonder what got the little witch riled up," Fat Earnie said. He was always saying rude things in an affectionate way.

"God knows," James Spakes said. "She's always riled up."

"The lady is new at the school, and maybe blind people are too much for her," Oather said, opening a Coke for Anna Belle Morris.

That night in the sleeping hall, the boys wouldn't leave Charlie alone.

"Bull, why are you so quiet?" James Spakes asked.

"Leave me be," Charlie said, from his bed, and then he blurted out, "She got me thinking in a religious way."

There was a general buzz. Charlie was known at the school for outdoing practically everyone in cursing.

"You see, yesterday she called me into an empty classroom," Charlie continued. "She asked me about my beliefs—asked me if I led a good, clean, Christian life."

Oather rocked with laughter. "You rascal, you! You're about the worst Christian in Arkansas." He tried to stifle his laugh in his pillow.

"At first, I said no," Charlie continued. "But then she lectured me about all those hot coals and such in Hell. Then somehow she got me down on my knees. She kneeled beside me and prayed for my soul."

A few boys guffawed. Most, however, remained quiet. Perhaps they were touched by Charlie's story— by the picture of huge Charlie and little Miss Holt kneeling on the floor of a classroom.

"What could I do?" Charlie was saying. "I wish you boys could have seen her there, her so young and beautiful. She was praying, praying over miserable me. I promised to quit cursing, quit taking God's name in vain. I never meant to curse at the vending stand—the words just came out."

Oather laughed, and set off many of the other boys. But I began wondering how many of them had had an experience similar to Charlie's, and whether they were laughing now as a subterfuge. Although I hadn't got on my knees, I couldn't laugh.

"I tell you, gentlemen, that Little Miss Dove's religious work in our school will come to an end when word about her activities gets to Mr. Woolly," Bruton said.

"But even Mr. Woolly can't stop secret prayer meetings behind closed doors," Oather said.

" 'I am not come to call the righteous, but sinners to repentance!' " someone shouted from under the covers. The voice was purposely disguised, so I couldn't tell who it was. All the boys fell silent, as if they thought that the voice was right in terming us sinners—or feared that the outburst would bring Mr. Clay to chastise us for talking after lights-out.

❧

SOME entries from my journal:

September 21

Mr. Woolly again wrote to the Immigration authorities in New Orleans that my temporary-stay visa had expired August 15th, and that he had had no word from the Service about their either extending it or converting it to a student visa. I am without any status at all.

October 31

Today was Halloween, a strictly American holiday, when ghosts and goblins come to the earth and everybody dresses in weird, fancy costumes. Each class had its own booth in a different classroom, and we took turns manning the booth of our particular grade and visiting the booths of other grades. The sixth graders were selling airplane rides—we sat in chairs and listened to their imitations of airplane noises. The seventh graders were operating a horror house under their desks. For the price of a ticket we could crawl around and feel slimy and disgusting things. The twelfth graders had a faculty graveyard. There were tombstones with funny sayings on them in Braille. Our booth, I think, was the most disgusting of the lot. It was called "Wound the Coon." Wayne Tidman, whose idea it was, had brought a stuffed-cloth Negro, and everybody could buy a chance to throw darts at it.

November 18

We had an outing at the airport in the pelting rain. It was on the invitation of Mrs. Emma Dell Mitchell, who had taught at our school and was now employed at the Braniff ticket office. She showed us through a Braniff DC-6. Except for me, no one had been on a plane, and all the students were thrilled just to walk up and down the aisle and touch the seats.

Mrs. Mitchell said that painted on the outside of the plane were "S.M.U. Mustangs" and "Hogtie the Hogs." How strange to think that Southern Methodist University horses are supposed to tie up pigs, and, anyway, why should the University of Arkansas have named its team the Razorbacks, after a special kind of bad pig? At home, "Swine!" is just about the worst insult you can throw at a person.

November 23

Mrs. Wilkes opened the annual Thanksgiving program of music and reading with a passage from the

Scriptures: "Every creature of God is good, and nothing to be refused, if it be received with thanksgiving." After the program, the boys ran up and down the corridor gobbling like turkeys.

November 24

I finally received a letter today from the Immigration Service. For some reason, it came from Miami. It said that my status had been changed from a temporary visitor to an immigrant student as of October 31st, and that my student visa was good until October 31, 1951, when I had to apply for another year's extension. I couldn't believe my ears when Mrs. Hankins read to me Form I-124, setting out the conditions and privileges of my new status. More than a year of correspondence has paid off.

December 21

I have just come back from a beautiful Christmas program in the auditorium. Vernelle sang "The Holy City." Her sombre voice echoed over our heads. Wayne read the Christmas Story to the sound of horns playing "It Came Upon a Midnight Clear." Treadway, Oather, and Bruton sang "We Three Kings of Orient Are" as they walked slowly across the little stage. Little Sue Harrison and Raymond Rodgers came in talking to the Holy Baby.

Mr. Woolly told us to remember in our prayers the Van White Pontiac Company, the Forrest City District of the Arkansas Federated Women's Clubs, the Altrusa Club, and the Capital View Methodist Church. They had given to the school a bushel of nice

pecans, a cover for the wrestling mat, wrestling hel-
mets, kickballs, and punching bags, as Christmas presents.

I wish I had gone to this school from the time I
was six, like so many of the beautiful performers; then
I would have grown up acting and singing, too. As it
was, I had to sit in the audience without any part in
the program. I wish I were a Christian, too. All we
Hindus ever do on our festivals is light some candles
and mud lamps, eat sweetmeats, and exchange clay
gods and goddesses.

MAX CARY, who was considered the most fascinating boy in the school, because he was always tantalizing us with stories of his adventures with girls, had
dropped out for the year to do some mysterious business in Louisiana—no one knew what. One day while
he was visiting the school, he invited me to spend the
first few days of Christmas vacation at his home, in
Springhill, Louisiana, saying that he would be leaving
from Little Rock and I could go with him. (Springhill
was near the Arkansas border, and so he was allowed
to go to our school.) When I asked Mr. Woolly for his
permission, he said, as if he were thinking aloud, "Now
that you've had mobility training, I guess you can
manage to get back by yourself—I know there's at least
one change of buses. It might be good for you to learn
how one of the other boys lives. And Max Cary may
be about the only boy here who can afford to invite
you home. I don't know much about his folks, but he

certainly dresses as if he'd got a little money to spend."

The bus trip to Springhill was very tiring; we had to leave at five o'clock in the morning and then change buses, with a three-and-a-half-hour wait. Then it turned out that Max lived with his mother, four sisters, and two brothers in a four-room house, and he hadn't told them that he was bringing me home. His mother seemed truly put out.

I took from my suitcase a little present I'd brought along for Mrs. Cary, and gave it to her. "It's the three 'no-evil' monkeys," I said. "It's made of ivory from India." Mrs. Cary didn't seem to know what ivory was, and I told her about elephants' tusks. She seemed impressed, but still a little cold.

Max launched into a big fat tale about how I was a rich, high-caste Hindu prince and we were going to go into business together.

"Max, you cut out your tomfoolery," Mrs. Cary said, and she added, "You knowed we were short on beds."

"I'll sleep on the floor," I said hesitantly. I was afraid that I might be lowering myself in her eyes, since people probably didn't sleep on the floor in America, but I felt I had no choice.

"Mama, we can move my bed into the boys' room, and I can sleep with Baby," Pat said. She was Max's seventeen-year-old sister, and Baby was their infant sister.

Mrs. Cary reluctantly agreed to the plan, and Pat's bed was moved into the little room where Max and his brothers slept.

I got practically no sleep that night. Pat's bed

smelled tantalizingly of face powder and a floral shampoo.

There was little to do in Springhill but kill time. I remember that Max and I spent the whole first day sitting around the house or standing on the street corner in front of it—the house was on a main street. The following morning, Max got himself a job as the projectionist at a local movie house for the day. I kept him company, and we spent eight hours cooped up in the little booth loading fifteen-minute reels on two machines, quickly switching to the second machine when the reel on the first machine ran out.

The only memorable part of the time I spent with Max was my meeting with the town's mayor, whom everybody called Uncle George.

"I know your face right well," Uncle George said to Max. "You're one of the Browns—Jim Brown, right?"

"You know me, Uncle George. I'm Max, Max Cary."

"Well, glad to see you, Max."

"I brought down an Indian friend from school to meet you. His name is Ved Mehta."

"Well, glad to meet you, Ved."

"You know India is a big place, Uncle George," Max said.

"Sure do."

"You want to ask my friend any questions about India, Uncle George?"

"Can do. How are you folks all getting on over there? Fine?"

"Uncle George, they got a caste problem over there—it's really bad, just like our Negro problem,"

Max answered for me, out of the blue.

"You could knock me down with a feather—I didn't know you got the Negro problem over there, Dave," Uncle George said. "You say they ain't behaving themselves over there? They sure ain't doing it here."

I tried to explain to him what the caste system was and how it was different from the American Negro problem.

"Uncle George, I'm going to take Ved to the senior high school tomorrow, so that he can explain the caste-system problem to them," Max said.

"They still in school?" Uncle George asked.

"Tomorrow's their last day," Max said.

"I guess you two aren't in school," Uncle George said. We said we weren't, and left.

There were a lot of questions about the caste system the next day, following my high-school speech. Then the students presented me with a hundred sticks of chewing gum. Since I didn't chew gum, I later gave them to Max.

❦

I HAD been invited by Mr. Chatterjee to spend a few days of the Christmas vacation in Yellow Springs, Ohio, and I had decided to go there after I got back from my visit to Max's family. A sighted friend, Jimmy, whom I'd met at Little Rock High School when I made a speech there, was going to Chicago for a little sight-seeing. Since it was on the way to Yellow Springs, I had arranged to go with him and see Chicago, too. I didn't know what we would do in Chicago, exactly. I just wanted to go there, because I'd heard that Chicago was the second-biggest city in the country and was on a lake that was almost a small ocean in itself. I had heard that it was very cold there, and I had bought my first overcoat—an event that added to my excitement.

❧

We were in Chicago. It was Christmas Day. I woke up and looked at my Braille watch. It showed twelve o'clock.

"Jimmy, it's noon!" I called across to his bed. "Get up!"

He turned over. "It can't be," he mumbled through his sleep. "It's really dark."

"It has to be," I said. "My watch says twelve, and we went to bed after midnight."

I got up and opened the window, and was practically thrown back by a rush of snow.

We had arrived in Chicago by bus the night before and checked into the Y.M.C.A. (Remembering that Daddyji had stayed at a Y.M.C.A. when he was a student in London, I had arranged for us to stay at one in Chicago.) I had never dreamed that the finest hotel—let alone a hostel for men—could be a little city in itself. There was a men's-clothing shop, a dry cleaner, a laundry, a baggage room, a barbershop, and a battery of machines that dispensed candy and cold drinks, stamps and fresh fruit. The hostel had a huge lounge, with a piano, a radio, and a phonograph; an auditorium, with a big television set and a movie projector; a typing room; and no fewer than two thousand rooms for travellers. For a moment, I had the illusion that the hostel *was* Chicago. Our room was on the fifteenth floor. It was carpeted and soundproof and had its own bathroom and its own huge closet. It had a writing table, a dresser, and two nice beds. I had never stayed in a hotel room before, and I basked in the room's comforts.

"Hey!" Jimmy now cried, and I quickly shut the window.

"My Lord!" Jimmy said, sitting up in bed. "It's snowing like crazy. I've never heard of snow like this in Arkansas. This is really big time. God, I'm hungry!"

The Y.M.C.A. had its own cafeteria, but the food there was too expensive for us. We set out for the nearest cheap restaurant, which the receptionist had told us was two blocks away.

The rush of the wind and the thick silence of the snow were disorienting. Indeed, the snow underfoot was so deep that I had no idea whether we were walking on the sidewalk or in the street. I had the strange sensation that I was floundering in a sea of cotton.

"Hey, let's have a snowball fight," Jimmy said. He was a couple of years older than I was, but he acted, I thought, much younger.

I resisted the temptation. "It's a temporary pleasure."

"What the hell is that?"

I was walking alongside him, touching his arm. Suddenly, he raced ahead and threw a snowball at my chest.

All at once, I was on the ground picking up snow,

patting it into a snowball with my gloved hands, and aiming it at Jimmy. I had never had a snowball fight before and didn't know what the rules of the game were, but I took care to aim below his face. How my sisters and my little brother, Ashok, would enjoy playing in the snow, I thought. I was spellbound by the delicate *plok* of the snowballs off our clothes and the almost noiseless way in which they fell back into the snow. But my facial vision was nearly deadened by the snow all around me, and for the first time I thought I knew what it was like to play blindman's buff.

I remember that we spent one whole day in Chicago visiting my first-ever planetarium, my first-ever aquarium, and my first-ever museum. I hadn't even known that such things existed. In the planetarium, I was so dazzled by the description of the heavens, accompanied by ghostly music, that I thought, If I could see, I would become an astronomer.

"What kind of fish are behind this glass?" I remember asking Jimmy when we were going through the aquarium. "I wish I could touch them."

"They're fish. You know what fish are, don't you?"

"I know, but what kind?"

"The most beautiful kind—much better than what you see in Arkansas."

Jimmy thought everything was the most beautiful or the best. But how, and in what way—and where and why—he couldn't explain. I felt depressed, and wished that Daddyji were there to explain everything to me.

Our last evening in Chicago, I typed a letter to Daddyji on a rented typewriter in the typing room, saying, in part:

A big city has a lot of its own charm. It has huge industries and subways and numerous movie cinemas and night clubs. This place is known to have the most gambling houses and criminals. In a city like this there is crime going on every minute—so says the Federal Bureau of Investigation. In a small town you get to know a lot of people and you live in a homey atmosphere. In a big city people mind their own business and are so abrupt. They have very little time to worry about others.

Here is a bit of unpleasantness which happened to me yesterday. I had ten dollars stolen from my pocket. I felt pretty sorry about it, but I did not let it spoil the pleasure of the trip.

We have to leave Chicago—it is pretty expensive. But then, we have seen everything.

I remember little about the trip to Yellow Springs. I recall that Jimmy showed me to the train and left to take a bus back to Little Rock. I recall that in Yellow Springs there was, if possible, more snow than there had been in Chicago, that Mr. and Mrs. Chatterjee and I sat around in uncomfortable chairs trying to think of something to say, and that what little talk there was while I was with them was about Marxism—Mr. Chatterjee turned out to be a Marxist. I recall that I couldn't get over the fact of the Chatterjees' mixed marriage: Mr. Chatterjee was Indian and Mrs. Chatterjee American, yet they seemed to be as happy as any traditional middle-aged Indian couple. I recall, too, that on my way back from Yellow Springs I visited yet another place. I stopped over in Louisville, Kentucky, and met with Mr. F. E. Davis, the superintendent of the American Printing House for the Blind, to see if I could get a job working at the press for the summer. His answer was no.

In retrospect, what I think was most important about all the travelling I did that Christmas, in Arkansas and Louisiana, in Illinois and Ohio, was that I was often forced to travel alone, in the cheapest possible way, in a combination of buses and trains, with several changes and layovers. At each place, I had to manage mostly on my own, or try to get help from bystanders and porters, taxi-drivers and bus drivers, even as I had to steel myself against panic if the help wasn't immediately forthcoming. I had to develop the knack of unobtrusively getting them to guide me to the proper train or bus, the rest room or the soda fountain, and of conveying to them at the same time my essentially self-reliant, independent nature, so that they wouldn't fear for me at every step. The boon of my Christmas, then, was neither the hostel's luxuries nor the snow fights, neither the treasures laid up in museums nor the experience of a mixed marriage flowering in the Midwest, but that knack—the dream of dreams, the prayer of prayers, the gift of gifts for a blind man.

VIII

BROOM CLOSET

This . . . is the news.

—*Edward R. Murrow, evening news broadcast.*

ONE DAY, MR. WOOLLY CALLED ME TO HIS office and said, "So you've been writing letters of complaint to your dad about our dormitory life here."

My forehead twitched guiltily. For some time, I had been writing to Daddyji saying that I needed a little room of my own, that my hints to Mr. Woolly were getting me nowhere, and that I wanted him to write to Mr. Woolly on my behalf.

"I can't live in the dormitory any longer," I said. "Living in Mr. Chiles's room over the summer spoiled me. I got used to my privacy." It had been hard to readjust to dormitory life—even just to the baseball and basketball broadcasts on the radio in the lounge, which seemed to go on all day long, with their roaring crowds and their non-stop patter.

Mr. Woolly was reading from a letter Daddyji had written to him: "As you have found out, Ved is a very hardworking and studious boy. If I may, I suggest that Ved be allotted a single room to himself, where he could quietly work in his own way." Mr. Woolly put down the letter and waited for me to say something.

I sat across the desk from him fearing that my letter home had upset him by going behind his back, and wondering what I could say to mollify him.

"As you know, son, the school was not constructed with any private rooms for students," Mr. Woolly finally said. "We don't have enough single rooms here to house the members of the staff. Even someone as important as Mr. Chiles doesn't have his own private bathroom. I've been after the legislature for some money to build a cottage for the older boys on the model of the one we have for the older girls, but nothing is likely to happen in your time."

In the adjoining room, Mrs. Hankins was opening and shutting filing-cabinet drawers and Mr. Lord was noisily moving some files around. In the corridor, people were walking by. Not even Mr. Woolly has any privacy, I thought.

"You see, probably not one of the students who

come here has ever lived in a room by himself," Mr. Woolly continued, lowering his voice. "I see from your dad's letter that you are different—that you are used to a corner of your own. You want a place where you can shut the door and be by yourself, keep on with your typing and reading, listen to Indian music and think of home. Am I right?"

I nodded. He's able to read my mind, I thought. He's so sympathetic. He's not upset with me after all.

"At Perkins, they would surely have put you in a private room right away, but we are a little old state school in Arkansas." Mr. Woolly shifted in his chair, and I took it as a signal that our talk was over—that I should go back to the infernal boys' dormitory. But he went on, "I've gone through the whole building, room by room, closet by closet, in my mind, and I can't come up with a single thing for you—or, maybe, with just one thing."

I sat in my chair as still as a mountain lake. I felt that I was in the middle of a very important dream and if I so much as moved my foot the dream would slip away.

"It's that broom closet just outside your sleeping hall. I believe it's about the size of the telephone booth you boys use at Stifft's Station and doesn't have so much as a darn window, but it has a door that you can shut. Since you live and sleep in the dormitory, it just might do, just might give you that little bit of privacy. I can't promise it to you right now, because there is the problem of what to do with the brooms and mops and buckets that are in there, but maybe I can persuade Mr. Clay to keep them in his rooms. He's an easygoing bachelor and might not mind having some cleaning stuff in one corner."

I had never been inside any closet in the school. From Mr. Woolly's description, the broom closet was a far cry from Mr. Chiles's room. Still, it's something, I thought.

"Mr. Woolly, is there room for my radio-phonograph in there?" I asked hopefully.

"Well, I've never actually been inside it, but I'm sure there's room for a record-player and your typewriter."

❦

IN the evening, Mr. Clay stopped me as I was going into the sleeping hall, and opened the door of the broom closet. "Here, tiger, get a whiff of this," he said, and added, "Yea, Lord, there ain't no justice."

I stuck my head in. The broom closet was as close as a coffin and smelled of mildew and Ajax. Cobwebs brushed my face. I could hardly take a step inside for all the cleaning paraphernalia on the floor.

"You ain't got room to turn around in there," Mr. Clay was saying. "Lordy only knows what you got in your mind. Boy, I'm asking you—you really want this thing?"

I couldn't imagine lasting very long in the broom closet, even with the door open, but I said yes.

"Then I'll haul this cleaning stuff to my room tomorrow and you can have it."

The broom closet was emptied out, but the smell

and the cobwebs seemed to cling to it, as if they were part of the four imprisoning walls. I at once wanted to set up my radio-phonograph, but there was no electrical outlet. The only electrical connection was a bulbless light socket dangling from the ceiling, and it didn't immediately occur to me that I could use the socket as an outlet. Moreover, I found that I couldn't set up my typewriter, because there was no spare table to be had in the whole school. I concentrated on getting a chair.

Every boy had a rush-bottomed straight-backed chair by his bed, which was used to hold his clothes at night and his Talking Book player. (The Library of Congress arranges for a player for every blind person in the country who asks for one.) I got permission from Mr. Clay to put my Talking Book player on the floor and keep my clothes at the foot of my bed, and to move my chair into the broom closet. After that, I would slip into the closet, close the door, sit in my chair, and read a Braille book or just think.

Mr. Woolly had told me not to trumpet the fact of the broom closet, in case it stirred up jealousy among the boys. But I discovered that the boys, far from being jealous, made fun of it.

"Old Whip is burying himself alive—burying himself upright, like Miss Holt's little piano," McNabb once said to the locker room, in my hearing. "I hope he's said his prayers, so he'll be saved."

Everyone laughed.

Partially sighted boys would start when they saw me coming out of the pitch-dark broom closet, and then cry, "It's Mr. Woolly's bat coming out of his black hole!"

Although I didn't need a light, I bought a bulb and put it in the light socket.

❧

ONE evening, I wasn't feeling well and I went straight upstairs from supper without going to the night session of study hall. Someone had forgotten to switch off the radio in the lounge, and a man was speaking on it. His voice was so hypnotic that it drew me the way the magnet I used to play with as a child drew steel pellets. The man was giving a few items of the news of the day. He went on to comment on one of them in sensible but foreboding tones. At first, his voice reminded me of the rising of the east wind in the Himalayas during my early-childhood walks, then of the grave, regal voice of the BBC newsreader speaking about the worsening war as if he were the King himself, broadcasting from under the weight of his crown. Perhaps it is really Daddyji's voice speaking to me through the vastness of oceans and deserts that now separate us, I thought dreamily.

There was a commercial for Campbell's soup, and the man signed off with a quotation for the day from Mark Twain and a sort of benediction: "Good night and good luck." The announcer came on and invited the audience to "listen to Murrow tomorrow."

Since the broadcasts of Edward R. Murrow clashed with the night session of study hall, I could hear them only on Fridays. Still, I came to think of those Friday broadcasts as my private weekly newspaper and would

feel sad if I missed a word between the opening "This
. . . is the news" and the closing "Good night and
good luck." Murrow came to fill a vacuum in my life
in Arkansas which I hadn't realized existed until I started
listening to him. I came to hear in his broadcasts echoes
of servants and neighbors, family and friends of my
childhood discussing the crash and bang of the world
war, the rumble and tumble of the British Empire, the
rise and fall of Hitler, Hirohito, Churchill, Gandhi,
Jinnah. In Arkansas, I realized, until I began listening
to Murrow I had been—except for Mr. Chiles's world-
history class—cut off from world events, almost like a
boy on the moon. Now, thanks to Murrow, instead of
thinking about my own problems and my own failures
I came to think about world problems and world failures. I came to believe that Murrow's sombre comments and light grace notes were a perfect way to
describe the world. I came to honor and venerate him,
idealize and identify with him to the point where I
wouldn't know what to think of a flash bulletin on the
radio, for instance, until I had heard him discuss it.
After listening to him, I would sit in my broom closet
feeling the burden of the world on my shoulders and
thinking solemn thoughts and wondering how I could
become another Murrow.

❧

TAPE recorders had recently come on the market,
and the school had somehow acquired a professional
model—a Magnecorder single-track machine that took

a five- or seven-inch spool and ran at the speed of seven and a half inches per second. It was used for recording band practice. I couldn't get over the idea of a tape recorder—the possibility of recording and erasing and rerecording. Then I read in the catalogue of the American Foundation for the Blind, in New York, about a special clock that the blind could set to turn tape recorders and radios on and off so as to record music and commentary off the air. (I had never heard of timers.) Although I had no money to buy even a tape, I began dreaming of buying a portable version of the school's tape recorder and my own special clock; of building shelves and putting in electrical outlets for the equipment in my broom closet; of recording, with the aid of the clock, Murrow's broadcasts off my radio-phonograph while I was in study hall and listening to him in my own time. I thought that if I could some-how fit my typewriter, too, into the broom closet, I might be able to use my as yet nonexistent tape recorder as a Dictaphone and type Murrow's taped comments directly into my journal, along with my glosses. Then I would have my own newspaper files, as it were, of world events, which I might use in later years when I became a journalist. This dream, in part as real as the tools in the shop and my bent for simple carpentry and electronics, in part as fanciful as a trip home on a magic carpet, bewitched me. It held out the promise of trans-figuring the broom closet and my whole experience at the school—a change as revolutionary in its way as the one that Miss Holt said baptism brought about in one's soul. On Saturdays, I would haunt electronics stores, retail and wholesale, asking about tape recorders and their accessories, and learning about their models and makes, their operations and applications, their performance and prices. But when I got back to school I would always come up against the same question: Where could I get the money for all the things I wanted?

MOST of the money that Daddyji was able to send me from India was used to pay for my tuition, room, and board. What little was left over was kept for me in the school office for incidental expenses. If I wanted a dollar for a pair of woollen socks, I had to apply to Mrs. Hankins. She recorded the sum and the explanation in an account book she kept for me, and gave me the money. The difference between what Mrs. Hankins could give me and what I now needed for a transfiguration of the broom closet was the difference between a pair of socks and a year's worth of education.

Then, one day, after I'd missed hearing Murrow for several weeks, because we were having Friday-night dances, a bank draft for a thousand dollars arrived from Daddyji. It was accompanied by a note saying that he'd been able to convert some rupees into dollars through unofficial channels, and that he wanted me to open a bank account and draw out money as I needed to, remembering that there were always rainy days and that he would need money for his visit to America the following year, after he retired. "I would like you to learn to manage money," he wrote. "You're certainly old enough." He's trusting me with his savings, I thought, just as his father trusted him when he was only twelve to supervise the construction of a house in a distant village. But he has forgotten that I can't sign my name, or he wouldn't have sent me the draft and asked me to open a bank account. (I had obtained documents like my passport by using my thumb impression, as if I were an illiterate.)

Daddyji's wishes were so clear that Mrs. Hankins, who had read the letter to me, handed over the draft without a word. I walked back to the boys' dormitory trembling, the draft in one hot hand, without knowing exactly why I was so wrought up. I put the draft in my locker under some shirts and did nothing about it for many days. I would, however, walk over to my locker again and again, at odd times of the day, and touch the draft, to make sure that it was really there—that it was not a part of my Murrow–broom-closet dream.

It happened that about this time the school acquired a new, magical slate for the blind which made letters written on it with a steel pen rise up so that one could touch and examine them. I got McNabb to write out my name on it. I can scarcely put into words the experience of touching for the first time the letters that formed my name—letters that sighted people saw almost from birth. The circles and loops, the ovals and lines, the hills and slopes, the tops and tails under my fingers reminded me of the labyrinth in an amusement park in Rawalpindi in which I used to run around to test my facial vision. Learning to distinguish the letters was rather like learning to match the stuffed birds in birds-and-animals class in my Bombay school with the doves and nightingales that I heard cooing and singing in the trees. Touching the shape of my name made me a small boy all over again. Even the "V," whose shape I was familiar with from making the V sign during the war, felt, under my fingertips, wholly new—two vibrant, twittering lines flying up and out into infinity.

It took me some time to learn to sign my name. That involved practicing on the slate and eventually writing my name on an ordinary piece of paper, using the edge of an index card to keep me writing in a straight line.

It was then that I finally removed the draft from my locker and, playing hooky, took a trolley to the Commercial National Bank downtown. There I sought out the manager, a relaxed, good-natured man who inspired instinctive trust, and got him to open a checking account for me.

"Sir, I'd like to withdraw half of the money immediately," I said, almost unable to find my voice.

"Fine," he said. "Do you want me to write out the check?"

I said I did, and after he wrote the check I signed it—my first check ever—using an index card and a bank pen.

"How would you like the money?" he asked.

I realized in a rush that for the first time I would be handling money alone, without Mr. Woolly or Mrs. Hankins looking over my shoulder and telling me which bill was which—which was a one and which was a five. I wished that different denominations were different sizes, as they were at home, because, short of asking for the five hundred dollars in dollar bills, there was no way I could be certain of what I was getting. But then I told myself that blind people could not get along in life without trust—trusting bank managers to fill in the correct amount on checks, trusting salespeople to tell the right price on price tags, trusting drivers to stop at stop signs and traffic lights. But then I remembered, with a pang, that Daddyji had trusted me with the draft. Was I doing the right thing in taking out the money? Would he approve of my plans to use the money for the purchase of a tape recorder and a timer and some lumber and wire? What would he say if he knew? I could have written him and told him that I felt I needed these things to become a journalist someday, and he would probably have given his permission. Yet lately I'd been noticing that it was difficult for me to write home about certain things, some of them as simple as the thrill of playing with the school's tape recorder, others as confused as my on-again, off-again attitude toward girls and dating. Certainly what Murrow meant to me, what he was worth, was hard to put into words. In my withdrawn state, I felt that I couldn't possibly justify to Daddyji spending five hundred dollars on a voice and a broom closet. And then there was another problem in conveying my feelings. I felt for a tape recorder what Max Cary, for instance, felt for a car: a passionate, all-consuming longing. In novels, characters had such emotions about people, but I had them about a machine—a machine I could control, a machine I could get to record and repeat anything I liked ad infinitum, whenever I chose, in the total privacy of my broom closet. How could I explain this embarrassing interest to Daddyji—especially over the distance of thousands of miles?

I now gulped and quickly told the manager that I would take the money in twenties, tens, and fives. When it came, I got him to tell me which batch was which, and arranged the bills by denomination in my three trouser pockets. I thanked the manager and started out of the bank.

"Hope you're going straight back to the blind school," the manager called after me. "That's a lot of money you got there. Just don't do anything with it that I wouldn't do."

Once I was out on the street, my trouser pockets bulging with Daddyji's money, my cheeks burned with shame and my heart beat like a drum signalling impending disaster on a radio program. But the wish to have, in Murrow, a daily newspaper of my own, beautifully written and beautifully read aloud, propelled me on, toward what I believed was an illicit goal.

❦

I THREW myself furiously into transforming the broom closet into an electronic listening post cum dictation-and-typing room. I bought some planks from a lumberyard and lugged them to the school's shop, where I sawed them into shelf lengths and cleats; I then installed the shelves in the broom closet in tiers—one broad shelf at table height for equipment, a narrower shelf above it for tape-recorder accessories, and a third, still narrower, above that for typing paper and other stationery. I bought from Woolworth's some electric wire, some male and female plugs, and some switches and switch boxes; brought an electric line down from the light socket in the broom closet; and built myself a veritable panel of half a dozen outlets and switches. I bought the latest-model Revere portable tape recorder, which had two tracks, took a five-inch spool, and ran at a speed of three and three-quarters inches a second, and along with it I bought a foot control, earphones, a tape splicer, and tapes. I ordered and received the special clock from New York. After what seemed like an interminable time—I could do my shopping and carpentry work only on weekends—I was able to hook up all my equipment through the clock and arrange my typewriter on the tablelike shelf beside the tape recorder so that I could operate both of them at once.

At all hours of the day and night, I would slip into the transformed broom closet, sit among a network of dangling wires and cables, listen to tape-recorded Murrow, and, with the aid of the foot control and the earphones, type his interesting comments into my journal. The journal grew rapidly, not only with Murrow but with quotations from other radio programs, with my own comments, and with passages from Talking Books; I had moved my Talking Book player into the broom closet, too, because when I was listening to books in bed I frequently dropped off to sleep, but when I sat up in my chair I was able to keep myself awake, no matter how sleepy I was. I could, in addition, tape Western classical music (something never heard in the lounge) off the air and listen to it and to my Indian records over the earphones—and nobody would know what I was doing. (I had hardly ever played my Indian records when my radio-phonograph was in the lounge, because the other boys laughed at the "caterwauling.") I felt that my broom closet was now a little spaceship, like the ones on the "Dimension X" radio program, and that I, its captain and sole passenger, was surveying events in the present world and back in history and, as it were, logging them for unknown generations. I felt that only one thing was missing to complete my happiness: some miraculous way of making Daddyji's money whole.

❧

From the day I withdrew the money from the bank, I had trouble sleeping. In the past, I had been able to sleep through an earthquake; now Joe's snore, the softest in the dormitory, or a boy's turning in his sleep many beds away would wake me up. Night after night, I lay under the terrible curse "Sleep no more."

I had taken out from the school library a correspondence-course textbook that prepared amateur radio operators for the licensing examination. I had the fantasy that one day a radio transmitter and receiver would arrive at the doorstep of my broom closet and I would be able to talk to my people at home at will. As I was reading along in the textbook late into the night, the idea for making Daddyji's money whole hit me. There must be correspondence courses for high-school subjects, I thought. If I took a few of them during the coming summer, I might be able to compress the high-school education of four years into three, so saving

Daddyji my school expenses for a whole year. That would take care of the problem of what to do with the summer, and after it I would skip the eleventh grade and enter the twelfth. All my best friends—Oather, Bruton, McNabb, and Treadway—would then be in the twelfth grade. I would go to classes with them and graduate with them. I wouldn't have to stay around after they left, and, as for my broom-closet equipment, I could use it for my correspondence-course work and in that way justify the expense. The correspondence-course idea had everything to recommend it.

I went to Mr. Woolly and asked him about correspondence courses for high-school students.

"There is the well-known Hadley Correspondence School for the Blind, in Winnetka, Illinois. But why do you want to know?"

"I want to do correspondence courses and skip a year and save Daddy some money," I said. "Would you have any objection to my writing to the Hadley School and doing some correspondence courses over the summer?"

Mr. Woolly didn't say anything for a few moments. He seemed to be turning the idea over in his mind. I had been so caught up in my plans that I hadn't stopped to think how they would strike Mr. Woolly. Now that the words were out, I realized that I shouldn't have broken the idea to him so abruptly—that I should have prepared the ground first. What if he takes my wish to leave the school personally, I thought. A simple no from him now will put an end to all my hopes. I had already invested so much emotion in the plan that I felt on the verge of desperation.

"I've been hearing that you've been spending a pretty penny fixing up that broom closet," Mr. Woolly finally said. "I suppose that first your dad encouraged you to spend his money and now he's putting the screws on you to graduate early and save him money—is that what you're telling me?"

"Not exactly," I said, trying to fudge the issue. I was afraid that he would ask me more questions about the money.

"The idea of doing correspondence courses has never come up at the school before," he continued thoughtfully. "But then we've never had anyone from India before, either. I think that all we care about is that you successfully complete our requirements for graduation. You already have some extra courses, and you can take some more next year. Maybe a couple of good, solid correspondence courses would do the job. I think I can get the faculty to go along with that. By the way, how old are you now?"

"Almost seventeen."

"If you skip a year, you'll be eighteen when you graduate—just the right age for college."

❧

THAT summer, I moved into Mr. Chiles's room with all my equipment and enrolled, for a nominal fee, in two correspondence courses offered by the Hadley School. One was in American history and was taught by Mr. B. W. Shearer; the other was in industrial geography and was taught by Mr. Donald W. Hathaway. The teachers wrote to say that I was to read "A

History of Our Country," by Muzzey, and "Industrial Geography," by Whitbeck—the standard high-school textbooks in those subjects, which were available in any Braille library—and was to type out or tape-record my answers to the test questions at the end of each chapter and post the answers to them, chapter by chapter. They would grade the tests and send me their comments in Braille. (Like many of our school's sighted teachers, both Mr. Shearer and Mr. Hathaway could apparently read Braille.)

I got the textbooks out of the school library and looked through them. Although each course would have taken a year of regular classes, I decided that if I could keep up the pace of a test a day I might be able to complete the courses by summer's end. So every day that summer, weekdays and weekends, I was at my textbooks, typewriter, and tape recorder from eight in the morning until five or six in the evening; after that, in order to keep myself fit and to have some diversion, I would take the trolley and bus to North Little Rock for a little swimming and chess at the Boys' Club. Every morning, I attacked the work afresh, finding an almost mystical pleasure in the discipline of solitary labor. Sometimes I read the book with one hand and typed with the other, and at other times I read with both hands until my fingers were numb; sometimes I fidgeted with but did not strike the keys of the typewriter as I ordered my thoughts, and at other times I typed so fast that I would be typing the roller before I woke up to the fact that I had come to the end of the page. (Although on occasion I recorded my answers on tape, somehow I was never able to talk my thoughts out under the pressure of the reels turning, and was constantly stopping the tape, backtracking, and rere-cording.) Reading through all those tests now, after so many years, has shown me what the academic part of my education was really like, stripped down to the bare bones, without the give-and-take of the class-room, the idiosyncrasies of teachers, and other human touches of school in session. The tests, which are a sort of mishmash of parroting the textbooks and voicing my own thoughts, are a record of the process of my Americanization—in a sense, all my schooling in Arkansas was directed to that end—and it is apparent that I accepted unquestioningly the position of the American-history textbook: that America was the greatest country on earth, with the most energetic, adventurous people and the best form of government. Similarly, I accepted the position of the industrial-geography textbook: that America was the richest, most bountiful, and most efficient country, with the great-est natural resources, the most varied climate, and the most advanced scientific methods. Indeed, the tests often read as if I looked upon the textbooks as scripture and the questions as part of a catechism. That is no surprise to me, because I remember how the courses spoke to my deepest feelings about America, how they helped to crystallize my views of the land, its people, its his-tory. I remember that, gradually, I came to identify with the country—so much so that I came to feel that the themes of American history and my personal his-tory were intertwined, as if I were a latter-day Columbus exploring the New World. Below are sample test questions and my responses, plucked almost at random from hundreds of pages of that youthful record.

American History:

What influence did the invention of printing have upon the discovery of America?

The mass production of books on geography and books on other literature educated the people of Europe. More people were exposed to views of the adventurous and educated people. This encouraged longer voyages. When those adventurers got back, their adventures were more widely related. All these factors, in my opinion, helped the discovery of God's own country, America. I would imagine the printing of more maps would also have a great deal to do with it.

Show on the map the voyages of Columbus, Vespucci, and Magellan.

This statement or question has to be left blank because of the obvious reasons. I would appreciate hearing from you, Professor, if you have any directions on how to deal with such statements or questions.

What is believed to be the origin of the American Indians?

They came from Northeastern Asia over a solid land bridge which connected Siberia and Alaska. The bridge is now the Aleutian Islands.

Give some examples of the arts practiced by more advanced Indians.

These Indians lived in big apartment houses and wove beautiful rugs and made wonderful pottery, glassware, and silverware.

Distinguish between the present meaning of the terms "Flor-

ida" and *"Virginia"* and their meaning as used in this chapter.

Ponce de León went looking for some youth when he discovered a beautiful place on Easter morning. He named this place Florida, or "flower land." The first American settlement was Jamestown, in Virginia, which was named after the Virgin Queen, Elizabeth I. Nowadays Florida and Virginia are just small parts of the United States. But as it is mentioned in this chapter, they covered much larger territory in the seventeenth century.

Why was the gold and silver brought from the mines of the New World harmful to Spain?

It started enriching the country through investment in industry and so made the haughty Spaniards despise work as beneath the honor of a gentleman. It led Spanish explorers in the New World to search with redoubled hope for imaginary kingdoms of gold instead of founding settlements. The Spanish noblemen spent fortunes and many people lost their lives. Finally, the gold and silver was squandered by the Emperor, Charles V, on his European wars. All these factors combined were harmful to Spain, as can be readily seen.

What were some of the evils of the Spanish government in the New World?

Only a few of the nobles possessed the wealth and authority, so the wealth was not well-stimulated and distributed. When the wealth is not in circulation the system of capitalism is very unbalanced, which is bad. To climax all this, the native Indians and the Negroes were frightfully treated under the lash of the slave drivers.

Why did the people in England leave their home to come to America?

The cost of living was going up, and the country

gentlemen could not quite afford to live as they wanted to. Many of them became poor. Englishmen were too dignified to beg like the blind. They would rather be adventurous and look for something new. When adventurous people are not satisfied with the present status, they always look for something new, may it cost their home or even their lives. Then, too, James I was persecuting the Puritans. These people wanted to escape from the pigheaded monarch who was so despotic, and a foreigner from Scotland, at that. They would not be conformed.

How did the education of girls in colonial days differ from that of girls today?

Colonial girls learned only how to cook, sew, and keep house from their mothers and older sisters. There were a very few wealthy girls who learned something about painting and music. Today's girls are equal to men in a lot of ways. They go and attend school with them and have massive general knowledge. When they are married they can have better understanding of the husband's problems because of their education. They can even live independently, if they choose.

Compare a colonial newspaper with a modern one.

In colonial days the newspapers were dull, and more like a school paper today. They were only published once a week and carried things like a letter written by a traveller abroad and some stale news. They also had very crummy advertisements compared with papers of today. We have papers published every day, and a lot of people depend on them for important news. This kind of uncensored news is only possible in a democracy. Democracy is a marvellous thing. I cannot imagine what our modern democracy would be like without our newspapers.

Why was the Stamp Act more irritating to the Americans than the Trade Acts?

Because the Stamp Act affected the life of every individual, even those who lived in the remotest part of the country. If an individual wanted to sell a newspaper or horse, or to make a will, he was forced by buy a stamp. Every time you picked up a newspaper you saw that stamp and it just burned you up. And the Stamp Act was put into effect without the consent of the colonists.

Do you think that the men of Boston were justified in destroying the tea?

No.

Why did Washington call the new American republic an "experiment"?

It was the first of its kind of government, in which people were to choose the officials who would govern them. Would people be patient? Could the law be a cure for people's difficulties? Would people resort to revolution again? Would people elect intelligent public servants and peacefully oppose them at the ballot box when necessary? The answers to all these questions would determine the fate of that experiment.

Would you have been a Federalist or a Republican in 1793? Give your reasons.

I would have been a Federalist. My reasons for this decision are enormous. Republicans believed in following the Constitution to the letter. Well, I don't believe that can be done. At best, we can follow the spirit of our Constitution. Also, the Republicans' claim that the Federalists were trying to establish a tyranny of the federal government was ridiculous. The Federalists just wanted to encourage capitalism—and after all, we do need some capital for investment in big industries. I am also a great admirer of the Federalist Hamilton. I think the world of him. Without him we might have had mobocracy in America. He helped to win the confidence of his countrymen in their government and the confidence of other countries in America. However, I would not let my admiration for people affect my judgment.

What was the origin of "The Star-Spangled Banner"?

The British were holding Francis Scott Key in a fortress outside Baltimore. After watching the night's fight he saw the signs of dawn and saw that the American flag was still flying. That was when he wrote the national anthem of the United States, "The Star-Spangled Banner."

Industrial Geography:

Give examples of countries whose commerce is aided by good government and of other countries whose commerce is retarded by bad government.

The commerce is aided by the better governments of the following countries: America, England, France, Australia, Japan, and so on. These countries have had steady, stable governments, which has led to prosperity. They have done it by being democratic and promoting open economic activity and capital investments. These countries have had more time to educate their citizens, and as a result, have more industrious and better citizens. Russia, Hungary, and China have had bad, despotically centralized, unstable governments which have retarded their economic growth. Their despotically centralized systems have discouraged investment and industry. It is true that Britain has recently adopted a socialist form of government, but it is not communistic and it has not discouraged investment.

Point out specific ways in which commerce and industry are aided by education and science.

Science puts at our command accuracy, standardization, speed, and new methods. We therefore can produce more necessities and luxuries. It provides us with medicine and so helps us to stay fit and well and working. Education provides us with better citizens with more thinking power, a more stable way of life. Educated people maintain good government, which in turn encourages more investment in industry and commerce. Educated people aspire to more things. Education helps us to produce better and better homes.

Why has the United States been able to make very rapid progress?

It covers three-fourths of the area of the twenty-seven European countries combined. It possesses a great quantity of agricultural land and so has huge food-producing power. Its mineral wealth, its forest wealth, its invigorating climate are unprecedented. Its people have descended from the most energetic European stock. All these factors have made America prosperous and a model for other countries.

Why is the United States regarded as, in a peculiar sense, "a land of opportunity"?

Because of the generous terms under which the United States Government sold the public lands to the settlers, because of the freedom of its people, because of all kinds of opportunities that attracted immigrants from different parts of Europe and allowed them to make their fortunes here.

We may assume that the average wheat crop in the United States is 800,000,000 bushels, and that about one-eighth of is consumed within two hundred miles of where it grows; the remaining 700,000,000 bushels travel considerable distances to markets. Assuming a carload to be 700 bushels, how many carloads of wheat must be moved considerable distances annually? Suppose these cars were made up into trains of fifty cars each, and that the trains passed a given point at the rate of one every ten minutes, how long (in hours and days) would it take the entire 700,000,000 bushels to pass this point?

One million cars. It would be 3,333 hours—139 days.

The two books together had dozens of tests, with twenty or more questions in each test. When regular school started, I still had half of the industrial-geography course left to finish, but Mr. Woolly and the faculty, after reading the reports of my correspondence teachers, placed me in the senior class and told me that I could graduate in 1952, provided that by the end of the Christmas vacation I had finished the correspondence courses, receiving a grade of A in both. This I was able to do.

IX

LIBERTY AND GENTLEMEN'S CHOICE

MEHTA SUCCEEDS ELAM AS PRESIDENT

In a close race Ved Mehta won the hotly contested race for Student Senate president over his lone opponent, Oather Brown. In accordance with the Senate Constitution, Oather Brown automatically becomes vice-president. . . .

The Student Senate was started only this year and has, from all respects, been highly successful.

—*Little Rock (Ark.) Arkansas Braille News, May, 1951.*

I T WAS THE END OF THE SCHOOL YEAR 1950–51. On the stage, at the lectern, was Mr. Woolly. Seated on Mr. Woolly's right, at a long table, were the three outgoing senators, including Jackie Elam, the president of the Student Senate, a popular boy I didn't know very well; standing on Mr. Woolly's left were the nine of us, the first senators to be elected for a full-year term. Seated below in the auditorium were the entire student body and the faculty.

Mr. Woolly went along the table lighting candles set in front of the outgoing senators and so beginning the installation ceremony. What strides our student government has made in the few months of its existence, I thought as the candles sizzled and sputtered. This ceremony is worthy of the Senate in Washington. I was about to be installed as president of the Student Senate, and I couldn't have been more excited if I'd been about to become the President of the United States.

"Don't you forget you were born in India, Whip, and people who aren't born in this country can't become President of the United States," Oather, my vice-president, whispered, as if he'd been reading my thoughts. He laughed under his breath; I tried to keep a straight face.

"The outgoing senate has done a fine job," Mr. Woolly said, returning to the lectern. "Your senators have assisted us in preparing the *Arkansas Braille News*. Your senate has set up a social committee for each of the six upper grades, to plan your parties and activities. It has also set up a student suggestion box."

Clapping filled the air.

As had been arranged, Mr. Chiles, the senate's faculty sponsor, walked up onto the stage and went to the piano. While he played "My Country, 'Tis of Thee" at a stately pace, Jackie Elam got up from his seat with his lighted candle in his hand, walked over to a stand near us, set down the candle, its holder making a little *clack,* and walked off the stage. One by one, the outgoing senators followed him, leaving their candles on the stand, while Mr. Chiles played the melody through for the second time. The Sons of Liberty are relinquishing their torch to the next generation, I thought portentously. Six of us were succeeding ourselves, so Mr. Woolly hastily put some extra lighted candles on the stand.

Mr. Chiles started the melody for the third time— Mr. Woolly's cue to swear me in. He called me to the stand and handed me a candle. The flame burned in front of my face, warming me all over.

"Repeat after me," Mr. Woolly said. "I, Ved Mehta—"

"I, Ved Mehta—"

"—solemnly pledge myself to fulfill to the best of my ability—"

"—solemnly pledge myself to fulfill to the best of my ability—"

"—the duties and obligations—"

"—the duties and obligations—"

"—entrusted to me as president of the Student Senate of the Arkansas School for the Blind."

"—entrusted to me as president of the Student

Senate of the Arkansas School for the Blind."

"I will at all times strive to uphold and honor the Senate Constitution—"

"I will at all times strive to uphold and honor the Senate Constitution—"

"—and to further the interests of this school."

"—and to further the interests of this school."

I thanked Mr. Woolly, and then he stepped down and joined the audience while I walked a couple of steps to the chair where Jackie Elam had sat, put my candle on the long table in front of that chair, and returned to the lectern to administer the oath of office to Oather, Bruton, McNabb, James Spakes, and the other newly elected senators. After they had all been sworn in and had taken their places at the long table, with candles glowing down its length, I made a short speech about our hopes for the future. I closed the installation ceremony by asking everyone to join in singing the national anthem.

THE idea of setting up a student government went back to the beginning of that school year, when we students were having a lot of trouble with Miss Holt, Mr. Lord, and other new teachers; we felt they were behaving capriciously. One day, Treadway, Oather, Bruton, and I had the idea of drafting a constitution for the junior-senior high school; we had all studied civics with Mr. Chiles and had been influenced by what we learned from him about democracy. But when we tried out the idea on the other boys in the sleeping hall that night they roundly attacked it.

"I ain't had your civics yet, so I don't know about constitutions," Charlie Wren said. "But I bet Mr. Woolly will just tell y'all to go jump."

"That he will," McNabb said. "This is a state school, and Mr. Woolly has to answer to the governor and the legislature. He'd have to be crazy to take the power away from the teachers and give it to the students."

"We'll fight Mr. Woolly and win, because we are the Sons of Liberty," Bruton said.

"You crazy boys ain't got even the bows and arrows of the Red Indians," Charlie said. His remark was as deflating as if he had inspected the clothes of us totally blind boys before a dance with his one good eye and announced, "Crazy boys in Booneville wouldn't be caught dead in *those* colors."

The next day, Treadway, Oather, Bruton, and I cornered Mr. Chiles and told him about the students' discontent with some of the new teachers and about our idea for a student government.

"I don't want to pass judgment on my colleagues," Mr. Chiles said. "But it's a sorry state of affairs when students and teachers draw battle lines. We live and work in the small community of the school, and we should live like a family." He added thoughtfully, "It might be a fine idea, though, for the junior-senior high school to have a student government under a constitution. Your government couldn't change who your teachers are—that's Mr. Woolly's domain—but it could give you a voice in the running of the school. Still, your government could work only if it had full faculty support and participation. What I'm saying is that if you drafted a constitution on these lines you could go to Mr. Woolly with it and present it not as a manifesto of your rights but as something designed to teach you— and your teachers—about government and civic responsibility. I'll be glad to go to Mr. Woolly on your behalf and ask his permission to work with you on drafting that kind of constitution."

We immediately agreed to Mr. Chiles's plan, and after he had got Mr. Woolly's permission we set about framing a constitution, imagining that Mr. Chiles was George Washington and we were Madison, Franklin, Hamilton, and Gouverneur Morris. It took a couple of months of steady work—mostly by Treadway, Oather, Mr. Chiles, and Miss Harper, who was called in because we needed a sighted reader—to prepare the final draft. The preamble stated that the purpose of the constitution was "to establish better understanding between students and faculty and to develop a sense of responsibility and leadership among the students." Article I set up the Student Senate. A section of Article II provided for the election of senators and apportioned the seats in such a manner that the eleventh- and twelfth-grade senators constituted a majority. Other sections and articles provided for the election of senate officers, the procedure for impeachment and removal of senators and senate officers, the procedure for amending the constitution. Finally, the bylaws called for weekly meetings of the senate and set forth its order of business. The whole constitution, however, was at the sufferance of Mr. Woolly: he had the power to veto any and all senate actions.

The constitution was presented to the school by Mr. Woolly at a weekly assembly in January and was immediately adopted by voice vote. The first senate could sit for only a few months, since the seniors would be graduating in May, so elections for senators and senate officers were held quickly.

The first meeting of the senate was held in February, in Mr. Chiles's classroom. Jackie Elam, who had been elected president, took Mr. Chiles's chair on the platform, while the rest of us who had been elected senators sat at desks, as did Mr. Chiles.

"As your president, I call the meeting to order," Jackie Elam said. He fell silent and shifted in his chair.

"Well," Mr. Chiles said, "I think that your first order of business should be to decide on rules of procedure. You could adopt Robert's Rules." He outlined them for us as if this were his class.

We all said, "Yes, yes," and the rules were deemed adopted.

"Mr. President, I make a motion—" Bruton began.

"Kenneth, you don't make a motion," Mr. Chiles said. "You say, 'I move that . . .'"

"I move that Senator Mehta be elected as secretary-treasurer," Bruton resumed. "The constitution says that we have to elect a senator for this office."

"I second the motion," Jackie Elam said. Mr. Chiles informed him that, as president, he had to stay neutral, except in the case of a tie vote.

"*I* second the nomination, then," Oather said.

Mr. Chiles told us that now anyone who liked could speak to the motion.

Bruton made a speech about how he thought I was good at handling money.

"Where would our funds come from?" Oather asked Mr. Chiles.

"Mr. Woolly will give us some funds for organizing parties and other school activities," Mr. Chiles said. "The faculty has also decided that vending-stand funds should be handled by the senate. But, as in recent years, those funds will have to be earmarked for silver class rings for seniors, the printing of graduation invitations, the senior banquet, and the senior formal dance."

"Since Mr. Woolly wants to publish our minutes in the *Arkansas Braille News,* we should have someone as secretary-treasurer who can write," McNabb said, speaking to the motion. "Anyone who's heard Whip typing knows that he can write—and, man, write fast!"

A voice vote was taken, and I was elected. I was as apprehensive as I was excited, but I immediately started taking minutes. Though I'd developed a private Braille shorthand, people talked much faster than I could write. After a while, I realized I was only putting down names and a few key words for the writing of a draft later on.

Bruton and I, along with one non-senator, Joyce Boyle, were elected to the editorial board of the *Arkansas Braille News,* which was published by the school three times a year in regular print and went to families of students and to friends and patrons of the school. From now on, the board members were to appoint student reporters, assign them various school beats, and receive their Braille or typed copy. Since we couldn't proofread the typed copy or the print version of the *News,* Mr. Chiles told us that Miss Harper had agreed to serve as our faculty adviser and help us with all the non-Braille tasks.

"I think that you should consider devising an installation ceremony for the president and all the senators who'll be elected in the spring," Mr. Chiles said near the close of the meeting. "Your ceremony should have a lot of pomp and circumstance, so that your senate will be invested with significance."

It hadn't occurred to us that we should have some kind of ceremony, but we put the item on the agenda for the next meeting.

❧

IT was April, and spring was in the air. Everywhere there was the fragrance of new grass and blossoming flowers. Except in Mr. Chiles's tenth-grade world-history class, little work was getting done. We whiled away the school hours teasing our women teachers, playing cards using French numbers and French suit names, so that Mr. Woolly would think we were practicing French, and, above all, talking school politics.

The election of the first full-term senate was a few days away. Oather and I were running neck and neck for president. Because school politics was relatively new to both students and teachers, we all seemed to be in a fever over the election. Wherever I went—to the locker room or the lounge, the sleeping hall or the vending stand—it seemed that students were discussing Oather and me. Blind people hate to be overheard, so I always made a point of clearing my throat when I entered a room. Once, I wasn't fast enough.

"Aw, don't you know that Barbara is old enough to be Ved's mother?" Billy Tabor was saying to Joe Wright as I walked into the lounge. "The only reason he's going with her is so he can get all the girls' votes."

Barbara Worthen (that's not her real name) had come to the school in the middle of the year. She was very studious and she could see better than almost any other girl in the school. She had been placed in the tenth grade with me, and I had just assumed that she was more or less the same age as the rest of us. I had had a date with her—the first date of my life—a few weeks earlier, and a couple of dates with her since, and they had had nothing at all to do with my running for office.

I wanted to shout at Billy that he was lying, but, thinking that any show of anger would be bad politics, I held my tongue and walked rapidly through the lounge.

"Boy, I don't know what to do—Oather and Ved are both nice guys," I heard Joe say as I went out.

The next morning, while Bruton, my campaign manager, and I were taking our showers, I told him what Billy Tabor had said. I counted on the noise of the water to keep boys who might come into the bathroom from overhearing our talk.

"I've heard Charlie Wren say that Barbara really looks old," Bruton said, "and boys have asked me why a popular guy like you should suddenly start dating someone like her. I didn't bother about it much, but now I'm wondering if it might turn out to be the sleeper issue of the campaign. Do you know how old she *is?*"

"Not you, too, Bruton!" I exclaimed.

"But I'm running your campaign. I have to know."

"I don't have the slightest idea." There are so many things a blind person can tell from a voice, I thought. I can often tell the height, the weight, and sometimes the age of the person. I can usually tell how attractive the person is. But there are always occasions when the voice is misleading. Barbara may be like one of those older actresses on the radio who sound young.

"It looks like the question of Barbara's age has gotten mixed up with your motives," Bruton was saying. "Did you or didn't you start going out with her to get the girls' vote? Everyone knows that the girls like Barbara because she can see, and help them with their clothes."

"I started dating her before the idea of my running came up. Why is everyone thinking such nasty thoughts?"

"Why don't you just ask her how old she is? It may turn out she's your age. Then I can contradict the charges. But if she's really old, then no one's going to believe it's just that you suddenly found her attractive. They're going to say you had ulterior motives."

"But—"

"No buts," Bruton broke in, turning off his shower. He added, "You shouldn't have gone into politics if you didn't want your toes stepped on."

❦

"YOU all jump up and you all come down. Swing your partner right around," Miss Harper called over the public-address system that evening at our square-dance club. The fiddle music on my tape recorder speeded up. (I provided the music for the square dances.) I swung Barbara, my partner, around.

All about us there was a continuous shuffle of feet, punctuated by the shouts of some clumsy students who had missed connecting with their partners.

"Is this too fast?" Miss Harper asked, without interrupting the rhythm of the call.

"No, we can go faster!" many of us cried from the floor.

Miss Harper quickened her call until her words were hardly distinguishable, but most of us knew the dance so well that we had no trouble following it. We moved faster and faster, until the floor under our feet seemed to be spinning like a turntable. Why is it, I wondered as we whirled, that so many of us master square dancing so much more easily than we do ballroom dancing. Is it easier to lose ourselves in a set pattern of group activity than to strike out on our own, like a sighted person, and lead a partner on the dance floor? Is there something in the condition of being blind that militates against bold initiatives and assertive action? I wished that the square dance would never stop—that I would never have to ask Barbara her age.

"What next, boys and girls?" Miss Harper asked, barely breaking the flow of her call. Maybe we never will stop, I thought.

"Texas Star!" people cried. We switched to that dance so smoothly that I imagined someone watching us might have thought we were professionals. For a moment, I had Barbara's hand in mine. She flew past like a scared bird.

There was a muffled sound, like gloved hands clapping. Miss Harper's calling stopped, and we froze in the middle of a step, a foot and an arm raised. It was as though a drive belt turning the gymnasium floor had snapped.

"Lois, are you all right? Kenneth, are you all right?"
Miss Harper asked, rushing over to Lois Woodward
and Bruton. They had collided head on. Maybe we are
not good at anything, I thought—neither ballroom
dancing nor square dancing. Maybe we are just deficient.

"Let's have a break," Miss Harper said.

"I'm so dizzy," Barbara said, coming over to me.

Everyone started toward the only water fountain,
near the punching bag. Barbara and I went along. "How
old are you?" I asked abruptly. I had her hand in mine,
but she pulled it away as if I had given her an electric
shock.

"Why?" she asked.

"I have to know."

"You see, for a long time I didn't go to school—"
she began evasively.

"How old? I really must know," I insisted.

"Twenty-seven," she said, with great effort.

She's ten whole years older than I am, I thought.
They're right—she's almost old enough to be my
mother. It's terrible.

"No one knows," she continued. "I've kept it to
myself." (She never did tell me why she hadn't gone
to school.)

We were right next to the punching bag. I wanted
to hit it.

"I knew I was ten years older than you," Barbara
was saying, in a shy, dying voice. "But you looked so
lonely sometimes."

I pressed her hand. She is really nice, I thought,
and, after all, the authorities almost actively discour-

age any long-lasting relationship between boys and girls at the school. They're always hinting that the real function of social-adjustment activities is to enable us to find a sighted partner out in the world. So, in a sense, whether Barbara is seventeen or twenty-seven makes little difference. We are just birds who are temporarily taking shelter here together and in the end are destined to fly our separate ways.

"How old you are doesn't matter to me," I said. "The issue just came up in the campaign. But I won't say anything about it, and you shouldn't feel you have to, either."

"Whip, did you ask Barbara how old she is?" Bruton demanded when I got back to the dormitory.

"No, Bruton," I said. "And I'm not going to. We'll have to fight this election without knowing that."

❧

I'D had my first encounter with Barbara on the first day of that school year. We were in Mr. Chiles's world-history class, and he introduced Barbara as a new student. I liked her voice, and liked the thought of a brand-new girl with no school past, no ties to any boy.

Mr. Chiles then handed each of us a new Braille textbook.

"I already have the book, in 'sight-saving' print," Barbara said, in a tentative voice, to Mr. Chiles.

Mr. Chiles asked Barbara how good her eyesight was. One of the first things that blind students and teachers want to know about any new student is whether he or she has some sight, I thought. Anyone who has even a little sight automatically has a certain standing.

"I can read print," she said.

The revelation made her seem exciting to me. She is only legally blind, I thought. She's almost as good as a sighted person.

I had never had a date, and I immediately thought of asking Barbara to a Saturday-night dance, but I imagined, as I had so often with other girls, that I didn't have a chance. I just assumed that Jackie Elam, Bruton, or some other really popular boy would soon ask her for a date and that she would become his steady. But weeks and months went by and no one asked her for a date. "She's just too doggone shy," Bruton confided to me. "She hardly ever opens her mouth."

It was true. In classes, she rarely spoke up, and Saturday after Saturday, whenever she was my dance partner—most of our dances were gentlemen's choice— I had trouble getting two words out of her. Boys said that she was just boring, but I thought that she was simply reserved—too good to indulge in gossip and small talk.

During that school year, my role in drafting the constitution, my election as senator and then as secretary-treasurer, and my position on the editorial board of the *News* gave me a certain self-confidence. One afternoon in spring, I happened to be alone with Barbara in the English classroom before the bell. I had just come from a senate meeting, and I recalled that she had run for the senate and lost. I felt sorry for her. I found myself saying, "Barbara . . . Barbara, will you come to the Saturday-night dance with me?" I felt breathless, as if I had run a mile. In asking Barbara for a date, I am going against my Indian moral training, I thought. I am giving in to temporary pleasure. I am seeking the company of a lady who is not a relative. I am pretending that my interest in her is something other than infatuation and animal lust. It's not so long ago that I was criticizing Cousin Yog for having dates. I am a hypocrite.

"I'd be glad to," Barbara said. I could feel my ears burning. She added—uncharacteristically, I thought—"I've been waiting for months for you to ask me."

Her acceptance made me feel let down, somewhat depressed. Perhaps because I didn't really respect myself, I imagined that now that Barbara had accepted me *she* wasn't worthy of respect. The boys are right, I thought—she's boring, and I should never have asked her for a date. If I had to ask someone, I should have tried for a girl more appealing and popular with the boys. (Quite aside from my moral qualms, as I realized much later, it was as if I had got so used to rejection that I didn't value acceptance when it came—as if I had come to feel that the only things worth having were things I couldn't have, like sight, and the things I could have were not worth having.)

All the same, when Saturday arrived I eagerly got dressed up for the dance and then walked over to the girls' side of the building with Oather, Bruton, and Jackie Elam, feeling—for the first time, it seemed—like a one-hundred-per-cent American and a one-hundred-per-cent-socially-adjusted blind person.

I even enjoyed waiting for Barbara. I am gaining self-confidence in so many areas of life, I thought. I am acting like someone in command of himself. The boys are right when they say that that's the key to getting dates—to being successful with girls.

It was a marvellous sensation to be stepping along the hundred or so yards to the gymnasium with Barbara, unchaperoned. Her hand, soft but firm, felt wonderful. I had held girls' hands before at the school, when we were dancing, but never while walking on the lively grass, under the still sky. And she was an American, and my date. Having a date is like being free, I thought. It's being self-reliant and democratic, using one's own judgment rather than leaning on that of a parent, as one does at home, waiting for a marriage to be arranged.

In the gymnasium, however, dancing with Barbara, to the record "Mona Lisa," her hand lightly resting on my shoulder and a bracelet she was wearing tinkling in my ear, I had a new attack of an unpleasant old thought: Would I be better off with a more desirable date than Barbara? Then it occurred to me that everyone now and again thought the grass was greener on the other side, but that our grass was without color. At that moment, more than ever, I wanted to see grass—also to see Barbara's face. Our ability to choose and be happy with our choice, it seemed, was damaged with our eyes. I no longer trusted the pleasure I took in Barbara's hand on my shoulder and the tinkling of her bracelet in my ear. The whole dance floor seemed to move to the rhythm of discontent.

Yet as the evening went on I came to feel that having any girl for a date had many pluses. Now I didn't have to stand by the wall listening to the couples out on the floor and making excuses to myself for not tapping a boy on the shoulder and cutting in—taking his partner's hand and waist, as we had been told to do in our social-adjustment classes. Now I didn't have to end up dancing with teachers, or sitting out dances, huddling with other boys who didn't have dates, feeling like a second-class citizen, jealous of boys who were dancing. It was so comforting to have my own date to stand with and to look after—to get punch and cookies for during the break.

As I was saying good night to Barbara on the girls' side, I found myself asking her—my heart beating wildly—"Can I have another date? We could go together to the school picnic at Boyle Park next Saturday."

"Yes," she said.

I stood there awkwardly, facing her, not knowing what I should do, what was expected of me. "Good night," I said, and, with my hands in my pockets, did an abrupt turn and walked rapidly to the boys' side, as if I could see the way.

❧

BARBARA and I were at Robinson Auditorium, in Little Rock, on a school outing. It was our third date; we had spent our second date at the picnic, walking, talking, and eating. At school, there was always a girls' side and a boys' side—in the dining room, in the auditorium, even in the gymnasium during wrestling meets—but for some reason the school authorities allowed students to sit with their dates on outings, and here I was, sitting next to a girl at a concert. I felt

happy and shy, and had difficulty concentrating on the
music, because I was thinking of Barbara breathing
next to me, with only an armrest between us.

The orchestra finished playing a familiar piece of
rousing music, and there was an intermission. I longed
to know what the piece of music was. I also wanted to
know the seating arrangement of the orchestra; I hadn't
even been able to tell which side the strings were on,
or the horns, because the sound had been all mixed
together and I hadn't been completely alert. Barbara
had the program in her hands and she was fidgeting
with it, making the paper crackle. I can easily ask her,
I thought. But that will be admitting to her what I
feel—that I am less than she is, because she can read
the program, can see the stage and the seated musi-
cians.

All around us, the boys and girls from the school
seemed to be talking animatedly. I must think of
something to say, I thought. It looks very odd for Barbara and me to be sitting like two silent telephones in
the middle of a public place.

Abruptly, Barbara said, her voice exploding like a
little firecracker, "I love you."

I felt frightened —more frightened than ever before
in my life, I believe. If someone had thrown a net over
me, as we used to do to catch butterflies, or had put a
pillow over my face and sat on it, as Cousin Rajinder
had once done, I couldn't have felt more trapped. I
wanted to run out of the auditorium and go back to
the boys' dormitory—to the familiar, ordered world of
the lounge, the locker room, and the sleeping hall.

"No, you don't," I snapped. I knew my voice sounded harsh and belligerent, but I felt I had to fight her off.

"I do," she said. In contrast to my voice, hers sounded weak and faint.

"No, you don't."

She was silent—so silent that the people in the auditorium suddenly sounded very loud. I've crushed her, I thought. I'm a brute.

"You don't know my family," I said, as gently as I could. "You don't know Punjabi." I tried to explain to her that she couldn't love me, because she couldn't possibly know me, all the while thinking that *I* couldn't possibly love anyone who didn't have my parents' approval, who didn't fit into our family system, who wasn't an Indian, who wasn't Punjabi, who wasn't of our caste and class.

She didn't respond. I thought of reaching over and taking her hand but decided that that would be encouraging her. I held myself in and said sententiously, "Love grows like a tree—it takes years."

"I love you. I'll always love you," she said again, quietly but with determination.

I am on dangerous ground, I thought. I may slip. Besides, the boys might overhear us and make fun of me. But they all seemed to be preoccupied with their own conversations. I was trying to think what to say or do next when there was a hush, people applauded, and the orchestra resumed playing.

The rest of the concert and the bus ride back to the school are hazy in my memory. I think Barbara and I were mostly awkward with each other.

It was a couple of days after the concert that I overheard Billy Tabor's remark that I was dating Barbara only to get the girls' vote.

❧

IT was election day. The sleeping hall was nearly empty, but I wanted to go on sleeping. The night before, I had stayed up late reading, in the broom closet. Anyway, I didn't want to wake up to election day.

"You have the election in the bag," Bruton was saying from somewhere above me. "You heard the steampipes this morning, didn't you?"

"No. Why?" I said, sitting up.

"Oather and a couple of the boys went down to the lounge at the crack of dawn and started banging on the steampipes," McNabb said, coming over. "The noise woke up practically everyone in the hall."

"I thought you were woken up, too, Whip, but, as a good politician, were just pretending to be asleep," Bruton said.

"But you must have heard Jackie say from his bed that you'd be a better president, that you wouldn't do something as irresponsible as wake everyone up just for fun," McNabb said. "I'm sure that every boy who was woken up by the steampipes is going to vote for you now."

"Besides, everybody knows that Oather is a country boy and doesn't have your style," Bruton said.

"I don't give a damn," I said petulantly—I was still half asleep. "I hate politics—steampipes and all."

"This is America. And what is democracy without

politics?" Bruton asked rhetorically.

"Politics is a dirty, disgusting business," I said.

"When the election's in the bag, every politician says that," McNabb said. "It's called eating your cake and having it, too."

I was furious. It wasn't the election results I was thinking of so much as Barbara's reputation.

That evening, Mr. Chiles came to the lounge. "I've counted the ballots," he announced. The ballots were in Braille. "Ved is the new president of the senate. I'm off to tell Miss Harper, so that she can announce the result in the girls' dormitory."

The few boys in the lounge clapped, but Joe Wright, who, as usual, was listening to the baseball game, asked, "What he say?" Without waiting for an answer to his question, he started cheering a hit.

I felt oddly sad. I thought that I had probably won because of the steampipes. I also thought that Oather was a much more deserving candidate than I was. My education had been sketchy, while he had been at the school since the school building was completed—in 1939, when he was eight. He had always been first in his class, and probably had the best record in the junior-senior high school. He was one of the most sociable, friendly, and good-hearted of the boys. There was another element in my reaction, which took me years, even decades, to grasp. I had worked flat out to be elected president, but now that I was president I felt that my success was not worth having, precisely because it was *I* who had succeeded.

Someone ran in through the side door of the lounge and flung his hairy arms around me.

"Oather!"

"Congratulations, V.P." My friends often affectionately called me V.P.—my first two initials. "V.P.,
now I'll be your V.P.," Oather said, laughing rau-
cously.

"I'm sorry, Oather," I said. "I really wish you had
won."

"To win and feel sorry for your defeated opponent—that's a privilege of democracy." He began to
spit some tobacco over my shoulder, but he quickly
stopped himself, doubtless realizing that he was in the
lounge, not in the tobacco room.

"But the steampipes—"

"Hell's bells!" he exclaimed, shifting the tobacco
in his mouth. "I did that knowing what I was doing.
I wanted to be sure that you won. Besides, who said
the steampipes had anything to do with it?"

We had been good friends before, but we were
inseparable from that day on. He even helped me to
free myself from Barbara. In my rather Indian way, I
had got it into my head that my three dates with her
were tantamount to a marriage proposal and that I
couldn't possibly jilt her after that. But when I spoke
to Oather about this he said, "Just don't ask her for
another date, and she'll get used to being without you."

"But she'll be heartbroken," I said. "She'll think
that I'm a cad—that I've taken advantage of her."

"The girls here don't think like that," he said. "You
try out my technique, and, Whip, you will know that
I'm as right as Joe Wright is wrong when he says the
St. Louis Cardinals will win the World Series."

Oather *was* right. I didn't ask Barbara for a date

again, and although she wrote me some powerful love letters from East St. Louis, Illinois, where she was spending the summer, she always concluded by saying that she knew in her heart of hearts that we were meant to be only friends.

❧

WHAT I felt about girls and dates after the debacle with Barbara—as I thought of it— was influenced in some measure by a series of scandals during my last year at the school. The first day of that school year, as I was sitting in the lounge, idle, Oather walked up and asked me if I had heard that Arlie Treadway and Vernelle Stewart got married over the summer. "Vernelle already has a baby, and Treadway isn't coming back to school," he added.

I was shocked and horrified, but then I thought, It's nonsense. It's malicious gossip. Treadway is one of my closest friends. He would never have kept something like that from me. He is so intelligent. He couldn't possibly have blundered into marriage. Anyway, Vernelle would have had to be pregnant for most of the last school year. How could she have fooled everyone and graduated, as she did?

"It's not like you to repeat such a terrible piece of gossip," I said to Oather, a little angrily. "I thought you were a good friend of Treadway's."

"I don't spread gossip," he said simply. "I had it from Mr. Hartman. Vernelle has a little boy."

I was stunned. The news had come from Mr. Hartman—it had to be true. Then I became disgusted—

disgusted with Treadway and Vernelle for doing this dirty thing, with Oather and Mr. Hartman for bearing the news of it.

Soon everyone in the school was talking about the scandal. None of the boys could figure out how Vernelle's pregnancy was kept secret, or how Treadway, one of the most open and best-natured of the boys, could have been so cunning as to stop dating Vernelle for several months in the late winter and spring—as he did—and make us think that he was breaking up with her. Then Miss Harper volunteered the information that some of the sighted teachers in the girls' dormitory had known for part of the school year that Vernelle was pregnant but had helped her to hide it, because they wanted to see her graduate—she had been one of the school's star students. I was glad that Vernelle had been able to graduate. But she lacked any qualifications that would help her get a job. And Treadway had only finished eleventh grade. Moreover, she was nineteen and Treadway was only eighteen, and they were both totally blind. How would they manage? Who would give him a job? How could he ever support a family? The more I thought about it, the more my original disgust turned into sadness and into fear for their future.

I confided my feelings to Bruton and McNabb.

"It may be worse than you think," Bruton said. "Maybe they're not married at all. Maybe they've got an illegitimate son on their hands and are just saying they're married, so the school won't get a bad name."

"I don't want to hear such talk," I said. "I won't have my friend's reputation ruined."

"But Treadway's reputation is already ruined," McNabb said, sounding like a judge. "You can't get away from that."

A couple of days after the scandal broke, Mrs. Hankins came and got me out of class, because Vernelle wanted to speak to me on the office telephone.

"Hello?" I said, scarcely able to keep the receiver steady on my ear.

"Ved, I just wanted you to know that we were secretly married last Thanksgiving," she said forthrightly. "The baby is fine."

"Why hasn't Treadway called me?" I asked. "I would have thought he'd tell me all about this himself. I had to hear everything in the dormitory as gossip, and I had no way of shutting people up."

"Didn't you know? Arlie was very sick all summer. For a while, he was on his deathbed. He just got up last week."

Vernelle didn't know exactly what Treadway's sickness had been, but she told me that he was well now and that both of them and the baby were off to Houston, where Treadway was going to look for a job as a piano tuner.

Here is Treadway, settling for just piano tuning, I thought. And he is so intelligent—much more intelligent than I am. Here is Treadway, throwing away his chance for education and a better life, and I had to wait so long and travel so far for that chance. But then I remembered that he had come from a broken home. Maybe he just needed some love and couldn't wait, I thought. I'm lucky to have my family behind me. Still, I have lost one of my closest friends. Who knows when, or if, we'll ever meet again? But, as Daddyji used to say, there is no sense in crying over spilt milk. At least, Treadway and Vernelle are married. Maybe they are more courageous than all of us, trying to make a family in spite of their blindness.

Searching for something comforting to say to Vernelle on the telephone, I now told her I was glad that Treadway had a skill he could turn to. I wished them the best of luck and hung up.

❧

WHEN everyone got back from Christmas vacation that year, I learned from Mr. Chiles as we were coming out of the dining room that Billy Tabor, a tenth grader, and Evelyn Worrell, an eleventh grader, had eloped and got married in Benton. Billy and Evelyn would never have thought of doing this on their own, without the example of Treadway and Vernelle, I thought. They are not leaders, like Treadway and Vernelle. Teachers are always after them for not studying.

In the lounge, many boys were gathered around Mr. Hartman. "Do you know what?" he was saying gleefully. "Billy and Evelyn planned to keep their marriage secret and continue in school as if nothing had happened. The plan almost worked, but after what Treadway and Vernelle did I've been looking carefully at the papers, and, sure enough, I saw their names on the list of people who had taken out marriage licenses, and I showed it to Mr. Woolly. I'll bet they didn't know that things like that are published in newspapers. Billy doesn't have any special skills, and Evelyn has a temper. This is one hell of a marriage." Mr. Hartman fastened on me and said caustically, "You should be glad you don't have a girlfriend."

I blushed. I had been thinking about trying to get myself a girlfriend someday soon.

"Mr. Hartman, what's going to happen to Billy and Evelyn?" Fat Earnie asked. "They don't have a baby, and they live in Little Rock. We going to have married students in school now?"

"Billy and Evelyn? Why, they've been expelled," Mr. Hartman said. "And anyone else who tries a trick like that will be expelled, too." He really has a voice as penetrating as a siren, I thought. No wonder he is so good at drilling us in calisthenics.

But Mr. Hartman's words were belied almost at once, because, as it turned out, the parents of both Billy and Evelyn came to Mr. Woolly and pleaded with him to let their children continue in school while living in one of their homes. Although such an arrangement was unheard of, Mr. Woolly agreed. I decided that he didn't want to punish the two by depriving them of their education. Oather said to me philosophically, "Let's face it, Whip. Marriage is no crime, and Mr. Woolly is no judge. This here is the only state school for the blind in Arkansas, and any person who lives in the state and is legally blind and is not too old has a right to study here. If you got married, you wouldn't want Mr. Woolly to throw you out, would you?"

"What if Evelyn has a baby?" I asked, ignoring his question but unable to leave the topic alone. "Would

Mr. Woolly let her continue at school then?"

Oather was stumped.

The next day, Mr. Woolly announced in assembly, "I've made an exception for Billy and Evelyn, because there may be some confusion about what our policy for this kind of behavior is. Well, now I'll tell y'all our policy. The next time this kind of thing happens, the people involved will be expelled and I will hear no appeals. School is no place for marriage."

In the days and weeks that followed, I noticed that Billy and Evelyn didn't talk to us much and never stayed around for after-school activities. In fact, they stuck out among the students like two aliens. What a difference marriage makes, I thought. I feel sorry for them. Their love can only be an infatuation. They should have had enough self-control to resist the temptation. Look at me—I might have got involved with Barbara, but I didn't give in to the temptation.

❧

BARELY a month after Billy and Evelyn's marriage, George Conner asked me to go with him for a walk in the woods in back of the school. He was nineteen and in tenth grade. He put an arm around my shoulder and drew me closer, and whispered, almost as if he feared that the trees would overhear him, "I'm going to tell you something that I haven't told a soul, because I knowed you could keep a secret. Phil and I have decided to go off to Benton and get ourselves married—we're on fire for each other." Mariann Phillips, his girl, was nineteen and in eleventh grade.

"I wish you hadn't told me," I said, and I instinctively drew away from him, but George continued to keep his arm around my shoulder. "You know Mr. Woolly will find out and expel you both."

"We're going to do it, sure as I'm standing here."

I was horrified. George was from a poor family, and although Phil was the only child of well-off people, she was adopted, and I feared that she might be disowned. How will they live, I thought. How will they manage? They are both likable, but George is unambitious and Phil is strong-willed. They are headed straight for disaster.

"Damn it, George, I'm going to tell Mr. Woolly," I said.

"No, you ain't, Whip," he said. "You'd never do that to a buddy.

I argued and pleaded with him, but George's mind was made up—or, rather, I thought, had been made up for him by Phil, since I had never known him to take a strong stand on anything before. Anyway, I got nowhere with him.

That night and the next night, I didn't sleep at all. I felt indignant because George had burdened me with a confidence I didn't want. At the same time, I fretted about going to Mr. Woolly with it and informing on George. Yet I was the president of the school senate, and I felt responsible to the authorities. In the end, I went to Mr. Woolly and blurted it all out, trying to tell myself that I was being virtuous and doing my duty.

Even before I had finished, Mr. Woolly jumped out of his chair and left the office, saying, "Boy, I'm going to find George Conner and stop him if it's the last thing I do at this school. You sit right there."

I sat in Mr. Woolly's drafty, empty office, feeling as exposed as a shorn sheep. I wondered what Mr. Woolly would say to George, what George would say to him, and whether I had done the right thing. "I shouldn't look back," I told myself. "But this whole dating business won't leave me in peace."

"Son, you all right?" Mr. Woolly asked, coming back after what seemed a very long time.

"I think so," I said, my mouth as dry as if a dentist had his draining tube in it.

"I'm sure George told you what you told me," Mr. Woolly continued, sitting down. "But when I taxed him with it he denied everything. But now that he knows I'm on to him I don't think he'll try anything. I don't think so at all."

I didn't completely believe that George could have given up his plan. Everyone said that Phil could lead anyone into doing anything when she put her mind to it. But I kept quiet and left Mr. Woolly's office quickly.

I walked around the dormitory guiltily, avoiding George, thinking he must know that I had told on him. But later that day he came up to me on the little terrace outside the lounge and said, "Phil went and told some of her girlfriends. One of them squealed on us to Mr. Woolly."

I stood there, lacking the courage to own up. I thought about the honest cow that Bhabiji, my grandmother, used to tell us about when we were growing up. The cow had kept her appointment with the tiger even though she knew that he planned to devour her.

George was no tiger. Still, I said nothing.

"Phil and me won't let nothing stop us," George was saying. "We just got to find a good time to sneak out of the school. Once we're married, Mr. Woolly will take us back, just like he did Billy and Evelyn. If not, we'll head west, like Treadway and Vernelle."

George sounded utterly in earnest. But carrying a tale once is enough, I thought. I did nothing about his fresh confidence.

A couple of weeks later, as I was coming down from the night session of study hall I heard a commotion from the direction of Mr. Woolly's office.

"You boys and girls were headed for Benton, weren't you?" Mr. Woolly was saying, in his normal voice. I marvelled at his calm manner; I found myself shaking all over.

"You were going to get married, weren't you?" Mr. Robinson said accusingly. (Francis L. Robinson had succeeded Mr. Lord as our principal at the beginning of the school year.)

"Yes, sir," four—not two—voices said, one after another, as if answering a class roll call. To my horror, I recognized the voices not only of George and Phil but also of James Spakes and Peggy Stevens.

"Y'all didn't know—did you—that I had alerted the night watchman after I talked to you, George. We were ready for you."

I hurried away.

A few minutes later, George and James came into the locker room and started packing. When they were asked what they were doing, they said that Mr. Woolly had expelled them and their girls, and that they were all being put on buses to go home. They wouldn't say more—they seemed determined to keep their own counsel. The sounds of their locker doors opening and their suitcases hitting the locker-room bench crashed in my ears like so many shouted reproaches. I am partly responsible, I thought. It's awful. I consoled myself by thinking that if Mr. Woolly had made an example of Billy and Evelyn the new scandal might not have happened. Then George, James, Phil, and Peggy would all have been able to graduate in a year or two. Now they had lost their chance for an education, along with their reputations.

I walked out of the locker room and out of the lounge. I wanted to be by myself. Treadway and Vernelle, Billy and Evelyn, George and Phil, James and Peggy—what can they possibly know about life and marriage, I thought. American teen-agers can't have much foresight. They let one event lead to another. They don't think about consequences. They might as well set out on life's road with their legs in irons. Such thoughts made me feel older and different, underscoring my feeling of separateness from people in the school, in Arkansas, in America.

❦

EVEN before this latest school scandal, Daddyji had given me the shocking news that my first cousin Surinder Mehta, Yog's younger brother, who was studying in Corvallis, Oregon, had eloped with a nineteen-year-old American coed named Jackie. Both Surinder and Jackie were underage, and to get married they had had to travel to another state, where parental consent was not required.

Surinder was scarcely a year older than I was, and had come to America just a year before I did, over the objections of many relatives, who had said that he was too young to go to the West and if he did go he would be corrupted by the loose Western morals. The same relatives had made similar objections to my coming. (They had not objected to Cousin Yog's coming to America, precisely because he was over eighteen and so, they thought, had a firm grip on Indian values.) Although Surinder and I hadn't been much in touch with each other in America—Oregon seemed as far away as another country—we had so much in common that I felt almost as if I myself had fallen desperately in love and eloped. I felt the ground underfoot giving way, shaking my belief that Surinder was mature and I was mature and American teen-agers were not; that a mature person eschewed temporary pleasures for permanent ones; that love was not an act, like falling out of a boat or running away and getting married, but a process, like the growth of a tree or my own parents' marriage, which had taken years of sacrifice and adjustment to become serene. It was that ground to which I had clung tenaciously, as to a piece of India, while I was buffeted by the winds and waters of the New World. I felt that I knew nothing about anything anymore, that now I would always be adrift on an uncharted sea.

❧

ALTHOUGH it was April, there was no hint of flowers. It had been raining continuously for days. There was no letup in the head cold I got in Arkansas every fall and had until the spring. Surinder seemed to be always on my mind, and I had a premonition that something bad was about to happen to me.

I was at the annual party the juniors gave for the seniors—I was to graduate in less than two months. The party was being held in the Home Economics Cottage. To my surprise, Lois Woodward, who was Raymond Rodgers' steady, arrived at the party alone.

"Where is Raymond?" I asked, going up to her.

"We've broken up," she said sadly. So she has finally realized that that childish Raymond is not right for her, I thought. She should feel happy.

She stayed around me, as if I were her date. It's natural, I thought. Oather and I are the only ones here without dates, and she wouldn't want to be around Oather, because he once dated her and then quit her. Poor Lois! She hasn't had good luck with boys.

I recalled that when I came to the school she had been Big Jim Pickett's girl. Big Jim was a senior then, and she was in the ninth grade with me. Months before he graduated, he had quit her. After that, she had no dates for almost a year. Everyone could tell that she was depressed. At parties, she would dance the minimum number of dances required to get good character marks in social adjustment, and during the punch-and-cookie time, instead of standing around the punch bowl and laughing and talking, as the rest of us did, she would stand alone by the wall until a teacher went up to her and made her join us. She was a small person with a small voice, and had always sounded a bit squinched up and sad, but during those dateless months her voice sank still lower. She was a clarinettist, and even her clarinet playing lacked her old energy. It was around that time that Oather, in his good-hearted way, had asked her for a date and taken her to a few parties. After that, Pat Thennes, who was sixteen and in the fourth grade, started dating her. We'd never heard of a tenth grader dating a fourth grader. Moreover, Lois was smart and likable, and Pat was lazy and quarrelsome. But Pat, too, soon quit her. Fat Earnie said, "Now she'll never get a date again. Who wants to date a girl who's been thrown over by Pat Thennes?" My heart went out to her then, but there was nothing I could do; I was already becoming interested in Barbara, and wrestling with my Indian morality so that I could get up the courage to ask her out. Then McNabb had got the idea of getting Raymond to ask Lois out. Raymond griped all the time (no one griped more), and McNabb thought that if he got a girl he would have something else to think about—or maybe McNabb was just being mischievous. But Raymond, who was sixteen, was in seventh grade and very immature, and McNabb was afraid that he wouldn't ask Lois for a date if he thought other people wanted him to. So McNabb put the idea into Raymond's head in such a way that Raymond thought he himself had come up with it. Anyway, Raymond asked Lois to a dance, and before anyone knew it they were going around as a couple. And now, after going steady for nearly a year, they had broken up. I was sure that it was the best thing that could have happened to Lois.

Presently, Miss Shults put a record on the phonograph, and I raised Lois's hand, took her firmly by the waist, and stepped out on the floor. She felt easy to dance with—even more so than she had at other parties. She was slender and had a good sense of rhythm, and she seemed relaxed, for her.

Before I knew it, it was time to go home. Boys and their dates started filing out to walk back to the girls' side. Assuming that Lois would walk back with Mr. Chiles, the chaperon for the party, I started toward Oather, in order to walk back to the boys' dormitory with him. But he said, "Whip, why don't you walk Lois home?" Oather had a voice that carried, and Lois had heard him. I have no choice but to be a gentleman, I thought. I went over to her.

The half-dozen other couples walked ahead, with Mr. Chiles following at a discreet distance. As chaperon, he had to make sure that there was no hanky-panky; at the same time, he had to allow couples some privacy along the way in which to say their good nights. He let Lois and me follow him, perhaps because we were not going steady and he knew we were not likely to do anything improper.

In order to make the most of the few minutes' walk to the girls' side, everyone dawdled, taking a few steps and then stopping to whisper and kiss. Although the footsteps and whispered endearments sounded loud in the still night air, and Mr. Chiles had very good hearing, I wondered how much he could really tell by just listening—I certainly couldn't tell who was kissing whom. Yet I reflected that Mr. Woolly couldn't entrust chaperoning only to sighted teachers, for that would make Mr. Chiles a second-class citizen in a school for the blind.

Since Lois and I had never walked together, we felt awkward.

"My hands feel cold," Lois said. The rain had stopped, and the air was cool.

"Here, put your hand in my pocket," I said, wondering as I said it if my bluejeans were too tight.

She slipped her hand in my pocket. It was so thin and small that I could scarcely feel it.

A dog barked somewhere. It must be Fritz, I thought—Mr. Woolly's watchdog. Fritz is never off duty.

I put my arm around Lois's waist and leaned toward her. Her hair was lightly scented. She is a small, slight girl, I thought, so she probably has a small, compact face. If I am going to get a kiss from her, I'll have to do it quickly. Why should I not avail myself of the chance? But the idea of touching her lips filled me with terror.

We were almost at the door of the girls' dormitory. With my facial vision, I sensed a sound-shadow—a slim lamppost looming a few inches ahead. I stopped abruptly. Lois walked smack into it.

She cried out and jerked her hand out of my pocket. A pain went through my heart. If only I'd been more careful, I thought—if only I hadn't been thinking about her lips. Yet I tried to tell myself that the lamppost was right in front of her door and she must have known about it almost from the day she arrived at the school.

I touched her face. She had not hit her forehead, as I'd feared, but had taken the blow on the cheek, which was more resilient. Still, it was swelling up.

I blew into my clean handkerchief and got it as warm as I could, then gently pressed it to her bump. She drew back from me as if she thought I was being forward, or as if she blamed me for not saving her from the lamppost in the first place.

I squeezed her dainty hand with my free one, and

she relaxed. I even thought she gave my hand a squeeze back. Oh, what bliss, I thought. I again pressed the handkerchief on her bump. My heart started beating rapidly.

I let go of her hand and felt her shoulder through her blouse. I stroked her soft neck, ran my fingers through her soft hair. I thought of how smooth her skin was, how small her waist was, how dainty she was in every way, how pretty. I tried not to think of the fact that she was Raymond's longtime steady, and told myself that she couldn't have cared for him—that she must have dated him to save face after being dropped by Pat Thennes. Suddenly, reason left me. I moved to kiss her, but the act of kissing on the mouth was so foreign to my upbringing that I had a fit of trembling. I tried to master my trembling, but "temporary pleasure, temporary pleasure," Daddyji's warning refrain, beat in my head.

Mr. Chiles cleared his throat, as he was known to do when he thought that couples were misbehaving. "Ved and Lois!" he called. "What's keeping you two?" He added kindly, "Y'all know Mr. Woolly wants good nights to be short."

It had begun to drizzle. Tiny raindrops flew about our faces in a thin spray of disapproval.

"We're coming, Mr. Chiles," Lois and I said, almost together.

I had missed the chance to get my first kiss. I had an overwhelming feeling of sadness, like a wave breaking inside me.

Back in the dormitory, I couldn't go to sleep. I didn't know how my love had happened. I had always thought of myself as a realistic person, who had better sense than to give in to such things. Like Oather, I had often felt that I was lucky not to have a girl, not to have the extra worry and the extra burden, but, rather, to be independent and concentrate on my studies. I used to lecture my blind friends, saying that we, even more than sighted people, had to look to permanent pleasures. Now here I was, just after my eighteenth birthday, within reach of my graduation, so much in love with Lois that I would have eloped with her, like Surinder with Jackie, and married her right then and there, come what might—even if I were expelled, like George and Phil, James and Peggy, or just left school, like Treadway. They say opportunity knocks only once, and I've missed the opportunity to kiss Lois and make her mine, I thought. I've missed the boat. I'll never find anyone like Lois again. I will always be a bachelor, like Mr. Chiles—and a lonely foreigner besides.

❧

I WAS in the locker room getting dressed for a band engagement in Benton—I played accordion in the band. I was wondering why it was that I had been tongue-tied around Lois since the night of the party the week before.

McNabb walked in. "Raymond, you've got lip-stick on your shirt," he said, in his most mournful voice.

"What about it?" Raymond said. "It's Lois's lip-stick. She must have got it on me at the square-dance club last night."

My legs practically collapsed under me. I had missed the square dance, and Lois had apparently gone back to Raymond, just as if she and I had never taken that momentous walk. If I had only been able to tell Lois what was in my heart, if I had only been able to tell her how much I loved her, if I had only sealed my love with a kiss, she wouldn't have done this to me, I thought.

I managed to finish dressing and carry my accordion out to the school bus.

Lois stepped in just ahead of me with her clarinet. Once I was aboard, I waited to see whether she would sit alone or with another band member. She sat by herself next to a window. I somehow fitted my accordion under the seat and slid in beside her.

We were sitting fairly near the back, away from everyone else. Perhaps I haven't missed out altogether, I thought. Perhaps I can create another opportunity. Benton is twenty miles away, and the bus ride will give me plenty of time. People elope to Benton—it's a romantic trip.

I had a reckless urge to reach over and grab Lois—to kiss her, and hang the school rules. I said to myself, "If she doesn't coöperate, I'll do it anyway, even if I have to force her." At the same time, something in me wouldn't let met forget the lipstick on the shirt, the morals I'd grown up with, the little time I had left till graduation. Yet that urge to possess her anyhow wouldn't leave me. I felt wretched. I had never experienced such strong feelings before, and they were so contradictory. *Yes, kiss her. No, don't kiss her.* I prayed to God to give me will power, to let me pass my remaining weeks at the school in peace and purity of thought, to keep me from doing something untoward that would ruin my record at school and the reputation of the girl I loved, to let me graduate with glory. I suddenly found that I had discovered real faith. I redoubled my prayers, telling God that I needed His help more than ever before, that I had no one to turn to but Him, because the days of face-to-face confidences with members of my family had ended forever when I left home for Arkansas. Still, I felt lost and lonely. To try to get strength from on high, I kept repeating to myself, "God, I won't kiss. I won't kiss Lois. God, this is my age for education, not sex."

"Lois, can I take you to the dance next Saturday?" I finally asked weakly, telling myself that I was striking a compromise between my physical urges and my principles, even as I moved closer to her, so that our hips and legs touched.

"No, thank you," she said, without a moment's hesitation, primly moving toward the window. "You know I'm Raymond's girl."

I was crushed and angry at the same time. I wondered whether I would be able to get through the band program, whether I would ever be able to concentrate in class again. I had a sinking feeling that something grave, troublesome, and irksome had permanently settled in my soul.

To hide my feelings, I got up and started walking up and down the aisle, cracking jokes with everyone on the bus. For all anyone knows, I thought, I'm hail-fellow-well-met, but inside I'm dying. O poet, if I had your pen I could express my grief!

That night, as I was going to sleep, I said to myself

that I wasn't going to let my romantic love get the better of me. I wasn't going to allow myself to love. I had too many responsibilities. I would marry for more solid reasons than love. Yet I felt that sighs were concealed in my breathing, that tears were in my eyes. I wished I didn't have to see Lois every time I turned around. My mind was in a million pieces.

OATHER stood behind me at the sink, the rough fingers of one of his hands running down my cheek and the cold steel of the safety razor in his other hand following the path traced by his fingers. I rinsed the shaving brush under hot water, swished it around in a mug with a little cake of scented soap in it, and applied more lather to my face as he told me to, being careful to apply the foamy film evenly.

"You're eighteen and you never shaved before," Oather was saying. "Man, we got boys here shaving at thirteen and fourteen."

"How did you learn to shave?" I asked, mumbling through the soap.

"Just like you're doing—but hold still, don't talk."

Ever since I could remember, I had been eager to have a beard to shave. I remembered taking Mamaji's little scissors from her sewing basket and running them across my upper lip when no one was looking—snipping and hoping. I got a fuzzy mustache when I was fourteen, but the beard wouldn't come. It had just sprouted over the past weekend, like the tender grass outside with the arrival of spring. It made me realize that I didn't even own a razor, let alone know how to hold one. The night before, I had stayed awake wondering whom to turn to, whom to tell about my predicament. I wished Daddyji were there. I wished for any male relative at all. My face felt itchy and grubby, as if it were caked with mud. I felt I couldn't let it go for another day. Finally, I took Oather into my confidence.

"Whip with whiskers!" he cried, and laughed and laughed, but not at all unkindly. He accompanied me to Stifft's Station and helped me buy the shaving things. Back in the locker room, he made me strip to the waist and marched me to the sink. It was late afternoon, and the locker room was mercifully empty.

The razor in Oather's hand seemed to slither around my ear, and I jumped.

"Whip, when you shave you have to keep your face steady," Oather admonished.

I tried to keep my head still, and touched Oather's hand holding the razor in order to get a sense of its tilt and movement. I noticed that he was pulling my cheek taut with one hand and following its plane with the razor. I wondered how it was that people shaving didn't cut themselves up, and whether I would really be able to finish shaving myself, as he'd said I would. Shaving seemed at once an extremely easy and a frighteningly difficult task.

Shaving at a locker-room sink is so different from the way Daddyji shaves at home, I thought. Now and again, as he sat in his pajamas and dressing gown, a bath towel tied around his neck and his shaving things arrayed on a folding table in front of him, he would shake his razor in a glass of hot water; the sound would remind me of Blackie—a dog we'd once had—shaking herself, making her dog tags clink and her ears flap. There was something very comforting about the gentle brushing sound of his razor against his skin—as comforting as the sound of Mamaji's knitting needles clicking through the day. We children would gather around him and have perhaps the most relaxed conversation of the day with him.

"You see, you've got to pull the razor along quickly, or the lather will dry out and the razor will catch at your beard," Oather was saying, even as the soap was drying on my face. I applied more. As Oather continued shaving me, it seemed that sometimes I had too much lather on my face and sometimes not enough. Sometimes the razor in Oather's hand seemed to skid over the soap without shaving the beard. Sometimes it dragged, as if it would shave my cheek off.

I now tilted my head to offer a better surface for the razor, but at the same time my cheek seemed to twitch and jump involuntarily. Now, though, Oather insisted that I should try to shave myself. He handed me the razor and showed me how to shave first one side of my neck and then the other, how to push my tongue behind my upper lip and then my lower lip to shave the corners under my nose and then the crease between my lower lip and my chin—his hand guiding me all the while, helping me to move the razor in little, well-aimed strokes. Now he praised and now he corrected, now he laughed and now he whistled, giving the task a certain lightness.

Under his direction, I rinsed off my face, splashing water on a few spots where I'd nicked myself. Then I examined my face to make sure that I had left no patch of beard unshaved. Running my fingers all over its tingling, fresh surface, I felt I was "seeing" my face for the first time, as if my fingers had the reflecting power of the shaving mirror that I couldn't use. I am finally a man, I thought. I have a beard and I know how to handle a razor. I felt almost as if I could see.

"I WANTED to know what it feels like not to see," she said, fiddling with her umbrella and nervously tapping it on the floor of the bus. "So I blindfolded myself an hour or so at a time—oh, not every day at first, but once a week or so. You see, I work at the rehabilitation center for the blind, and I'd seen these people coming and going, day after day, and really had no idea what it felt like. It—I mean blindfolding myself—was the strangest experience of my life. I got vertigo. The world seemed to be turned upside down. Every little noise was amplified, became irritating. The typewriter next door sounded like elephants stomping. And then there was this panic that rose up in my chest like a huge glob of phlegm and practically choked me. I couldn't stop crying, actually sobbing. All I had to do was take off the blindfold. I knew that. But I wanted to see how long I could stand it—how many hours at a time, how many days in a row." Although we were in public, her way of talking was so discreet and soft that I felt we were having a conversation in private. "You won't believe it, but the simplest action, like opening a Coke bottle, took me five minutes. And I had no energy. It was as though a steamroller had run over me, flattened me out—left me feeling like a corpse. Now, at the

rehabilitation center I'd heard other social workers speak
about people experiencing blindness as a form of death.
I couldn't understand it—why the loss of eyesight should
be felt that way. But blindfolding myself made me
realize how total that loss must be, how much like
death it must be. Taking the blindfold off was almost
like experiencing resurrection. I think all blind people
must need to have some kind of daily spiritual resurrection to keep going."

I listened to her spellbound, without nodding,
without making the usual sounds of acknowledg-
ment, for fear of stopping her flow. Listening to her, I
felt that she was verbalizing thoughts that I had had,
but thoughts so shadowy I could scarcely articulate them
to myself. I felt that she had somehow managed to
bridge the gulf between the seeing and the unseeing—
that in some way she had become one of us. There
wasn't a hint of "you blind people" in her way of
speaking.

"Well, goodbye, then," she said. The bus was at a
stop and she got off. A few minutes later, I couldn't
be sure whether she had been a real person or an appar-
ition, whether she'd been sitting there next to me or
I'd fallen asleep and dreamed her. I just heard her wispy
but clear voice in my head, and had an urgent sense of
longing to speak to her more, to learn more about my
experience through her.

I never saw her again, but I remember the conversation as if it were taking place today. Although she
spoke to me only because I was blind, she happened to
put in crystalline form certain of my elusive recurring
thoughts—thoughts I had then and still have.

X

A LEAF, A STEM

TO A BLIND SON

Because I cannot tilt your head and say,
"See! Those are stars—and that a moon—
And this is twilight, when a dying day
Slides gray and silent like a fading tune
From memory. And there, across the sky,
In wide, gay arching is a rainbow. See
How gold it is, how lavender, how shy
And pastel is its color. Look, my son, with me."

Since this I cannot do, I take your hand
And teach it how to touch a leaf, a stem,
And how distinguish snow or grass or sand,
And tell you, as I can, of all of them.

And somehow, you and I can learn how much
Of beauty like the stars there is to touch.

—*Anonymous, Arkansas Braille News, February,*
1950.

S OME EXCERPTS FROM THE LAST YEAR OF THE
journal I kept while I was in Little Rock:

September 9
Oather and Bruton were suddenly here, as
if they'd never been away for the summer.
Oather had brought some wieners from home, and we
three struck out for the woods at the back of the gymnasium to cook them. Bruton got hold of a piece of tin
and hammered it into shape to put under the fire, while
Oather and I scrambled about looking for firewood and
roasting sticks. Within a few minutes, we were sitting
around the fire roasting our wieners, our sticks touching.

Bruton said that he had met a woman back home
who had asked him why he needed sleep since his eyes
were closed all the time. Oather said that he'd met a
woman in his home town who thought that blind people had to have strings running from their forks and
knives to their mouths to eat. I don't think we've ever
laughed so much.

September 12
Miss Harper told us that over the summer she had
done some more square dancing and learned some new

square-dance calls—Four-Gent Star, Cowboy Loop, Down the Center, Paul Jones, Sally Goodwin, Swing in the Hall. I am in charge of recording good fiddle music off the radio on my tape recorder and bringing it to the square-dance club gatherings in the gymnasium every Wednesday.

September 15

Oather read out to us a dumb poem from an old issue of the *Arkansas Braille News* that a father wrote about a blind son. We decided that the father couldn't have had a blind son—just made him up for the poem.

September 17

Mr. Woolly told me that a Dr. Ray Penix has given the school a white wolfhound called Igor. No one at school has a Seeing Eye dog, and Dr. Penix wanted the school to get interested in the Seeing Eye dog program. Mr. Woolly appointed me to try out Igor.

I was utterly astonished by Igor. He was almost as tall as a little donkey and was fitted up with a harness and a stiff handle through which I could feel practically his every movement. I took him to Stifft's Station. He stopped when we came to the intersection and didn't move until the light was in our favor. Yet I found having him along somewhat awkward. On the sidewalk, people made a show of giving us a wide berth, or complimented me for being his owner. I felt as if I had a performing bear on a chain. Igor is not much use to me, but he would be a great help for people like Norman Penix [no relation] who have a hard time getting around, because they lost their sight later in life. I told all this to Mr. Woolly.

September 18

I am now one of the twelve vending-stand operators. We get one dollar a week. We have just worked
out a schedule for manning the stand. I am learning
how to keep a daily record of purchases and profits,
reorder stock, pay the bills.

September 20

It was a lovely autumn day. Joe Wright got hold
of a softball and a bat. Oather, Bruton, and I went out
and stood in the open space under the locker-room
window and took turns batting. Joe aimed at the bat—
he has just enough sight for that. We listened to the
sound of the ball, calculated its speed as it sailed through
the air, and tried to hit it. I thought that we would
get tired of the monotony of just standing there and
batting, but we didn't. After an hour or so of playing
our version of baseball, we hardly missed a pitch.

September 21

Today I became a full-fledged member of the band.
There are nine other members. We will be playing
simple swing music, and sometimes someone will sing.
For every public engagement each of us will be paid
five dollars in cash.

October 15

The city council had this terrible idea of taxing
Seeing Eye dogs and banning them from city buses. I
represented Mr. Woolly before the city council, along
with the members of the Little Rock Braille Club, and
lobbied against the measures. So today, Dr. Ray Penix,
with his Dalmatian, Susie; Elsie Arnold, with her Ger-

man shepherd, Shep; Paddy Driscoll, a war veteran, with his boxer, Tina; and Igor and I presented our case. The council members were much impressed, and pictures of us and our dogs will appear tomorrow in the *Arkansas Democrat*. I found the whole experience exciting but humiliating. I like politics, but people have to do embarrassing things to get ahead in it.

October 18

Igor was sent back to Dr. Penix today, because we have no good place to keep a dog. The faculty decided that no one needs a Seeing Eye dog to get around the school.

October 25

Mr. Woolly announced in assembly that every Wednesday at the noon meal two students would eat in the faculty dining room and two teachers would eat in the student dining room. In that way, every student would have a chance to eat among sighted people at least twice a year.

November 15

I've been thinking about Uma Vasudev. She was Sister Nimi's best friend. She used to come over in Simla and play chess with me until three o'clock in the morning. How I miss her! The old days will never come back. When I get back home I'll be too big to just sit with a girl and play chess late into the night.

December 8

I was standing in the office talking to Mr. Chiles when the phone rang. On the other end was Mr.

Robinson. He said that he could only find one teacher who could give blood for Miss Harper's father. He has a bleeding ulcer and a collapsed lung. He had already had thirty-five pints of blood. Since Miss Harper's family would have to pay for the blood if they couldn't replace it, I went to Mr. Woolly and asked if we students could help out. He said we could try. Twelve of us went down to the hospital. My heart was pounding. The thought of the needle in my arm was very vivid and frightening, but I had to be brave and set a good example. The nurse said I wasn't of age but that I could give blood anyway by diplomatically lying on the form, and this I did.

George Conner went in first and came out after some time, rubbing his arm. Then Bruton went in, but he came right back out—his blood pressure was too low. Then I was called. I went in feeling brave and strong. The nurse took some blood from my finger for a test and said that my blood was fine. She gave me a jab with a needle in my arm, to deaden it, then a jab with another needle. This time, she somehow strapped the needle to my arm. It was in for fifteen minutes.

After giving blood, I felt pretty low—I didn't have my old energy. But it was wonderful to do something for Miss Harper in return for all that she has done for us.

December 10

We senators decided today to take some of the vending-stand profits and buy an electric clock for the wall behind the stand. We felt that the clock would give the stand an air of prosperity.

January 1, 1952

I finished "Walls of Jericho," by Rudolph Fisher, today. I feel critical of its plot, its style. The author overdid everything. Perhaps it is necessary for writers to overdo things so that they may impress their readers and also so that they may write a long book. Most of modern literature seems disgustingly overwritten to me. Why can't people write like Dickens or Dumas?

I feel confident that I could write a book one day—not an ordinary book but a book that would reveal my deepest personal feelings and thoughts. I could write a book about my contact with the worst of human beings and the best of human beings. As it is, my thoughts and emotions are hidden in me without an outlet. I want to push them out into the world, let them be the property of the scraps of paper they would be written on. I would let the tragedy of the world be revealed through me. But the competition in the field of writing is great.

January 2

Practically all my morning was spent in Mr. Woolly's office completing the admissions form for Columbia University. As I sat in the office, millions of thoughts entered my head. I wished I were a child again so I could dress as I pleased, go barefoot, have fights, and have no restraints, no worries about tomorrow. I feel that I became mature at too early an age. I wish I had had a long childhood. If I am ever blessed with children, I will make sure they have very long childhoods.

I came to Little Rock when I was too young. My

first days here were terrifying, and my whole first year was spent trying to win acceptance, to make my name and reputation. Somehow or other, I made Little Rock my second home. Now I may be going to Columbia, where I'll know nobody. I will have to readjust, this time to a sighted place, to a big city. I will have to establish a new home. I will have to make my name all over again. To build up a reputation takes ages and requires patience and suffering, but a reputation can be destroyed in a moment.

Sometimes I wish I had never left India, because now I must live mostly in memories, like a man with no real home in this uncertain world. I have never had better friends than my family. My heart is only with them. God knows how much longer now I will have to live without them. Yet when I was a child I longed to leave them—longed to be a grownup and to gain my position in the world.

We finished the Columbia admissions form except that I have to retype my autobiographical sketch. We must struggle to exist at all times and prepare for all kinds of sacrifices if we are to achieve our goal. That's life.

January 3

This is the worst day we've had for more than a month. It has been raining since morning. Weather like this does not help the feeling of the individual. I spent most of the day reading in bed.

I have not received any letter from home for a month and a half. Each day I think a letter will come, but there is nothing. I don't think the holidays are good for me. Perhaps I will spend all of tonight reading. What else can I turn to? I wish that I could sleep better and get a letter from home.

January 4

This morning, I went to see a Mr. Freeling, the insurance agent. I have no health insurance, and Columbia requires applicants to have some.

We had excellent meals today. But I had no appetite. This was sad, because only once in a blue moon do we get a good meal here. But I made myself eat for the sake of the people who prepared it. Oh, Mother, you simply spoiled us with good food! Has anybody ever thought what a person has to put up with when he leaves the shelter of his parents' roof?

January 5

I spent all morning washing my clothes and cleaning out my locker and broom closet in preparation for the reopening of school tomorrow. I also wrote a letter to Sister Pom. I am really worried about her pregnancy. She's already had a stillborn baby.

Mr. Chiles came back today and I told him about the five books I read this vacation—"Walls of Jericho," "Treasure Island," "Oliver Twist," "The Count of Monte Cristo," "Lone Star Ranger." I also told him that I had finished my correspondence course, so I would be graduating this year after all. He took great delight in the news. He has the ability to take genuine pleasure in other people's successes.

I'm going to listen to the news now, and then go

to bed to sleep and dream. I can't ever go to sleep without listening to the news. I'm fascinated by it.

January 6

All the students are back. Once again, I had almost forgotten how noisy it is with everyone around. Students were very indignant and stunned to learn about Billy's and Evelyn's marriage. It was the subject of talk all day.

I spent some time talking with Mr. Chiles about the world situation and so on. The world is indeed in a great turmoil.

I helped carry a piano today.

I spent most of last night reading "Damon Runyon Omnibus." Damon Runyon was a genius. Critics say that the book is very true to life. It's the most interesting and revealing book about the underworld in and around the East.

It's eight-thirty, but I can't stay awake any longer. I have a hard and difficult day at school tomorrow.

January 9

We had a great piece of news today. Miss Harper's father is completely recovered.

At two o'clock I had a visit from two ladies whom I didn't know. They wanted me to speak on Hinduism to their ladies' club on January 20th, with four other speakers from different religions of the world, including a Muslim. I didn't want to speak with a Muslim in the room, since a great part of my speech is generally about Partition and it would be undiplomatic to talk about that with him there. But the ladies wouldn't take no for an answer.

January 10

Today I got a terrible piece of news about Surinder. How could he have fallen in the blinding mist of physical desire. I have always wanted to marry an Indian girl who shared my background, my thoughts and feelings about home, who loved Indian music, Indian food, and the slow Indian way of thinking. I wouldn't want my children to be uncertain of their nationality, not know whether they're Indian or American, Hindu or Christian. Yet all along, Daddyjee has discouraged me from going back, because he says no matter what I do, my blindness will always be an obstacle to leading a full and rich life in India. Is he right? Will a nice Indian girl marry me? A blind person is often tense. He needs some feeling of security, someone to rely upon. But if Daddyjee is right, I may have to resort to an American girl whether I like it or not. Also, if I am going to become a writer I'll need someone to read to me from the world of books. I would need to marry an educated girl who could help me in my work. Oh, how I wish I were more experienced in these matters!

January 11

Today I received two letters from home. Most of my sorrow and sadness has had to do with being away from home—as a child, and now in Little Rock. When one's feelings of homesickness flare up, one loses one's good sense and starts living in a completely private world. Depression clouds the mind, and one can't share his feelings of depression with even his closest friend, because then the mansion of friendship might go up in smoke. That's why I must suppress my feelings of depression with an iron hand, for friendship is not like parents' unconditional love for their child. It depends completely on putting up a cheerful front, especially if one is a foreigner. I therefore must learn to live with these feelings of depression that constantly invade me and keep them to myself. The best man is he who, when depressed, clenches his fists and bites his tongue and doesn't so much as let out a sound. In this way, the insanity can be controlled and made temporary. Still, I am afraid that these feelings will break out one of these days and I will destroy my reputation for being a good fellow. Oh, God, sometimes I feel so angry. What did they use to say at home—that there are five stages of temper? I feel I have them all at once. The best way to check temper is to turn it against oneself. But that only feeds depression.

January 12

I have just returned from the senior class party in the gymnasium. I took my tape recorder, and because of it we had some beautiful music to roller-skate to. Norman Penix and Carol Rowe [she was eighteen and a senior] wanted to skate, but nobody wanted to help them, because they are not good in mobility. So I took it upon myself to lead them around the floor on skates. They were really appreciative and showed their gratitude. I feel so satisfied when I can help someone. Perhaps because I know that I am going to need help in my life, I get great pleasure in doing things for others.

Or maybe this is inherited. My parents are the same way.

As I sit at my desk and type these few lines, my body is tired but I feel good. I would feel better if there was someone who could have shared the joy of the party with me—someone who was dear to me.

January 13

It is Sunday morning. Everyone has gone to church and the school is quiet. I am sitting in my broom closet typing and listening to Saigal sing love songs on my tape recorder. Tears are welling up in my eyes—eyes that cannot see but can picture. I am still a child made up of very delicate material. Listening to Indian music makes me especially sad because it recalls so many memories of home—Sunday mornings sitting with Sister Nimi in the drawing room, a blazing fire hot on my face, or typing letters to schools late into the night, with a raga on the radio. The letters of rejection would come back from those schools up and down, right and left, saying that I shouldn't come out of India at such a young age because I would become maladjusted, not fit to live either in the East or the West. Perhaps those authorities were right, after all.

Today Daddyjee again presented in a letter "the real facts" of what my life would be like if I insisted on returning to India. He said that I would lose all the independence I've acquired in America, that I would never be able to go out on the street by myself. But I am ready to face anything to go home, my memories are so dear to me.

January 14

Haste thee, Nymph, and bring with thee
Jest and youthful Jollity. . . .
Hence vain deluding Joys,
The brood of Folly without father bred! . . .
Hail, divinest Melancholy!

As I listened to Miss Harper read "L'Allegro" and
"Il Penseroso" aloud in our literature class, I felt the
urge to swallow these masterpieces whole. Oh, the
admiration I feel for these poems and for good literature is beyond anyone's imagination. I have hunger for
knowledge. I wish I were widely read. I wish I could
read without bounds. Oh, God, I wish that I had eyesight, only so I could read. Reading on records is not
the same as reading with eyes—you never know how
anything is spelled or punctuated, and you can't study
anything. Reading in Braille isn't the same, either—
it's much slower than reading on records. One summer, I am going to do nothing but read.

January 18

Today I read a biography of General MacArthur in
Reader's Digest. I had conflicting feelings about him. I
think he would have gone down in history as a greater
man if he had closed his career after his inspiring and
fascinating speech to Congress. But then again, like
him, I would perhaps have stayed on and sought more
glory and more recognition. Anyway, it's clear from
his background that he's not the kind of man to quit
under heat. I admire him for his firmness.

What a great democracy America is.

January 19

Today, as I read the first few lines of "The Long, Long Trailer" in *Reader's Digest,* my heart became heavy, because they revived the memory of the dream Daddyjee had of getting a trailer and driving the whole family from India to the West. Did I ever believe that his dream would come true? Yes I did, because I wanted to believe. It doesn't take a minute for me to leave the real world and fall into dreaming, something I must have got from him.

Perhaps I will be able to realize Daddyjee's dream and go on a tour of the West in a trailer with my children. Oh, God, will you bless me with a family? Will I be able to pass what I have learned from Daddyjee to the next generation?

January 20

It was a day of glory that I will remember for the rest of my life. I gave a very good speech in front of a very big audience [at the ladies' club]. The people there were anything but poor. Yet they all seemed unhappy and desperate. It seems Americans have all the material things, but they lack the spiritual bread.

The people in the audience asked so many questions. One lady wanted to know why I didn't become a Christian. I told her that I sometimes worried about not being a Christian, but that I couldn't stop being a Hindu. I said that I looked forward to the day when people will unite under one religion and have an international government. Until then, we will have to live in terror and agony.

January 23

I spent nearly all evening taking the radio-phono-graph combination out of its cabinet, which I am going to refinish. It was a lot of fun to fool around with the electrical equipment as I used to do at home. Oh, God, if I could see, I would study engineering and electron-ics. If I could see, I would own a car, a hunting dog, and a gun. But even if I could see, I wouldn't have the money. The best policy is not to want things that one doesn't have. I hope, though, that one day I can have a car and someone to drive it. This wish is childish but very strong.

January 24

Today we had a band engagement at a P.T.A. meeting at Wrightsell Primary School in Little Rock. We played such numbers as "Rhythm in My Nursery Rhymes," "An Apple for the Teacher," and "School Days."

When I got back to school, I went to Mr. Chiles's room and borrowed some beautiful classical records from him. As I type, I am listening to them and transferring them onto my own tapes. Oh, I wish I could own all the music in the world! I wish that music were eatable! My wishes are very silly and odd. They are the result of imagination, which makes up for my lack of eye-sight.

The world is full of tension which makes people moody and pessimistic, but music provides us with a refuge. In fact, the world could not survive without it. Because of it, I can sit back in my chair, detach myself from the doings of the world, and penetrate my whole past.

For the last couple of weeks it has been awfully springlike. I have been spending as much time as I possibly can outside, admiring and enjoying the flowers. They've already started blossoming. But Arkansas has really startling reverses in weather, and everyone is predicting a bitter cold wave. That'll put an end to the flowers.

January 27

Today I ran the vending stand for three hours. Then for two hours I did office duty—answering the telephone and receiving no end of visitors to the school. I'm feeling very sleepy.

January 28

I am relaxing in my broom closet, listening to "Branded" on Lux Radio Theatre. Once, Mr. Chatterjee remarked that he had met a writer who told him that if a person could not find a new short story every time he listened to the radio for five minutes, he would never become a writer.

January 30

It is about eight-thirty in the evening, and I have just returned from a session of the Student Senate. We discussed the planning of a party for the visiting wrestling teams from two other states ten days hence. It seems all the members of the visiting teams would want girls to entertain them. But the boys here who are going with girls won't let them be hostesses. They seem to think that these girls are their property. It's hard to entertain Americans, because all they want is girls. We spent forty-five minutes talking about it, but couldn't reach any conclusions.

January 31

I spoke today for two hours in Rosedale, which is about ten miles from Little Rock. I again had the impression that Americans, in spite of their great material wealth, are not happy. They boil within themselves like atom bombs. The Korean War is making them tenser.

February 1

Today I received a letter from Sister Nimi written after she got a job and took a room in Jamshedpur. She writes about loneliness in the steel town and about our lovely days in Simla. She's facing the same problems that I did when I came to Little Rock. Then, I wrote her a letter to relieve the pain I felt. Now, she's written to me to relieve her pain.

February 2

This has been the worst day of my time at school. George Conner and Mariann Phillips and James Spakes and Peggy Stevens were expelled for trying to run off to Benton and get married. I feel so guilty that I can't write anymore.

February 5

Today I received a letter from Daddyjee. He told me that Sister Pom had had a baby girl. It pleased me no end. Since she already has a son, she wanted a daughter. Now her family is balanced.

Daddyjee enclosed a telegram from the Watumull Foundation telling him that he had won a prize of six hundred dollars for his essay on India's population problem. It was indeed heartening to learn that he had made use of his gift for writing and been rewarded for it. He also enclosed a letter from Mr. Norman Cousins. [My father had got to know Norman Cousins, the editor of the *Saturday Review,* during Cousins' visit to India, and had been sharing with him some of my more descriptive letters home.] Mr. Cousins said that he thought my experiences in America could make a book. He said he was writing about me to a friend at Houghton Mifflin, which publishes books. Mr. Cousins' letter lifted my spirits. Ever since I arrived in the States, I have been thinking of writing a book about my experiences. Here at last is someone in the field who thinks I can.

Today Miss Harper tried to teach me more English grammar. I did not know any grammar before I came to America. I don't know how I ever did without it, but I did.

February 7
We had a pep rally for the wrestling team with a snake dance today. I had to make a speech to raise the spirits of the team and my fellow-students. Since I didn't know what to say, I was quite nervous, but the right words came to me spontaneously.

February 8

I read nearly all night, with the exception of a couple of hours which I spent lying in the arms of Morpheus.

February 9

Oather, Bruton, McNabb, and I served as hosts for the visiting wrestling teams from the Oklahoma and Kentucky Schools for the Blind. I had to look after five wrestlers and make sure that they got to the dining room and got plenty to eat, got to the gymnasium and the dormitories. It was an honor for me.

All through the matches, I had to run a makeshift vending stand in the gymnasium. But I was able to work and watch and enjoy and yell all at the same time. I ruined my throat. Our school won first place in the meet by four points.

I simply fell in love with the five boys I was looking after, especially Evans. He was sixteen, in the eleventh grade, and quite childlike. I got very attached to him. Now he has left, and I probably will never see him again. I hated to see him go—to make a friend in a day and then to lose him. We didn't even decide to write to each other.

February 10

The most eventful part of the day was a few minutes ago, at eight-thirty. I turned on the radio to see what was on and heard the announcer say that we would not hear "The Sixty-Four-Dollar Question" today because of a special broadcast. The special broadcast was someone named Chambers reading a letter to his children. The letter is the foreword to his book, called "Witness," which will be published in June. The letter dealt with the Hiss case. It was a most heartbreaking letter. I have a great hunger to find out more about this case.

February 11

Today was a great day for me. Thanks to Mr. Cousins, I received a letter from the Houghton Mifflin publishing house in Boston. They want me to submit some of my works on completion. My thrills cannot be imagined. I'm a long way from a book, but this could be my great chance.

February 12

Our calendar is usually crowded with paid engagements at this time of the year, but our first band engagement in 1952 was gratis. It was at the state mental hospital, for their Valentine's Day dance. We had to accept this engagement for Tuesday—the most strenuous day of the week for many of us in the band.

We had to carry our instruments, our amplifier, and the speaker to the school bus, in the pouring rain. At the hospital, when we started tuning up, we discovered that the piano, a beat-up old thing hardly worth the name, was half a pitch lower than our instruments. The band had had the same problem with the same piano last year, and the lady in charge of social life at the hospital had promised Mr. Woolly over the telephone that the piano was now in perfect tune. The lady now offered no excuses, but told Mr. Woolly that we should go ahead and play, since mental patients couldn't tell the difference anyway. She said that they just wanted to march around to the music and get some much-needed exercise.

Mr. Woolly lost his patience and Mr. Sykes absolutely refused to play the piano.

Mr. Woolly called the school and arranged for the school bus to bring over one of the spinets from a practice room. We had heard of pianos being trucked in for great pianists, like Rubinstein, but we were just a small state-school band. We were both flattered and disgusted.

The patients became restive. They started shouting that they wanted to dance, and some of them started marching around, calling "Band! Band!" They wouldn't stop till Mr. Sykes played them a Chopin grand march. He beat it out on the out-of-tune old thing as if he were whipping a dead mule. The patients really loved it.

The engagement was to begin at seven. At eight, we were still sitting on the stage, laughing. At nine o'clock a spinet arrived from the school, and we finally settled down to play. Then Mr. Sykes discovered that the pedal had been broken during the spinet's trip to the hospital. He got down on the floor and tried to fix it, but gave it up as a hopeless job. As he stood up, he caught the seat of his trousers on a nail on the hospital bench and tore a good six-inch-long hole in them. The pity was, he had put on a brand-new tan suit for the occasion. If I had been him, I would have packed up and gone home, but he just tried to laugh it off. I marvelled at his good humor.

We got down to playing, and played for about three

hours. We played "The Cradle Song," "The Doll Dance," "After You've Gone," "Mighty Lak' a Rose." The patients really pounded their feet and clapped with excitement when we played "The Doll Dance."

During the intermission, I danced with Lois to Mr. Sykes's piano playing. I complimented her on her clarinet playing. She was really pleased. I think I like her very much.

We had to carry the instruments back to the bus in the rain. What a day!

February 13

This evening I went to the Robinson Auditorium to listen to the two world-famous pianists Babin and Vronsky. They were great. How I envied them! I wish I had had proper training from my childhood to be a great musician.

February 14

Today has been a day of fatigue and disgust. I learned that there are some people who will never admit a mistake, who will never retract what they have said, even when they know that they're in the wrong. Such is their vanity. Mr. Robinson is one of these people. He's a fine man, but he has this fault, which sticks out like a sharpened pencil point. In three years we have had three principals, and each one has been a real winner.

February 15

This morning we had to get up at six o'clock and get dressed, because we had a band engagement at the Capital Club.

Mr. Woolly told some of us at the vending stand that he'd had a letter from the superintendent of the Mississippi School for the Blind, suggesting that we expand our annual competition in wrestling to include other activities and subjects. He thought that we would all benefit from getting to know another school in this way.

Miss Howard [the kindergarten teacher] asked me to come along with her to the Moses Melody Shop to advise her on buying a tape recorder. Usually we have band practice on Friday afternoon, but some of us had got Mr. Sykes to cancel it this week so that we could listen to the funeral broadcast of George VI. I set my special clock to turn on my radio and tape recorder to record the broadcast, and went with Miss Howard to the shop and helped her out.

February 17

Most of the day I spent thinking about home. Depression so often gets the better of me, but what keeps me going is the feeling that my family is behind me.

A little while ago, I heard an announcement on the radio that today is the silver jubilee of the City Service Band of America, and they were having a jubilee musical program. As I type this, I'm listening to the wonderful music of the band and recording it. The radio and the tape recorder have become my private companions, my American family that no one knows about.

February 19

As I sit at my typewriter with seven minutes to lunch, I am in a boiling temper. I was so eager to study journalism that when Miss Harper began to teach us the subject yesterday in English class, I could have blessed her. But today, without giving us any time to learn, she gave us a test. I made seventy-six, the lowest score I've ever made. As if the test wasn't bad enough, she gave us an assignment to hunt up six interesting leads in newspapers. This is a hard task for us, since we don't have any sighted readers here to work with.

Now I've just returned from lunch. Eating cooled me down some. I make a habit of being good-tempered and jovial at meals. That's good for one's digestion. I decided that I was worked up about a little happening, when in truth what I really care about are the big political problems of the world. But I suppose that I must educate myself by analyzing little happenings before I can understand big issues.

February 20

Mr. Hartman said at the square-dance club that he didn't believe in giving to charity. I became prejudiced against him right away. When I stop to reason, I can see his point of view—that he wants everyone to work for a living—but I reacted against him. I must learn to rise above my prejudices.

February 21

I have only thirteen weeks to go to graduation. I have to learn my long part for the senior play, rehearse, and perform in it. And that is just one of a hundred things.

February 22

This morning, the band went to Mabelvale High School. As usual, the students seemed to enjoy our music. Coming back, I found the last seat in the school bus and sat by myself. I felt very homesick. My heart cried for the old memories and wanted to be back in India. I don't know why, but I felt more lonely than I think I ever have before.

February 23

It's late in the evening. I am feeling rotten. I did not sleep last night. I am suffering from a terrible case of the flu.

February 25

We once had a dormitory supervisor, a Mr. Clay. He was chronologically old, but youthful in spirit. He woke us up every morning at six-thirty, saying things like "Come on, gentlemen, curry that mule," "Tickle that tiger—don't let him get away." He came to each bed and woke us up individually—shaking, pulling, or rolling us. Some boys didn't get up till five to seven, but they made it to breakfast by seven, because they knew that Mr. Clay had the power to confine us to the school building for two weeks.

Mr. Clay was heavyset, not over five and a half feet tall, and had a confident air. All the partially sighted boys commented on how blue his eyes were. He said he was learned in history, geography, and philosophy, and he took great pleasure in telling stories about Cleopatra. Unlike most men, he knew how to handle the eternally troublemaking and changing woman. Yet as far as anyone knew, he was a bachelor. He flirted with Miss Harper, Miss Wilson [Dorothy Wilson was the typing and girls' physical-education teacher], and the girl students, and they all took delight in his cute and cunning ways. He was famous for patting every young woman teacher before leaving the faculty dining room. His favorite food was white bread with sugar on it.

February 26

I wrote my last journal entry for Miss Harper's journalism class. Miss Harper admitted that everything I said about Mr. Clay was true, but she said that I hadn't considered how students' parents would feel when they read the assignment. [All the assignments were to be printed in the *Arkansas Braille News*.] I argued, but she insisted that I had to consider how the parents would feel when they came to know that such a man worked as a supervisor at the school. She cut out all the references to girls and women teachers and made Mr. Clay sound like a very ordinary, pleasant man. So I learned today that it's not at all diplomatic to tell the truth.

February 27

This is the first year that our school has had a French class, and during it, we are learning to read very elementary French, memorizing everyday phrases and common nouns, competing in spelling games, and playing cards in French. In the class, you may see our faces redden as we tackle grammar tests, or a faraway look come into our eyes as we dream of being in Paris and visiting the beautiful, historic places we read about. Learning this language has broadened our outlook on world affairs. Perhaps the time will come when we, the students of French, can play our part in solving the world's crises, because of our better understanding of our Western neighbor. Our school is playing its little part to avoid world destruction.

March 1

Today we had contests in Braille reading, sight-saving reading, spelling, music, voice, piano, clarinet, mental math, chess, and track and field events all day. All grades competed. The idea was to select our team to go to the Mississippi School for the Blind in Jackson. Then we went and had supper, and came back to the auditorium. Mr. Woolly announced the names of the lucky winners. I wasn't successful in any contest.

March 3

As so often, I have been wondering what I wish to become, what profession I should seek. I am sure I can't succeed in music. I didn't start studying Western music when I was very small, so I have no foundation in it. My model, Mr. Chiles, was playing classical piano music when he was in ninth grade, and he didn't succeed in making a career of music. I like the thought of law. I believe I have the power to think logically. I love oratory. Law is imperative for going into politics, and I would like to become one of the greatest statesmen. But the practice of law requires memory, and I have a very poor memory. Then there is writing. I love to read and write. I love good literature. I love to criticize books. I have the imagination and possess the talent to write, I think. I would also like my views to be known widely—all over the world. I think I could succeed in this profession, in spite of the great competition. But my foundation in the English language and everything else is so poor.

I must discuss my future with my father.

March 4

I just had my report card read to me. I was thrilled. I have made the honor roll again. This means that I have been on the honor roll the entire school year. Mr. Robinson, however, continues to give me B's in geometry. I don't understand. I work awfully hard in his class, but I must be at fault. I wish I knew what my fault was so that I could correct it.

March 5

Mr. Woolly just handed us our class rings in front of the whole junior-senior high school in the auditorium. I sat there, anxious to hear who our class valedictorian and salutatorian would be. Many a time in the past months I have wondered if I would be one of the two speakers. I have done well in the last two years, except for math. But my grades in ninth grade were simply awful. That was my first year in this country. Besides, I have had to carry heavier loads so that I could finish high school in three years rather than four. Then Mr. Woolly announced that Oather Brown would be the valedictorian and I would be the salutatorian. I couldn't contain my excitement. I am extremely ambitious. I can't help it.

Mr. Woolly then announced that he had an honest-to-God writer in the auditorium and that her name was Charlie May Simon. She was widely known as a writer of books for children and was married to Arkansas's greatest poet, John Gould Fletcher.

I listened, sitting on the edge of my chair, as Miss Simon said that what a writer needed most was experience—that when she was writing a book, she sought out experience. For one book, she went to live in a houseboat on the White River with three children. She and the children would go out on the river in a small motorboat every day for the experience of watching the fishermen fish.

March 6

I sit at this typewriter in my broom closet and I imagine that I am writing a letter to all those who would like to know the reactions of one student who is going to graduate from high school within three months. The pleasure of wearing a class ring for the whole day and feeling like a senior is beyond description.

March 7

I am alarmed at the world situation. Is there going to be a stable French government? Is General de Gaulle going to become the military dictator of France? Is the United States going to continue giving foreign aid to the poor countries of the world, or is the Senate going to let politics and public relations interfere with their responsibility, and cut foreign aid? Is there going to be a United European Army? Will the Korean armistice talks result in anything? Is Eisenhower, my favorite man for President, going to be nominated and elected? And is there going to be a Third World War? All these questions are rushing around in my mind.

The answers I come up with are all grim. But I suppose the show will go on.

March 8

There were two additional contests for the Jackson, Mississippi, trip, in typing and essay writing. I took part in both and won in typing. Hallelujah!

The more I go to school parties, the more I realize that social functions help lift people's morale. But a person at a social function should not try to attract attention or be jovial at the expense of his integrity. One iota of integrity is more precious than all the king's men or all their horses.

March 12

We all got cold shots this morning. Cold shots have never helped me. But one can't be particular when one is away from home.

March 17

We are reading the works of Shakespeare in both my eleventh- and twelfth-grade English classes. His plays are simply out of this world. They are so beautiful and so philosophical. Oh, my yearning is simply to become like this great man. I know that's impossible. But if one aims one's arrow at the sky, it will at least get to the top of the trees.

March 18

Evelyn Worrell made a remark today that really got to me. We were discussing a geometry problem in the classroom before Mr. Robinson arrived when Evelyn said that she didn't want to hear what a "darky" had to say. I don't generally lose my temper—Daddyjee gave me strict training in controlling it—but today I did. I have been called a Negro before and been mistaken for a Negro once, and it didn't bother me, but I was enraged because Evelyn dismissed my opinion on the grounds that my skin is darker than hers. Evelyn is a junior. She has this attitude, after all the education she has received! More than ever I am determined to write a book one day and discuss this attitude that many Southern people seem to have.

March 19
I have only eight weeks left till graduation. Oh, how thrilling it will be to leave this school behind!

March 20
The weather outside is simply lovely. I love early spring days. Nature enthralls me. It reminds me that there is some supernatural being who created all these beautiful things.

March 21
It's my birthday. It was just like any other day except that I received letters from home wishing me many happy returns. Mother asked me in her letter, "What are you planning to do for your birthday?" The answer, of course, is "Study."

March 27
We got back tonight from Jackson, Mississippi, tired but happy. I lost the typing contest to Viva Lou

McCravy. If I had to lose to someone, I'm glad it was Viva Lou. Her voice was as sweet and original as her name. I'll write more about the adventures of us Arkansas travellers in Mississippi, but now my head is nodding over my typewriter and I must go to bed. Good night, Viva Lou, good night.

XI

OUTSIDE THE GATE

Hail to thee, O A.S.B.,
  Our heads bow down before you;
Great numbers shall thy glory see,
  For those you've known adore you.

Though we attain life's highest goal,
  As one we all agree:
We'll be, as in the days of old,
  Thy students, A.S.B.

—*The alma mater of the Arkansas School for the*
Blind.

M R. CHILES OCCASIONALLY HELD OCCUPA-
tional-guidance classes, as part of the social-
adjustment program. He would invite guest
speakers from organizations like Arkansas
Enterprises for the Blind, the Vending Stand
Program, and the Department of Vocational
Rehabilitation, and they would tell us about what a
blind high-school graduate could do in the world outside—how he could become a piano tuner or a vending-stand operator or a Dictaphone typist. As a matter
of course, I was required to attend these classes, although
I had long since decided that I would go to college,
like my older brother and older sisters and Mr. Chiles
himself. Moreover, unlike the few graduates of the school
who had gone to college, I wanted to go to a world-
famous university—assuming, for some reason, that I
had only to decide which university I wanted to go to
and I would be able to go there. Mr. Woolly and the
faculty shared this rosy assumption. As they saw it,
ours was one of the best schools of the kind in the
country and I was one of its star pupils. Also, I was a
much written-about personality in Little Rock. They
thought that any university would be proud to have me.

Daddyji suggested that I go to Harvard, Yale, or
Princeton, which he called "the triple towers of American university education." But I ruled out Yale and
Princeton because I somehow got the impression that
the one was a nest of lawyers and the other a second-
class Oxford. I settled on Harvard, and told Mr. Woolly
that that was where I would be going.

"Then I'd better write and let them know," he
said.

One day in March, 1951, Mr. Woolly called me to his office and read me the reply he had received from Richard M. Gummere, the chairman of the Committee on Admission at Harvard:

DEAR MR. WOOLLY:

In the case of a young man who is blind, it is our regular custom here in the Admission Office to refer all the details of the case for study to our Hygiene Department. We have found that on account of differing degrees of blindness, the problems of getting around from one hall to another in a city, and the matter of dormitories and other such things, it calls for very intensive study ahead of time. We feel that the case of a boy who cannot afford to have someone pretty close to him as a guide a good deal of the time makes it more difficult for the blind boy to get along here with the conditions mentioned above. If you could enlighten us a little further on the degree of blindness and any other such details about the young man, I will be very glad to give the matter my attention.

I repeat that we are very glad to discuss the matter with you since we want to help boys who are able to deal with this handicap in our College, but we have very few because we are not like a small college campus where everything is nearby and within a certain circle and very accessible.

Mr. Gummere's letter depressed and puzzled both Mr. Woolly and me; Mr. Gummere seemed to have no idea that there were totally blind people who could get around by themselves—as Oather and I did, for instance. Yet Harvard was on the doorstep of Perkins, an institution for the blind without an equal in America.

"Boy, you can get around Little Rock and North Little Rock and you've travelled outside the state by yourself—Harvard isn't going to present you with any problem," Mr. Woolly said. "But maybe you should go to Hendrix, after all. People there know the capabilities of our blind youngsters. After all, Mr. Chiles went there."

But I had set my heart on getting the best education I could. Anyway, the more I thought about Mr. Gummere's letter, the more I came to think of it as a challenge to me to educate the Harvard authorities on our "capabilities," and I now said as much to Mr. Woolly.

"Well, then, we'll keep at Harvard," Mr. Woolly said. "I'm sure that's what your dad wants for you."

In due course, he wrote to Mr. Gummere, saying this about me, in part:

He has no vision, having lost it at the age of four. However, he travels very well, having made the trip from New Delhi without an aide. Also, he has traveled a good deal over the U.S.A. In fact, he travels as well as any blind person I know.

In order to buttress my credentials, Mr. Woolly gave Mr. Gummere a list of all the courses I had taken and would be taking before I graduated, and told him that if he thought I needed additional courses for Harvard I was prepared to take them through the Hadley Correspondence School for the Blind, in Winnetka, Illinois.

In the meantime, at Mr. Gummere's suggestion I got in touch with Mr. A. Howard Stebbins, Jr., an alumnus of Harvard who lived in Little Rock and often interviewed candidates for admission to the university. Mr. Gummere had said that the admissions committee set great store by his evaluation. I remember that I telephoned him for an appointment, got dressed in my dress trousers and my only jacket—a sort of nylon windbreaker—and went alone to see him. I thought that if I walked into his house without a cane, and without stumbling and bumping into things, he would at least be able to tell the Harvard admissions committee that I got around without any difficulty. I remember walking through his door, shaking his hand, and finding a chair unassisted, but the rest of the interview is a complete blank. It is one of the few episodes in my life over which memory has pulled down an impenetrable blind.

❧

IN addition to calling on Mr. Stebbins, I asked for a letter of recommendation from Lieutenant Colonel Dr. George M. Leiby, a surgeon serving at Moody Air Force Base, in Georgia. Dr. Leiby had met Daddyji during a visit to India in connection with the Indian government's attempts to control venereal disease; subsequently, he had spent a few hours with me in Little Rock on his way to a medical conference in Hot Springs. He was the most important person I knew in the country and was just the kind of man I was sure had gone to Harvard, although I was too shy to quiz him about it. (Actually, he hadn't.) He sent me a copy of a letter he had written to Harvard on June 21st:

DEAR SIR:

I am acquainted with the problems Ved has had to solve since his early childhood, and have been intimately acquainted with his family for the past two years. This young man's blindness . . . did not prevent him from riding a bicycle and leading a full life. He has quickly learned the environment in which he lives, and does not depend upon such physical aids as canes and Seeing-Eye dogs. . . .

One is impressed with the excellent scholarship record Ved has accomplished at school. In addition to his activities as a student, he has organized a student government, of which he is president. . . . Ved has a fine personality, a high moral character, excellent judgment, and is exceedingly tolerant in his thinking. It is indeed a privilege to be able to recommend Ved Mehta to the Committee of Admissions for consideration to be accepted as a student at Harvard University.

I didn't like reading about myself, and I remember wanting to correct certain impressions that Dr. Leiby's letter gave, such as that I had organized our student government. But I naïvely thought that the letter alone might swing the authorities at Harvard in my favor. Dr. Leiby got only a polite response from Harvard, however. Undeterred, I went to the lengths of filing a complicated application. Although I did not get a formal rejection letter from the university, in the end I was forced to conclude that the Harvard admissions committee was like the Great Wall of China, and there was no way I could scale it.

❧

LIKE all officials of the Indian government, Dad-dyji had faced mandatory retirement at age fifty-five. Although he had been given a year's extension—something that the government granted to officials it regarded as "indispensable"—by the summer of 1951 he was out of a job. Since he and the family had to leave his government accommodations, they moved in temporarily with some relatives, and Daddyji converted most of his modest government pension into ready cash, so that he could use the money to build a little house for the family. He had already bought a little plot of land in a refugee colony in New Delhi, with money that the government had paid him in compensation for our house lost to Pakistan. (All refugees who had lost property in the Partition were given ten per cent of its value by the government.) Daddyji's total resources at his retirement were barely eighty thousand rupees, or sixteen thousand dollars, and in addition to having to build a house, as Sister Pom wrote to me, he still had to support four dependent children: my brother Om, who was twenty and had just started a four-year marine-engineering course; my sister Usha, who was fourteen; my brother Ashok, who was seven; and, of course, me. Sister Nimi, who was twenty-three and had just got a job, was technically self-supporting, but, as Sister Pom pointed out, Daddyji would have the expense of providing a dowry and putting on a wedding for her one day. As it was, after his losses in the Partition he had already had to marry off Sister Umi.

Almost from the day I reached America, Daddyji had had the idea that, like other students in the West, I could perhaps "learn and earn." "In the West, there is no stigma attached to work," he had said. "Unlike us, people there attach a dignity to labor." We couldn't think of any work I could do, however, so he had come up with the idea of our carrying on a little trade in Indian hand-carved ivory pieces, imagining that there would be a great demand for them in Machine Age America. The plan was that he would buy the "curios," as he called them, in the local bazaars for a few rupees and I would sell them for thirty or forty times that in Arkansas. Neither of us stopped to ask how he could hope to buy enough curios from the shelves of local bazaars, how he would get them to me, what customs would say about them, or how much money we could really hope to net. Neither of us had any notion of how things were supplied and marketed. Anyway, practical questions seldom intruded on our dreams.

When the dozen ivory curios I brought along with me to America in order to test the waters were stolen from my bag en route, Daddyji replaced them with three sets of ivory "no-evil" monkeys, four elephants, an oxcart, and a few other such pieces, sending them over with an American friend. For nearly two years now, I had been trying to find some way of selling them. Once, I went with Mr. Woolly to a flower-and-gift shop, and we showed them to its owner. He admired them but turned them down as "too exotic." So they were redeposited in the school's safe, and remained there, in their cotton-wool and Indian-newspaper wrappings. I took them out only a couple of times, when I wanted to choose a piece to give someone as a special present. Now and again, I would mention them to Mr. Woolly, but he seemed embarrassed by the whole subject, possibly because he didn't know any more about business than Daddyji and I did.

Now that Daddyji was retired, however, the need to "learn and earn" seemed urgent. One Saturday when Mr. Woolly had gone to Florida for some meetings, I got Mrs. Hankins to take the curios out of the safe. I put them in a paper bag and set off for the trolley and downtown.

I went to Pfeifer's department store and talked my way into the office of the manager, a Mr. Strouse. I tried to get him to look at the ivory curios, but he showed me the door, saying grandly, "Pfeifer's does not buy goods from customers."

Then I went along to M. M. Cohn's, the other department store. I had no more luck there; the assistant manager said that the demand in America was all for glass knicknacks.

I gave up hope, but one day not long afterward Joe and Jean Red took me to a restaurant on the highway to Hot Springs. As I was telling them about my experiences at Pfeifer's and M. M. Cohn's, Jean said she had noticed a sign for a gift shop attached to the restaurant, and suggested that I try my salesmanship there. "This is a nationally famous restaurant," she said. "A lot of tourists stop here on their way to Hot Springs."

Jean accompanied me to the gift shop, and I spoke

to its owner-manager, Mrs. Adkins. "I have some very special handmade ivory pieces from India," I said, talking as I imagined good salesmen did. "I have a curio with a wooden base and three good-sized monkeys sitting on it. One has his fingers in his ears, the second has his finger pressed to his lips, the third has his hands over his eyes. I have a stock of three of them."

"It sounds a little delicate," she said. "We get a lot of handling here—and by children, too."

"The curios are not at all delicate," I said, telling a diplomatic lie.

Mrs. Adkins finally agreed to look the curios over.

The next day, the Reds drove me out to the gift shop with the curios. Mrs. Adkins cooed over the trunks of the elephants, the hands of the "no-evil" monkeys, the filigree work on the oxcart. She promised to give them a splendid display and sell them at her usual commission, of forty per cent.

"What price will you charge for them?" I asked, trying to contain my excitement.

She thought a moment, and marked the oxcart at twelve dollars, the monkeys at nine dollars each, the elephants at five dollars each.

I calculated that Daddyji and I would net more than thirty dollars, but the pieces sat in her shop for several months and she didn't manage to sell one. In the meantime, my concern about how I would stay on in America—how Daddji would pay for my college education—mounted with each passing day. Whenever I wrote to him and asked about this, his reply invariably was that my education was his responsibility, that I shouldn't worry, that something would turn up. But his vague optimism only increased my anxiety.

❧

EVEN before I began to lose heart about Harvard, I had turned my energies to getting admitted to Columbia—mostly at the urging of Daddyji, who on second thought, preferred it to Harvard, Yale, or Princeton, on the ground that New York was the commercial center of the country and so the best place to make contacts for my future. I wrote to Columbia and received a fifteen-page application form. It took some time to complete it, because I had to write a longish autobiographical sketch and get five letters of recommendation. Almost before I had recovered from that, I received a ten-page financial-aid form, followed by another form for foreign students. To strengthen my application, Daddyji appealed to Professor M. S. Sundaram, first secretary in the Indian Embassy's Education Department. He was sympathetic, saying that the Indian government would like to help me, since I was the only blind Indian student in America, and he undertook to write to an acquaintance, Mr. Lawrence H. Chamberlain, who worked in the admissions office at Columbia. Daddyji also got Norman Cousins, who had attended Columbia Teachers College, to write a letter of recommendation for me.

The Columbia application process took several months. Finally, Mr. Woolly, who had entered into correspondence with the university, received a letter, dated Febrary 21, 1952, from Mr. Bernard P. Ireland, assistant director of the Office of University Admissions, which read, in part, "You will understand, too, I feel sure, that Mr. Mehta's handicap raises a serious question about whether we shall be able to serve him here. However, we do occasionally admit a blind boy if the total evidence indicates that he is very strongly qualified to cope with the kind of program we offer." As part of that "total evidence," Mr. Ireland said, I would be required to take the College Board tests, which consisted of the Scholastic Aptitude Test and Achievement Tests in English Composition and two electives. He directed us to get in touch with the Educational Testing Service, in Princeton, to make the necessary arrangements.

I immediately wrote off to the Testing Service, and received this reply:

EDUCATIONAL TESTING SERVICE
20 NASSAU STREET
PRINCETON, NEW JERSEY

FEBRUARY 27, 1952

Mr. Ved Mehta
Arkansas School for the Blind
2600 W. Markham—Box 668
Little Rock, Arkansas

DEAR MR. MEHTA:

In reply to your recent letter I am enclosing blank form of application and Bulletin of Information for the March 15 College Board tests. . . .

I should perhaps add that it is unusual for blind students to offer College Board tests [for university admission], since these are timed examinations and no extra time is allowed. In the mathematical section of the Scholastic Aptitude Test diagrams and graphs are included.

We have prepared a Braille edition of the Scholastic Aptitude Test as well as a Clear Type edition (for partially blind students), which we should be glad to have your school administer to you. . . .

None of the achievement tests of the Board are in Braille.

Sincerely yours,

Justine N. Taylor

(Mrs. William V. Taylor)

Executive Secretary to the Director
of Test Administration

The Testing Service authorities later decided to administer the tests to me at Little Rock Senior High School on March 15th, when forty sighted students were scheduled to take them there. Some special provisions were made for me, however, which Mrs. Taylor set out for Mr. Woolly in these terms:

We are asking our supervisor in charge of the tests at the Senior High School, Little Rock, to appoint a proctor to administer the tests to Mr. Mehta. It will be the responsibility of [your] school to supply the amanuenses. No additional time will be allowed but the candidate may use a typewriter if he plans to offer the English Composition test.

ON the morning of the appointed day, when I arrived at the high school with Miss Harper, who was to serve as my amanuensis, I was full of trepidation but also of self-assurance. The prospect of taking the day-long College Board tests was alarming; still, it never crossed my mind that I would do badly, since I felt confident that I was as good as the sighted students trooping in for the tests.

The proctor gave Miss Harper an envelope and led us into a little side room, saying that it was nine o'clock and we had better get going.

"But there is no Braille copy of the Scholastic Aptitude Test!" Miss Harper cried, ripping open the envelope.

"I don't know about that," the proctor said, turning to leave, "But this is a timed examination. You'd better get going."

"But there are some very complicated diagrams and graphs here," Miss Harper objected, rapidly turning pages. "I can't possibly describe them to him."

"I don't know about that," the proctor said, almost out of the room. "But since he's registered and has now received the tests, he'll be marked whether he does them or not." The proctor left, locking the door behind him.

"The testing service promised a Braille copy, Miss Harper—this is so unfair!" I cried, trying to control the rage mounting inside me. I wanted to call Mr. Woolly, call Mrs. Taylor, call Mr. Ireland, and complain and shout.

"I know," Miss Harper said. "But we don't want you to fail because you didn't try. We had better get started."

The first test I had to take was the three-hour-long Scholastic Aptitude Test, and its first section was mathematical. It seemed to be full of diagrams, graphs, charts, and maps—for want of a better collective term, figures. Sometimes Miss Harper would take my finger and trace it over the figure on the cold piece of paper; sometimes she would trace it on my hand with her finger or the point of a pencil, pausing at a bisecting line or a side of a rectangle, at an angle or a corner to tell me how it was marked—in degrees or inches, in combinations of letters and numbers. I had to build a figure in my mind from everything that Miss Harper was showing and telling me. I got so rattled that I began to doubt whether any of my mental images corresponded to the actual figures, and began flubbing even questions to which I knew the answers. I remember that at one point there was a question with a map. I was sure I knew the answer, but somehow, with Miss Harper guiding my finger over an ordinary sheet of paper, without differentiation between the mountains and the sea, between plains and lakes, as on our Braille maps at school, I suddenly couldn't make head or tail of the map in the question. And it seemed that as soon as Miss Harper had shown me one figure and I had tried to visualize it and answer a question about it there was another, more difficult figure. Sometimes, when there was a group of connected figures with intersecting lines, I wasn't sure whether, for instance, a particular triangle in the group was isosceles or equilateral or a particular shape was a trapezoid or a pentagon. And then there were mathematical theorems to be proved and algebraic calculations to be done—all in my head. (There was no way I could have used Braille to work them out; the system simply doesn't lend itself to that.)

I kept on looking at my Braille watch and asking Miss Harper to go over the questions again. I realized that questions that should have taken me a minute to answer were taking me three or four times as long, but the more I tried to hurry, the more bogged down I seemed to get. I felt dizzy. It seemed that I couldn't concentrate, that I'd lost my ability to manipulate numbers and variables mentally, that my mind was a sieve. If someone had put my head in a vise and slowly started tightening it—its serrated lips digging into my skull—I couldn't have been more frightened or frantic.

Even the verbal section of the Aptitude Test seemed to be beyond me. "Agricultural implements were discovered . . . Choice 1 . . . Choice 2 . . . Choice 3 . . . Choice 4 . . . Choice 5 . . ." Miss Harper read evenly, expressionlessly, not giving so much as a hint, by a pause, of what she might think was the correct choice. I couldn't recall what an "implement" was. *Implement, implement,* I thought. I know what that is. I've heard the word somewhere—but where? I started to sweat.

"Do you want me to go over it again?"

"Yes, please." It was like trying to climb a pole covered with thick bicycle grease. I would start up it only to slip right back down. Three's a lucky number, I thought, and said, "Choice Three."

"Three," Miss Harper said, her pencil making a little scratch.

I would get Miss Harper to mark one choice, then change my mind and get her to mark another choice, and, when I was on the next question, ask her to go back so that I could change my answer yet again. And that would be only one question down, with dozens, scores, perhaps hundreds to go.

"True or false? . . . Blank 1 . . . Blank 2 . . . Blank 3 . . . Blank 4 . . ." I felt that my head was being squeezed by that tightening vise to the size of a skull on a headhunter's necklace.

The proctor unlocked the room and announced, "It's twelve o'clock." He swept up the half-finished Aptitude Test in the middle of the question that Miss Harper was reading to me. "Y'all have an hour off for lunch," he said.

As we came out of the room, Miss Harper whistled under her breath. "I'm a college graduate and I can see," she said, "and I couldn't have done many of those questions."

"But do you think I got some of them right?" I asked, trying to master myself—I was trembling all over.

A man joined us. He clapped me on the shoulder, almost making me fall. "You know, there's a trick to these tests," he said. "Like I tell the kids I teach, don't have second thoughts and change your answers, or the examination folks will sweep the floor with you—that they will." He laughed, making my heart sink even lower, if possible, than before.

Miss Harper began protesting about the missing Braille copy.

"I'm just an examination supervisor," the man said. "But I seem to remember that we had a blind fellow who came here and took the tests some years ago. He got a Braille copy, all right, but the dots were so worn down that he couldn't read much of it. The folks at Princeton must have decided that the copy wouldn't do you any good, so they just spared themselves the trouble of mailing it down here."

We were back in the locked room. We began doing the hour-long Achievement Test in English Composition. Part of it consisted of closely reasoned passages to test reading comprehension. I felt somewhat at a disadvantage, because I couldn't refer back to a word or a phrase by its place on the page. Instead, I had to get Miss Harper to read the whole wretched passage again. Similarly, another part of the test required rearranging scrambled sentences and clauses in a paragraph to make sense of it. Since I couldn't refer to all the bits and pieces on the page, I had to rearrange them mentally and then explain to Miss Harper how to mark them on the paper. Still another part of the test called for composing a little essay. I had brought along my typewriter for the purpose, and was able to type out the essay faster than I could have dictated it. Still, when I lost the thread of a thought, as I did on several occasions, there was no time to get Miss Harper to read back to me what I'd typed.

The composition test was followed by the Achievement Test in French. The French I had learned at the school was so rudimentary that I would not have offered it as one of my two electives if Columbia had not required proficiency in a second European language. I had learned French words less by their sound than by their configuration on a page of Braille, and this meant that sometimes the only way I could get the question was to ask Miss Harper to spell out the entire French sentence. I am an imbecile, I thought. Lower than an imbecile—an idiot.

My second elective was American history, and I went through the test on that rapidly. In fact, I got the impression that I gave the best part of my bad performance on it.

When we got back to school, Miss Harper and I told Mr. Woolly what had happened.

"Hell's bells!" Mr. Woolly exclaimed. "People at the Educational Testing Service will throw out the scores—we'll make sure they know they failed us. The people at Columbia won't bother about the scores even if they get them. They know that they'll be lucky to get you."

Mr. Woolly and I immediately wrote to the Testing Service and to Columbia, telling them the whole story, but their replies were far from reassuring; the Testing Service informed us, without any apology, that, just as the examination supervisor had surmised, its Braille copies of the Aptitude Test were too worn down to have done me any good, and that other blind students had managed without them. We objected. But the Testing Service stood by its method of testing me and—in accordance with its practice at the time—forwarded the scores to Columbia. Without disclosing them to the school or me.

I remember feeling in the aftermath of the tests that even if I had had good Braille copies of all the tests and had been given all the time in the world to complete them I might not have done much better. Anyway, because of my own sense of inadequacy I endowed the Testing Service with mysterious, almost supernatural powers of infallibly evaluating the intelligence of students. I felt that the Testing Service had exposed, as nothing before had, the big holes in my formal education, which everyone at school thought had been filled up with learning—that it had exposed, perhaps, the poor quality of my Arkansas education. I thought that I might have excelled at the school precisely because its standards fell short of those of Columbia and Harvard, the Testing Service and Perkins, and even, possibly, Little Rock Senior High School. During my three years at the school, I had often been depressed and anxious, but the depression that gripped me immediately after the College Board tests was different. It affected not only my sleep and appetite but also my voice and step. Even raising my hand to comb my hair was an effort. The simplest tasks, the simplest motions seemed to weigh me down, as if I were a coolie laboring up a mountain with a thousand pounds of someone else's luggage on my head.

What I remember even more vividly than the experience of taking the tests is dreaming about them. Sometimes the examiner was a dog, sometimes a bully from my childhood, and sometimes a Muslim village priest from my father's childhood who used to accept as donations little boys with impecunious parents and fit them with iron skullcaps, so that they would grow up with the heads and brains of children and walk around the village mindlessly giggling and begging alms for the mosque. The examiner, in whatever guise, would shout, "True or false?"

During this period, no one around me knew or

guessed what I was feeling, and the astonishing thing was that a few days after taking the tests I myself half forgot them. I bounced back, carrying on with my normal school life, which I had never really left off, and feeling like a mythical creature in a book. The more this creature was beaten up, thrown on the ground, jumped on, danced on, the more quickly it sprang up, as if the point of life were resilience in adversity.

ALMOST as soon as the Christmas vacation was over, our senior year had become a series of public rituals— or preparations for them—that had little to do with our studies, and even less to do with what awaited us on the other side of graduation. There was, for instance, the senior play. Miss Wilson, who was in charge of putting it on that year, picked "Bolts and Nuts," by Jay Tobias. One January day, she assembled the seven of us seniors in the auditorium, along with boys and girls from the other classes in the junior-senior high school who were to have parts in the play, and told us that it was set somewhere in Missouri and concerned a private sanitarium full of crazies—people who had cat phobias, contamination phobias, claustrophobias, and phobias about people with phobias.

"Miss Wilson, you want to expose our school as a crazy house?" Oather asked.

"Now, Oather Brown, would I do a thing like that?" Miss Wilson asked disingenuously, and continued, "But I know exactly which one of you is going to play which crazy."

Everyone protested that we weren't crazy. Miss Wilson laughed, and ran down the list of characters in the order of their appearance and told us whom she had chosen for which part. Carol Rowe was to play Benita Bolt, a niece of the manager of the Bolt Sanitarium for Mental Hygiene; Lois Woodward was to play Lutie Spinks, a flirtatious maid; Anna Belle Morris was to play Rebecca Bolt, the manager of the sanitarium; Barbara Worthen was to play Martha Grubb, a melancholiac cook; Max Cary was to play Twink Starr, Benita's megalomaniac fiancé; Oather Brown was to play Dr. Hippocrates Joy, a psychiatrist; Kenneth Harrison (he was seventeen and in the tenth grade) was to play Henry Goober, a porter with a phobia about lunatics; I was to play Phineas Plunkett, a lawyer with a humility complex; Pegie Johnson (she was sixteen and in the ninth grade) was to play Miss Prunella Figg, a claustrophobic patient; George McNabb was to play Cadwalleder Clippy, a patient who had a cat phobia; Joyce Boyle was to play Mrs. Gertie Glossop, a patient with a contamination phobia; Kenneth Bruton was to play William Glossop, her darling child; and Norman Penix was to play Jack Gordon, a young interne.

Since Braille transcription was very time-consuming and, in that period, couldn't be mechanically duplicated, it took us several days to put into Braille one complete script and copies of our individual lines. Since we could refer to the complete script only by turns, it was some time before we understood exactly what was going on in the play or how our parts fitted together. Then everyone seemed to have a quarrel with Miss Wilson over the part he or she had been chosen for. Lois said she couldn't wink and therefore couldn't play the flirtatious maid. I protested against being cast as the oily lawyer. But Miss Wilson was stubborn and unyielding. "I'm your teacher," she said. "You just have to do what I tell you, or we won't have a senior play."

I remember that we performed "Bolts and Nuts" on the first two evenings in May, playing each time to a full house of students, parents, patrons, trustees, and friends of the school, but even from a distance of decades the memory of the experience is excruciating. The puns we had to deliver seemed painfully silly, Lois and Anna Belle forgot their lines several times and had to be prompted in a loud stage whisper by Miss Wilson, and Norman Penix had to be practically led around the stage. Once, I was late appearing onstage because I couldn't change costumes fast enough. On top of it all, the play, with all its crazy characters, often sounded like our locker-room carryings on, recklessly put on the stage for everyone to laugh at.

❧

ONE day, we seniors all met in Mr. Chiles's classroom and talked out our Class History, our Class Will, and our Class Prophecy, sparking ideas off each other as if our words were steel and flint. The documents were slated for publication in the *Arkansas Braille News,* and I was the scribe, taking notes in Braille and reading them back to my classmates before typing out the copy for Miss Harper to get ready for the printer. Reading these effusions today makes me squirm, but back then we all agreed with what Oather said to me at the end of the session: "Whip, we hit every last nail on the head!"

CLASS HISTORY

Way back in 1939,
A new school was built for the blind,
And as the first term did commence,
Some bright young pupils entered thence.

There was George McNabb, only but a
   chap,
And sweet and timid Anna Belle, fresh
   from her mother's lap.
To add to this distinguished crew,
   There was Brown, Bruton too. . . .

On into sensational seniorship we did
   glide,
Blowing loud and bursting with pride. . . .

About this time, with sheepish grin,
The pride of the Orient came sneaking in.
He ascended from the below—
Either he left, or they made him go [a
reference to my skipping eleventh grade].

Some more misfortune befell us somehow,
For the north winds blew in Carol Lynn
   Rowe.
She drifted in like Iowa snow,
And set poor Norman's heart aglow.

CLASS WILL

The senior class of 1952, in its last will and testament, which has been duly signed, witnessed, and probated, do bequeath to the following:

Oather Brown wills to Bruce Wing his love for candy and girls. To Johnnie Bill Cole, his wrestling tights, in the hope he will fill them well. To Mr. Chiles, his guitar playing ability, and all the boys who have borrowed his hair oil and shoe polish do not have to pay them back. . . .

Ved Mehta bequeaths one windowless storeroom to Mr. Hartman for his use in the daring exploration of photography. It is his due warning that Mr. Hartman keep the rats chased out so they won't be annoying him. . . . To Kenneth Harrison, Ved leaves one bushel full of fifty-seven and one-half pounds of contempt for geometry. . . .

Norman Penix bequeaths his world history book to Mr. Chiles, who seems to be interested in that subject. He leaves his geometry book to anyone who wants it, provided the person has no natural tendency toward insanity.

CLASS PROPHECY

The scene is a wrestling arena in a large city in the year 1957. . . .

Two men enter the arena and sprint down the aisle between the cheering masses. . . . One man's name is Cutie Ken [Bruton]. . . . The other man's name is Unnormal Norman [Penix]. . . . The tall helper [Penix] then proceeds to give Cutie a brisk rubdown. He performs this rubbing with such skill one can tell he is well into his sophomore year at the Carver School of Chiropractics in Oklahoma City. . . .

As time draws near for the match to start, a young announcer at ringside [me] is getting his equipment in shape. To his right, he has two tape recorders, one loud speaker, and one amplifier. To his left, he has two Braille writers, one typewriter, one microphone, three letters to be read, four passports, two college entrance exams, five insurance policies, one plane ticket, a folder of senate activities, and a Coca-Cola. As he gets his gear in shape, a young piano-tuning politician [Oather] comes into sight. He is smoking his pipe full of Bull Durham, as usual.

The young announcer stops him for an interview. "Mr. Brown, what do you plan to do if you are elected mayor of Prattsville?"

The politician speaks, after several deep puffs on his pipe. "Well, lad, when I am elected mayor of Prattsville, I plan to have the city tune every piano in town—me doing the tuning, of course. You may quote me, lad."

ONE May evening, after supper, there was a baccalaureate service for us seniors in the auditorium, with the whole school present. The tenor of the service was lofty, as if we seniors were denizens of some great academy about to leave it forever. A sombre, mysterious piece was played by Carol Rowe on the school's organ, after which we all stood up and sang "Come, Thou Almighty King." The Reverend Dr. R. D. Adams, pastor of the First Presbyterian Church in Little Rock, gave a sonorous invocation, and while we remained standing the choir sang "Goin' Home," whose melody Dvořák used in his "New World" Symphony.

We sat down, and Dr. Adams delivered a sermon based on the parable of the feast to which the poor, the maimed, the halt, and the blind were invited. He commended to the Lord's care each of us graduating seniors—citing by name Oather Brown and George McNabb, Kenneth Bruton and Norman Penix, Carol Rowe and Anna Belle Morris, and me—as we stepped into the new, treacherous world outside the gates. Then we all stood up, and Dr. Adams led us in singing "Onward, Christian Soldiers." The hymn had never sounded more powerful and rousing to my ear, perhaps because the smallest child in the auditorium knew its words and tune, and all present threw themselves into its spirit.

Dr. Adams closed the service with a benediction thanking the school authorities for having brought the seven of us so far forward into the light.

WE were now in the middle of May, with only a week to go until graduation. Still there wasn't any definite word from Columbia. The tests, I thought—the tests have done me in. Yet the one or two letters we got back from Columbia in answer to our inquiries had seemed friendly. I would fret and console myself, only to fret again. Once I graduate, I will have to get out of the school, I thought. There won't be Mr. Woolly to turn to. Where will I go? What will I do? I don't even know exactly where and how I will spend the summer. I planned to go to Los Angeles soon after graduation in order to see Daddyji, who, a year or so after his retirement, had managed to get himself across to America as a Fulbright visiting professor at the U.C.L.A. Medical School. But the Fulbright people had paid only his passage; he was not earning anything, so there was no telling how long he could stay on in the country and I could stay with him. Besides, just being in Los Angeles doing nothing all day, having no definite college plans, was frightening. "The time for my graduation is growing closer," I had written to Daddyji in one of my many anxious letters. "I would like to be sure of my future. Nobody can be sure of the future itself. However, there could be some planning about it." There was the old worry: If Columbia did accept me, how would I pay for my education there? And the new worry: If I did get into Columbia and managed somehow to pay my way, would I have as much trouble settling there as people there said I would? It does take time for a blind person to settle in a new place, I would think. I have never been on a college campus. I have no idea what campuses are like—whether they are housed in one gigantic building or consist of many little buildings. I wrote to Sister Nimi:

I think of the life that's ahead of me. I have to go to college, where a new era of my life will start, where I will have to build a third home, where everything will be entirely new and on a much larger scale. All these thoughts create nightmares.

At my urging, Mr. Woolly wrote this letter to Columbia's admissions office in May 16th:

GENTLEMEN:

Some months ago I made application for admission to Columbia College for Ved Mehta, a blind Indian youth who will graduate from high school next week.

To date, he has not been advised as to whether he will be accepted. Since he is most anxious to attend a University in the United States, he would appreciate some word as to the possibilities, so as to know whether to make application to some other University.

Sincerely yours,

J. M. Woolly, Superintendent

I finally received this letter from Columbia:

May 20, 1952

DEAR MR. MEHTA:

We have now received your College Board scores, and I am sorry to report that it is our judgment that they are not of sufficiently good quality to indicate that you could be expected to do good work in the kind of program offered here. In view of this fact and the keenly competitive situation with which we have to deal, we have decided that we cannot admit you. Perhaps I should add that we have tried, in coming to this decision, to give appropriate weight to the special handicap under which you are laboring.

We sincerely regret the necessity of disappointing you.

Very truly yours,

Bernard P. Ireland

Assistant Director

I was crushed, but I immediately wrote to Mr. Ireland begging to be allowed to repeat the College Board tests and pleading for reconsideration of my application. Mr. Woolly wrote to him on my behalf. At the same time, he fired off letters to friends of Daddyji and friends of the school asking for their help. On May 29th, he wrote to Mr. Sundaram:

Columbia Admissions Officer Mr. Bernard P. Ireland has just informed me that Ved Mehta will not be admitted because his College Board scores do not seem to be adequate.

I am wondering if you could look into the situation to see if anything can be done for Ved.

You must be assured that Ved does have the mental ability to do satisfactory, if not outstanding, work at Columbia. The scores from the College Board are probably not too valid, in my estimation, since none were in Braille and thus all of them were read to Ved. No additional time was given him and he had only a week to prepare for them, since we were informed he must take the tests very shortly before the scheduled date.

I am enclosing a copy of his transcript which indicates the quality of his work. Our teachers are among the best qualified people and they feel he is adequately prepared to make a success there.

If you feel you can give him any help we will appreciate it very much.

And Mr. Woolly wrote in a similar vein to Norman Cousins and to Miss Georgie Lee Abel, an educational consultant for the American Foundation for the Blind, in New York.

Everyone at school who came to know of my rejection was unnerved by it. As for me, I remember that I was not at all comforted by the justifications, alibis, excuses offered by everyone around me or by the ones I could think up for myself. Still, I persevered in trying to get the Columbia decision reversed.

Finally, I received this letter, dated June 6th, over the signature of Bernard Ireland:

DEAR MR. MEHTA:

It is my understanding that friends of yours have raised a question about the possibility of our reconsidering your application for admission to Columbia College because you contend that the circumstances under which you took the College Board Examinations were not adapted to offsetting the obvious disadvantages imposed by your blindness. I understand also that you have asked about the possibility and desirability of your retaking these Examinations.

I have discussed the whole problem in careful detail with the authorities of the College Entrance Examination Board and it is their opinion that there are no forms of these Examinations available which would cast additional light on the probability of your success in Columbia College. If your request is to be reconsidered, therefore, it must be on the basis of the evidence now at hand. While I cannot encourage you to expect a reversal of the action already taken, I shall be glad to resubmit the matter to the Committee on Admissions if you care to write to me requesting that I do so and stating in careful detail why you believe you encountered more difficulty in making good scores on the Examinations than has been encountered by other blind boys who have taken these tests with more successful results.

I did what Mr. Ireland asked me to do, but as I enumerated all the extenuating circumstances for him it didn't occur to me to mention that my cultural background was so different from that of the Americans taking the tests that even if all the circumstances had been ideal I probably could not have done well.

❦

IT was the evening of our commencement exercises. The seven of us graduating seniors, wearing whatever dress clothes we had, were seated on folding chairs near the lectern on the small stage of the auditorium. The stage curtain was closed, as if we were actors waiting for our play to begin. On the other side of the curtain, seats were audibly filling up.

"I wish I wasn't graduating," Bruton said. "I can't imagine life without the school to come back to in September."

"One of the blind organizations is sure to find you a good vending stand," McNabb said. "You can't stay at the school forever."

"Mr. Chiles has done a good job of staying on here," Bruton said.

"Why do you fellows sound so solemn?" Oather asked Bruton and McNabb. "I've been looking forward to this day since I came here as a little boy."

"You can look forward to getting out of here," McNabb said. "You got piano tuning under your belt."

"I hear that in sighted schools they have beer and wild parties at graduation—we don't get to do any of that," Anna Belle said.

"Next year, Max Cary will be dancing with Pegie—
the bum!" Bruton said. Bruton had recently been dating Pegie Johnson.

There was general conversation about the difficulties of surviving outside the school—finding jobs and
places to live. For myself, I felt heavy in the heart for
a different reason. I didn't know when I would get
back to Arkansas, when, if ever, I would see my classmates again—they were going back to their homes in
Prattsville, in Newport, in Mabelvale, in Greenbrier,
in Fort Smith, while I was going out to California—
or any of the other people who had filled my life in
Arkansas.

"I wonder how many people are out there," Bruton
was saying. With some of our vending-stand profits,
Mr. Woolly had ordered for each of us seniors twenty
engraved invitations to the commencement exercises.
Each of the other seniors had sent out all twenty and
had received a number of acceptances. I hadn't sent out
any. Daddyji could not afford to come from California,
and I knew that no one else in my family could come.
To shield myself from feeling sad or having to make
do by asking Joe and Jean Red, for instance, I had
simply dismissed the whole idea of the graduation ceremony as a stupid tribal rite, something not worth
bothering with. But now that the ceremony was at
hand I felt twinges of pain, perhaps like those an old
classmate of mine in India had told me he felt in his
phantom hands—his forearms had been blown off in
the war. Even now, I thought, the families of my
classmates are gathering in the auditorium, waiting to
surround the new graduates at the end of the cere-

mony. I am all alone. There is no one waiting for me.

I noticed that Oather was suddenly quiet. I wondered if he was going over his valedictory speech in his head. I immediately felt that I had forgotten my salutatory speech, perhaps in my nervous worry over speaking in front of Mr. F. E. Davis, who was to be our commencement speaker. He was the superintendent of the American Printing House for the Blind, in Louisville, Kentucky, where most of the American Braille publications and Talking Books originated. As head of the Printing House, he was a nationally influential figure in the work for the blind and was therefore one of the first people I had appealed to when I was trying to come to America. He had opposed my coming, however, striking a theme all too familiar to me by then from my correspondence with educators in Britain—that blindness was a social maladjustment in itself, and that my coming to the West at such an early age would lead to cultural maladjustment as well, so that I would be a misfit in the East as well as in the West. Mr. Davis's opposition had almost proved fatal, for my letters to American schools for the blind were often referred to him for his advice. As it happened, he had been Mr. Woolly's predecessor at the Arkansas School, and I had often reflected that if he had been its superintendent when I applied I would not have won admission. Indeed, if Mr. Woolly, who had been unaware of Mr. Davis's opposition, had stopped to ask the simplest questions that Mr. Davis and other educators asked—such as what would happen if I got ill in America, and what I would do when school was closed for holidays, to say nothing of what effect my

Western education would ultimately have on me—he might have independently reached Mr. Davis's conclusion. He certainly would not have said (as he liked to tell the story), "Boy, come on over!"—as if he were speaking to me on the telephone and I were just a long bus ride away from the school. Now, sitting there about to share the stage with Mr. Davis, I wondered if he, in his commencement address, would refer to our correspondence, as he had politely done when I went to Louisville and met him at the Printing House. Would he take note of the fact that I was the salutatorian of my class and compliment Mr. Woolly for his boldness in accepting me? Or would he remain silent about me, perhaps taking the view that the evidence in my case simply wasn't in yet—would not be in for years? Perhaps he knew what negative opinions the authorities at the Educational Testing Service and Columbia had formed of me. The thought made me blush with shame. I tried to tell myself that it didn't matter what Mr. Davis thought—that I was going to California, a whole different world, and that there (if Columbia didn't take me in the end) I would somehow get myself admitted to a college where no one would even know who Mr. Davis was.

There was a disturbance in the curtain, and Mr. Woolly came onstage. "Boys and girls, y'all know your way to the lectern?" Mr. Woolly whispered. "Sure you won't stumble when the Honorable Mr. Prewitt calls you to come get your diploma?" Mr. T. A. Prewitt was the chairman of the school's board of trustees. Norman said he felt a little uncertain. Mr. Woolly walked with him the few steps from his chair to the lectern and back. "You're a fine-looking group," Mr. Woolly whispered proudly, moving back a few steps, as if he were going to take our picture. "You're the best class we've ever graduated from A.S.B."

There was another disturbance in the curtain. This time, it was Mr. Davis. He was introduced all around. He greeted me warmly, mentioning our previous meeting, and sat down with us.

Then came a rattle of curtain rings as Mr. Woolly drew back the curtain, and the commencement exercises were under way.

I remember the ceremony hazily. I remember that there was some organ music, and an invocation by the Reverend Dr. Jeff E. Davis. I remember feeling awkward when my turn to speak came. I remember that I stepped up to the lectern and mechanically recited the introduction, imagining that Mr. Davis was looking over my shoulder and judging me. "This day marks the end of many happy years we have spent in our second home," I said rapidly, and then made an effort to slow down. "I was fifteen when I came to America and was confronted with a rugged and monstrous mountain. Every member of the class has experienced a moment of depression in venturing out on this mountain. Yet there is no retreat from this climbing for people who are determined to aim high and keep on climbing. We will be climbing this mountain for the rest of our lives. And we are going to need your help and understanding. If we are to take our place in society, we must be accepted as intelligent citizens with good character and education. We are grateful to those who have aided us in starting our journey."

I sat down, and Anna Belle sang a solo. Oather gave his speech. Finally, Mr. Davis took his place at the lectern. I remember that at one point he turned to me and said, "Some years ago, I corresponded with this young man. I have to admit to you that Dr. Farrell, of Perkins, and I were dead wrong when we advised him to stay home." Far from gloating, I felt depressed, perversely thinking that he was wrong now and had been right before. And so often in the past, it seemed that once I had got the thing I wanted I wasn't able to enjoy it.

Mr. Prewitt now came to the lectern. As he called our names, we walked over and received our rolled-up diplomas. Miss Harper had described the diploma to us beforehand—it had on it an angel, a figure in a sunburst, and an eagle with a ribbon in its mouth saying "Regnat Populus"—but when mine was handed to me I was surprised by how big it was, and I walked back to my seat with it not knowing what to do with it or where to put it. It rattled in my hand, as if to draw attention to itself. Then, just as I had sat down and laid the wretched thing on my lap, Mr. Prewitt started calling some of us by name again. He presented Oather with a Certificate of Proficiency in Piano Tuning and Industrial Arts, Bruton with one in Typing and Industrial Arts, McNabb with one in Industrial Arts, Anna Belle with one in Typing and Home Economics, and Carol Rowe with one in Home Economics. Then Mr. Woolly took over and called my name. He presented me with the annual Stanley Medal for Scholarship, a little gold triangular leaf with a pin on the back. I considered my medal a good omen, thinking that it would help me get into a college, much as my classmates' Certificates of Proficiency would help them get jobs.

At the end of the ceremony, the families of my classmates rushed onto the stage. I quickly walked down its steps and up the aisle of the auditorium.

Waiting at the door was Mr. Woolly, like a pastor ready to offer a handshake and a few words for each of his parishioners as they leave the church. "That was a fine speech you made," he said, shaking my hand. "You and Oather were neck and neck for valedictorian, but you had to do your junior and senior classwork in one year."

Mr. Woolly turned to someone else, and suddenly Wayne Tidman was there. "You really swung it, Buster," he said. "I can't believe you're graduating a year ahead of me."

Lois joined us. "Wayne won the Stanley Medal the first year of high school, and now you. Two from our class!" I've finished a year ahead of her, I thought, but she still thinks of me as her classmate. Despite the fact that she went back to Raymond, I really do love her.

"Yes, it's quite an achievement to have the highest scholastic average in the junior-senior high school," Mr. Davis said, coming up to us.

"Among the boys," Wayne corrected him.

I thanked Mr. Davis for his words about me in his speech.

Oather walked past with his family. He heard my voice and came running back. He threw his arm around me. "Nice to have known you, Whip," he said, overwhelming me with his Bull Durham-chewing-tobacco smell. Then he rushed away.

With Oather's voice in my ear and his smell of tobacco in my head, I walked along the school's central corridor and down to the locker room, now empty— most people had packed earlier and taken their things out and put them by the side of the driveway or in the school bus. Oather was already becoming a memory. In fact, that was the last time I saw him, the last time I saw practically anyone from the school. Years later, in preparation for this narrative, I tried to find out what had happened to some of the people I'd known at school. Bruton and McNabb were running vending stands in Little Rock. Barbara, who had got married and now had a son in his twenties, was also running a vending stand in Little Rock. Anna Belle Morris was a telephone-switchboard operator for the Arkansas Highway Department. Oather owned a piano store in Shreveport, Louisiana. No one seemed to know the whereabouts of Carol Rowe or Norman Penix. Lois was teaching in a school for the blind in New Mexico. Wayne, who had given up preaching, was teaching counselling skills at a college somewhere. Mary Ann Lambert had worked for a time in a defense plant. Max Cary, when he was last heard of, had served a sentence in a Texas penitentiary for stock manipulation. Treadway, who had eventually come back and graduated from the school, was living in California; Vernelle had died. Mr. Woolly had retired. Mr. Chiles was still teaching at the school. Mr. Hartman had died. Miss Harper, who had taught at the school for some twenty years more, had got married, lived on a farm, and raised a family, but was now divorced. A few of the people I had known had not got married, but most of them had, and were fathers and mothers. From what I heard, none of them seemed to stand out from the mass of American humanity in the way every one of them had stood out in my school days. When I did seek a few of them out for myself, in the hope of comparing memories, our conversations seemed never to get off the ground; none of the people shared my interest in recollecting our past. All of them turned out to be, in a sense, as inaccessible to me as the familiar but now vanished landmarks I had known: the Boys' Club had burned down, and the club had moved to a new site; the ice-cream plant had gone out of business and been demolished; most of the stores on Main Street had disappeared with their old-fashioned buildings; the school plant itself had expanded and changed almost beyond recognition. Indeed, the people and the landmarks of my Arkansas seem to have left hardly a trace, except in my memory.

After graduation, my life took such a different turn—I didn't pursue my appeal to Columbia but, instead, started college in California—that my experiences in the school and in Arkansas fell away like feathers from a molting bird. The three years of my life I had spent in Little Rock became sealed in a compartment in my mind which I dreaded to open, not so much because they had been unhappy as because, in retrospect, the near-total submersion in a residential school for the blind seemed to accentuate my blindness, when all along my aspiration had been to be a well-adjusted member of the seeing society outside.

❧

"SON, we have a present for you," Mr. Woolly said. I was finishing a farewell dinner with him, his wife, and their three sons in their small apartment, on the third floor of the school building, which I had never before entered—nor, as far as I knew, had any other student, or any teacher, ever entered it. He gave me a silver tie clasp—a bar with two snake chains and a pendant with a raised "A.S.B." design on it, like the design on my class ring. "Son, I want you to have this keepsake, so that whenever you wear it people will know you went here. You won't forget us, will you?"

Mr. Woolly fastened the clasp on my shirt and pulled my tie through the snake chains. I had never worn a tie clasp with chains before, and the pendant, though small, felt a little heavy against my chest.

"How could he forget us, now that we've put our seal on him?" Mrs. Woolly asked.

"Mr. Woolly and Mrs. Woolly, I am deeply indebted to you," I said—stiffly, in spite of myself—feeling the blood rush to my cheeks. "If it had not been for you, Mr. Woolly, I might not ever have got to the States."

❦

IN the morning, a number of faculty members surrounded Mr. Woolly's car. I said my goodbyes and got in the front seat, beside Mr. Woolly. Mr. Chiles, Miss Harper, and my old arithmetic teacher Miss Mitchell—who were coming with me to the airport—got in the back, and we set off. These are the streets I rode through when I first arrived, I thought. Then I scarcely knew what direction I was travelling in. Now I know all the street names—I know practically every turn.

"Son, what's the most precious thing you're taking from us?" Mr. Woolly asked, breaking the little silence in the car—it seemed that none of us knew what to say.

"Mobility," I said unhesitatingly. I was surprised at the baldness of my reply.

At the airport, when I was taking my leave, Mr. Chiles said, "Who knows? You might come back after the summer and go to Hendrix after all. You could major in history there, as I did." And do what, I thought. Come back to the school, like Mr. Chiles, and teach there?

"Hendrix is a great place," Mr. Woolly was saying. "It's one of the best in the country. We could keep an eye on you there, and you could come and visit us whenever you wanted to."

"Hendrix and Arkansas are not quite right for me," I said. "I'd like to be in a bigger place."

"The orbit of influence of any one person is limited." Mr. Chiles said.

"Well, we'll help you get into any college you want to go to," Mr. Woolly said. "Just let us know."

"Amen," Miss Harper said.

"Amen," Miss Mitchell said.

I thanked them, and soon I was once more in an airplane—this time on my way to the new frontier of California.